THE FIELD OF
BLOOD

THE FIELD OF
BLOOD

● ● ●

The Battle for Aleppo and the
Remaking of the Medieval Middle East

NICHOLAS MORTON

BASIC BOOKS

New York

Basic Books
Hachette Book Group
1290 Avenue of the Americas, New York, NY 10104
www.basicbooks.com

Printed in the United States of America

First Edition: February 2018

Published by Basic Books, an imprint of Perseus Books, LLC, a subsidiary of Hachette Book Group, Inc. The Basic Books name and logo is a trademark of the Hachette Book Group.

The Hachette Speakers Bureau provides a wide range of authors for speaking events. To find out more, go to www.hachettespeakersbureau.com or call (866) 376-6591.

The publisher is not responsible for websites (or their content) that are not owned by the publisher.

Print book interior design by Amy Quinn.

Library of Congress Cataloging-in-Publication Data

Names: Morton, Nicholas.
Title: The field of blood : the battle for Aleppo and the remaking of the medieval Middle East / Nicholas Morton.
Description: New York, NY : Basic Books, 2018. | Includes bibliographical references and index.
Identifiers: LCCN 2017022600| ISBN 9780465096695 (hardback) | ISBN 9780465096701 (ebook)
Subjects: LCSH: Ager Sanguinis, Battle of, Syria, 1119. | Sarmadåa (Syria)—History. | Artuqid dynasty, 1098–1408. | Crusades. | Syria—History—750–1260. | Islamic Empire—History—750–1258. | BISAC: HISTORY / Medieval. | HISTORY / Middle East / General.
Classification: LCC DS99.S26 M67 2018 | DDC 956/.014—dc23
LC record available at https://lccn.loc.gov/2017022600

ISBNs: 978-0-465-09669-5 (hardcover), 978-0-465-09670-1 (ebook)

LSC-C

10 9 8 7 6 5 4 3 2 1

For Maria and Lia

CONTENTS

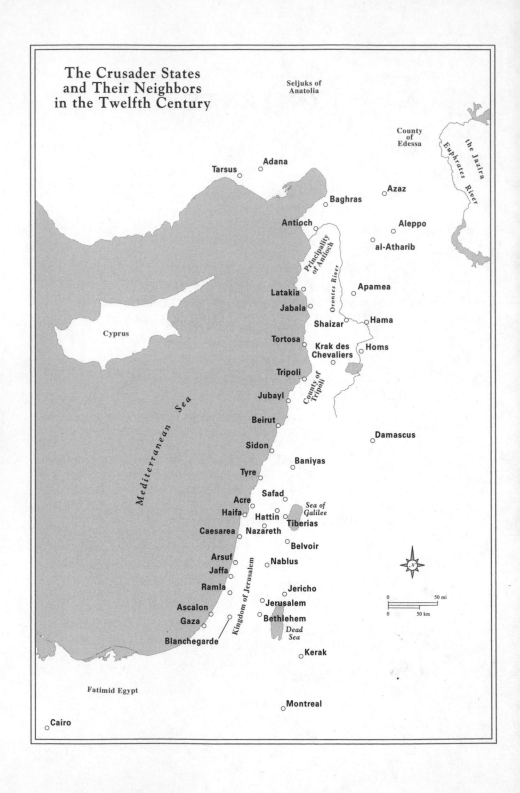

The Crusader States
and Their Neighbors
in the Twelfth Century

Seljuks of
Anatolia

County
of
Edessa

the Jazira

Euphrates River

Tarsus

Adana

Azaz

Baghras

Aleppo

Antioch

al-Atharib

Principality of Antioch

Orontes River

Apamea

Latakia

Jabala

Shaizar

Hama

Cyprus

Tortosa

Krak des
Chevaliers

Homs

Tripoli

County of
Tripoli

Jubayl

Beirut

Damascus

Sidon

Mediterranean Sea

Baniyas

Tyre

Safad

Acre

Sea of
Galilee

Haifa

Hattin

Tiberias

Caesarea

Nazareth

Belvoir

Arsuf

Nablus

Jaffa

Kingdom of Jerusalem

Ramla

Jericho

Ascalon

Jerusalem

Gaza

Bethlehem

Dead
Sea

Blanchegarde

Kerak

Fatimid Egypt

Montreal

Cairo

0   50 mi
0   50 km

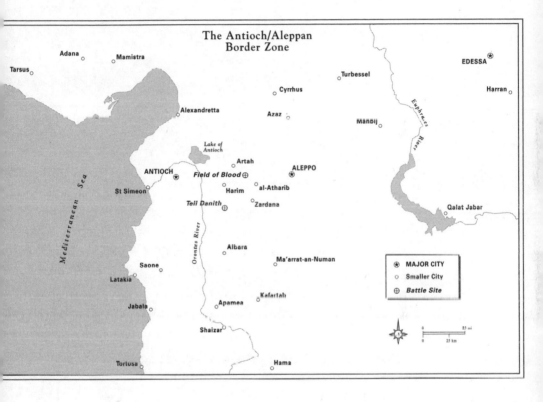

The Antioch/Aleppan
Border Zone

Tarsus

Adana Mamistra

EDESSA

Turbessel
Harran

Cyrrhus

Alexandretta
Azaz Manbij

Euphrates River

Lake of
Antioch
Artah

ANTIOCH Field of Blood ALEPPO

St Simeon Harim al-Atharib Qalat Jabar

Tell Danith Zardana

Orontes River

Mediterranean Sea

Albara
Ma'arrat-an-Numan

Saone
Latakia

Jabala
Apamea Kafartab

Shaizar

Tortosa Hama

⊛ MAJOR CITY
○ Smaller City
⊕ Battle Site

0   25 mi
0   25 km

PROLOGUE

THE SCREAM RANG out across the barren wilderness, the sound of a man in mortal agony. Corbaran, the Turkish ruler of Oliferne, sprang up at the sound, calling for his advisers and his crusader captives. He demanded that they listen in case the man should scream again. Corbaran did not know who had made such a cry, but the stranger's evident distress filled him with pity. Then Baldwin of Beauvais—Corbaran's prisoner—spoke up. He had recognized the voice. It was his brother Ernoul. The brothers had been taken captive a long while before at the disastrous Battle of Civetot, during the First Crusade, but even their long separation could not make him mistake his own kin. The dying man's screams became more plaintive and more distant, as though he were being dragged away. Ernoul was calling on Saint Nicholas and the Virgin Mary before his words were suddenly cut short.

Even before they heard those distant cries, it had been a strange day. Corbaran's Turkish army, along with its small band of captive crusaders, had not intended to be here. They had strayed into this stark land, which lay somewhere on the slopes of Mount Tigris, when the wind had flung a blizzard of dust into the air, disorienting them and causing them to mistake their road. It had been achingly hot, and they had made camp in a small orchard. Neither the Turks nor the Franks knew where they were, but they all feared that they knew what was causing the distant knight such distress. It was the great dragon Sathanas. They had tried to avoid its lair but had instead strayed directly into its hunting grounds.

Overcoming his terror, Baldwin demanded that his captor permit him to save his brother. Corbaran refused. He warned Baldwin that deep in the mountain was an ancient city that the dragon had ravaged long ago. Now it was deserted, save for the beast, and no man in his right mind would seek to enter those crags to confront him.

Still Baldwin would not be dissuaded, and Corbaran reluctantly yielded, granting his captive and friend the weapons he needed. The Turkish lord invited Baldwin to pick his own arms, and he selected a white chain-mail hauberk, a helmet, a shield, two swords with silver hilts, and a javelin. Then he confessed himself to his fellow captive, the bishop of Forez, who appealed to God that Baldwin might live to see Jerusalem. He set off on foot up the mountain, leaving both Turks and Franks grieving for him as though he were already dead.

Baldwin proceeded cautiously up the ruined road into the mountains. He climbed for many hours into the high places, feeling the weight of his weapons and sweating profusely. Nothing but toads, worms, and snakes lived in those desolate crags. By the time he reached the summit, he was reduced to crawling on his hands and knees. At the peak he commended himself to Christ in preparation for the coming battle and called out boldly to the dragon, challenging it to come out and fight. Then, rounding a boulder, he came upon the beast. It was asleep, having gorged itself on Ernoul's corpse; only the poor knight's decapitated head remained.

When Baldwin approached, Sathanas awoke and reared up, displaying the full length of its great scale-armored body. The spines on its torso bristled, and it raked its vicious talons against the rocks. Baldwin made the sign of the cross and, calling upon Christ and the saints, flung his javelin at the beast. It was a valiant throw, but it made no impression at all on the demon-possessed monster, and the shaft snapped. The dragon bellowed in rage. Far away Corbaran and the French knights heard the roar and, summoning their courage, determined to climb the mountain to aid Baldwin.

Baldwin and Sathanas flung themselves into combat, talon against sword, in a mortal struggle. Baldwin raised one of his swords, inlaid with a silver cross, but the beast seized it in its jaws and broke it in two, swallowing the fragments. But God caused the broken blade to grow in the dragon's chest so that it nearly burst out, causing the beast to writhe in pain.

Baldwin thrust his second sword into the serpent's mouth. Sathanas lurched, and the Devil flew out of the beast in the guise of a raven. Convulsed with agony, Sathanas battered at Baldwin, knocking his helmet from his head, leaving him bloodied. Baldwin then swung his blade down hard on the dragon's head, but it simply rebounded from the armored scales. The two were again locked in a deadly combat until, with a mighty thrust, Baldwin rammed his sword down the worm's throat and into its rocklike heart. The dragon was dead, and Baldwin collapsed from pain and fatigue.[1]

The great duel between Baldwin of Beauvais and the dragon Sathanas forms part of a dramatic tale known as the *Chanson des Chétifs*, which tells the story of a brave group of crusaders imprisoned during the First Crusade who had to fend for themselves in distant lands under their Turkish captors. The earliest version of the story was commissioned in the mid-twelfth century by Raymond, prince of the crusader Principality of Antioch (a large and well-fortified territory situated in the coastal region of northern Syria). The *Chétifs* is a work of fantasy, yet, like most fictional tales, it communicates a great deal about its intended audience.

This was the kind of story that would have been recited at feasts, when the guests had eaten their fill and were ready to set aside their cares to hear songs of war, heroic knights, mythical beasts, and beautiful maidens. Although the assembled dignitaries of the Antiochene court would undoubtedly have enjoyed the escapism of the dragon slaying—presumably shouting their approval and banging the table as Sathanas's body crumpled to the ground—there was nonetheless a great deal in this tale that spoke profoundly of the realities of their own lives on the frontiers of the known world.

The Principality of Antioch was a product of the First Crusade, the colossal military expedition that had carved a path across western Christendom (Christian Europe), the Byzantine Empire (the continuator of the old Eastern Roman Empire), and the Middle East to conquer the holy city of Jerusalem in 1099. In the wake of that successful campaign, most of the survivors took ship back for their homes in western Europe, but a small number of knights remained to defend the scattered pockets of land taken during the years of war. Their objective was to transform a handful of captured towns and cities into viable states that would guarantee Christendom's ability to retain and protect the holy places of the Near East. Initially there were three such "Crusader States," founded around the cities of Edessa, Antioch, and Jerusalem, and in time they were supplemented by a fourth centered on the city of Tripoli.

These early settlers were engaged in a perilous quest, conducted in the teeth of the most intense resistance. In their early years they lacked money, troops, strongholds, ports, governing institutions, and the infrastructure necessary for the creation of a stable country. They were surrounded by neighbors whose languages and customs were unfamiliar and who were far from reconciled to the newly arrived crusaders. Like Baldwin of Beauvais, they were a long way from help, and they were seeking to pioneer new societies in unfamiliar lands. Far to the east, beyond the Tigris River or across the Arabian Desert, lay . . . they did not know what. There was no reason for them to disbelieve the tales told by many cultures that terrifying beasts like dragons or griffins existed "out there." They were living on the borders of legend.

These were also lands steeped in thousands of years of history, and the fortified cities such as Jerusalem, Antioch, or Edessa, which secured the settlers' (known generally as "Franks") small territories, often had roots that stretched back into the Greek or Roman era, or even earlier to the Iron Age or the Bronze Age. They were living amid the ruins of former empires, just like the mythical ancient city inhabited by Sathanas.

In their determination to grow and consolidate their meager holdings, the Franks pursued many policies. They acquired commercial experience, learning to grow sugarcane for export, to yoke the Silk Roads from the Far East for tax, and to trade with a broad assortment of neighboring peoples. They fought wars across many theaters, conducting raids alongside the Bedouin on the margins of the Arabian Desert, fighting Egyptians in the fertile farmlands of the Nile delta, besieging Turkish fortresses in the highlands of southern Anatolia, and tackling enemy war fleets on the rippling blue waters of the Mediterranean.

They acclimatized themselves to the world of the Levant (the eastern Mediterranean region), picking up new customs and acquiring a taste for local foods, while sharing their own western European culture with the local peoples. They displayed a forceful energy in all they did, not least in their building work: producing huge numbers of strongholds, city defenses, churches, mills, houses, shops, and harbors. These were young, arrogant, devout conquerors constructing new countries for themselves from scratch.

———

On a strategic level, the Frankish conquest of the Near East essentially consisted of two overlapping phases. When the First Crusaders returned home, those who remained in the East held three important cities (Edessa, Antioch, and Jerusalem) along with a scattering of nearby towns. These cities provided the starting points for their future states, but on their own they were isolated and vulnerable. The first phase of expansion was therefore to build up the hinterland surrounding these cities, acquiring the unconquered satellite towns that would strengthen their defenses and bring enough farmland under their control to supply the food, resources, and taxes needed to maintain their armies. The most important of these towns were generally the ports strung out along the Levantine coast. These harbors were crucial to the creation of supply lines with western Europe, which could then provide the much-needed manpower, trade goods, and troops to guarantee the survival of the Frankish position in the East.

This was a vital first step, but if the Crusader States were to become permanent fixtures in the Near East, then they needed to successfully undertake a second phase of expansion: the conquest of their opponents' major centers of power in Aleppo, Damascus, and Cairo. Only if at least one (but ideally all) of these inland cities came under their control could the crusaders expand beyond the narrow strip of the Levantine coast.[2] This was the challenge that consumed the rulers of the Crusader States for decades. It was the conflict on which the success of the Crusader States would turn, the struggle that would ultimately decide whether the Franks would expand to achieve regional dominance or be driven back into the sea.

For academics in recent decades, it has been easy to write off the Crusader States as a doomed venture that never had any real chance of success. We know that the Crusades did eventually fail and that the Crusader States were overthrown, first in 1187 and then again in 1291. It might be observed that the Franks were consistently outnumbered by their enemies and could never have maintained themselves in the long term against such odds. It could be pointed out that hundreds of miles of sea divided the Crusader States from their major supply sources in western Europe. Historians could underscore the strangeness of the East, highlighting the efforts and ultimate failure of Frankish commanders to engage meaningfully with the complex mesh of ethnic and political alliances spanning the region, while their men and horses struggled to accustom themselves to a diet, a climate, and diseases with which they had no prior familiarity. On these grounds, the eventual demise of the Crusader States could be styled as a foregone conclusion—the crusader settlement was always going to fail, if not sooner then later.

Such a conclusion, however, fundamentally underestimates how near the Franks came to total success. This book will demonstrate, by contrast, how extraordinarily close the Crusader States came to achieving their goals through completing the second phase of conquest, seizing their enemies' capitals, and thereby entrenching their presence across the Near East.

In the heady, early years of the Crusader States, commentators from many civilizations viewed the Franks as an unstoppable force, whose eventual victory was all but certain. So, far from anticipating that the Christian invaders would inevitably be driven back to western Christendom, there was a serious concern that the regional capitals of Aleppo, Damascus, and Cairo would be engulfed by marching columns of Frankish knights. So what stalled this advance? When were they forced onto the back foot?

In any failed war of conquest there are generally two sets of turning points. The first are those key events that bring the conquerors' advances to a halt, forcing them to shift from the offensive to the defensive. The second set are those later moments when the final structural supports maintaining the conquerors' presence within their already-acquired territory are removed or destroyed, leading to the general collapse of their position. To date, historians of the Crusades have tended to focus their attention on the latter turning points, seeking to identify the moments that led to the final collapse of the crusading project. This book asks rather different questions: Why didn't they succeed?[3] How did the Franks' enemies manage to halt their steady initial advance across the Near East and prevent them from conquering further inland?

To answer these questions, this book focuses on one of the most hard-fought military struggles in the history of the Crusader States: the war for Aleppo in 1118–1128. This conflict effectively ended the Frankish advance in the north. In the preceding years, the Franks had been making dogged progress across northern Syria, and by 1118 they were poised to take control of Aleppo. Possession of this crucial city would have strengthened their position across the board, giving them the resources and strategic positioning to potentially conquer the entire region. Their ultimate failure to win this struggle stands as a major turning point in the history of the Crusader States and represents the high-water mark of their expanding dominations in northern Syria.

During this crucial decade, 1118–1128, the pace of conflict was relentless, and every year was punctuated by a persistent cycle of attack and counterattack. Nevertheless, in the midst of the ongoing slaughter, two encounters defined the course of the overall conflict. The first was the more important: the catastrophic crusader defeat at the Battle of the Field of Blood in 1119. This reverse broke the momentum of the Frankish advance across northern Syria, leading to years of chaotic fighting among the embattled factions. The second was the failed attempt to besiege Aleppo by an allied Frankish-Arab army in 1124–1125. These moments, more than any other, were the turning points when the crusader project to conquer Aleppo failed. This defeat represents the first and most important block to the Franks' strategic advance across the Near East.

This book re-creates this epic encounter. It begins, in the first two chapters, by exploring the early rise of the Crusader States following the victories of the First Crusade and the steady growth of Christian power in the Aleppan region of northern Syria. The third chapter then opens the great struggle for Aleppo, focusing specifically on the crucial battle at the Field of Blood, exploring why the Christians lost so heavily after years of steady progress. The fourth chapter turns to the battle's aftermath and the ongoing struggle for Aleppo as later Frankish rulers sought to reassert an aggressive military policy in the north and regain their former expansionist momentum.

The final chapter places this contest against the wider backdrop of the history of the Crusader States. The struggle for Aleppo was the moment when the Franks came closest to conquering one of their enemies' major centers of power, but in the following years the conflict would continue and later Frankish rulers launched their own unsuccessful campaigns to seize the other major Near Eastern capitals of Damascus and Cairo. This section deals with these later ventures, in which the Franks attempted to resume an aggressive policy and drive inland, and will suggest an answer for the much broader question of why the Crusader States ultimately failed in their war aims to conquer the entire Near Eastern region.

———•———

The Battle of the Field of Blood and the broader struggle for Aleppo was an intensely complex affair, drawing in many factions—Frankish, Turkish, Armenian, Arab, and Byzantine. Like so many of the Crusader States' wars, it was rarely a simple matter of Christians versus Muslims. It is a common misconception that the Crusades were a straightforward duel between two combatant religions. The sources underpinning this book offer a rather different—and much more sophisticated—picture.

In the story of Baldwin's epic combat against the dragon Sathanas, the Turks led by Corbaran may have been his captors, but they were also valued friends who marched to his aid when he needed help. The world of the medieval Near East was every bit as complex as this tale implies, and Frankish Christians often found themselves fighting as allies alongside different ethnic or religious groups. Friendships and alliances formed across cultural and spiritual divides, and coreligionists often went to war against one another. As we shall see, the world of the Crusader States defies easy categorization, and the battle lines were rarely simple.

Drawing out the diversity of the medieval Near East, this book will go beyond the interests of the Franks to consider the perspectives of other protagonists involved in the Field of Blood and the struggle for Aleppo. Among these, it was the Turks who were both the crusaders' greatest adversaries and the dominant force across the region. Like the Franks, they too were conquerors, newly arrived in the Near East. During the century preceding the Crusades, the nomadic Turks had departed from their homelands in the central Asian steppe region and had migrated south in vast numbers. They broke upon the Muslim world, conquering much of the Islamic caliphate and overthrowing those who stood in their path. In 1055 they took control of Baghdad, and later they moved west into Syria and the Jazira, displacing the Arab and Kurdish rulers who governed the major cities.

Soon afterward, the Turks invaded Anatolia (modern-day Turkey), staging a series of assaults on the great Christian empire of Byzantium. The Byzantine Greeks labored for decades to protect themselves against these attackers, but they steadily lost ground. Their most famous defeat was at the Battle of Manzikert in 1071, when the Turkish sultan Alp Arslan decisively defeated a major Byzantine field army, fragmenting the empire's defenses and paving the way for Turkish tribes to move permanently into the area. These defeats prompted the Byzantines to send emissaries to the papacy in Rome, requesting aid against this powerful foe, and these appeals helped lay the foundations, in time, for the First Crusade.

When the crusaders began their crossing of Anatolia in 1097— en route to distant Jerusalem—they were entering territory that had been under Turkish control for only a few decades. The Turks were determined to confront this new Frankish menace, and they became the crusaders' primary opponent during their long march. Still, the Turks' struggle against the First Crusade was complicated by the deep divisions within their own ranks. The First Crusaders arrived to find the Turks in the midst of a civil war that prevented them from unifying their efforts against the oncoming crusaders— some Turks even sought the crusaders' protection. The Turks and the Franks were the leading pugilists in the Near East, and they would continue to spar for control of the region during the years following the crusader conquest of Jerusalem.

The Turks may have dominated much of the Near East during this period, but they were minority rulers, governing a broad and diverse population of Arabs, Armenians, Syrian Christians, Kurds, and many other minorities, who often resented their Turkish masters. The victories of the First Crusade weakened the Turks' control over these peoples, encouraging many to resist their overlords.

These peoples all played their parts in the events surrounding both the Battle of the Field of Blood and the broader struggle for Aleppo. They rarely felt much love for the conquerors dividing up the region, whether Frankish or Turkish, but were guided, rather, by the desire to plot a safe course through the unfolding chaos. This was a complex world, molded by many agendas. Some fought for God, others for wealth or power, but many fought simply for survival.

Chapter 1 will lay the foundations for the Battle of the Field of Blood and the war for Aleppo, going back to the days of the First Crusade and its immediate aftermath and exploring how the Franks first established themselves on the shores of the Levant.

THE RIVAL ARCHITECTS OF THE CRUSADER STATES: BALDWIN OF BOULOGNE AND TANCRED OF HAUTEVILLE

1100–1110

THE FIRST CRUSADE was over. Jerusalem had been recaptured for Christ, and most of the victorious crusaders had returned to Europe. Against all odds, their hopes had been fulfilled. But for the handful of knights who remained to defend the lands conquered during the crusade, the battle had only just begun. Transforming their temporary conquests into viable states would be an undertaking every bit as challenging as the crusade itself.

Amid the lush ravines and steep-sided valleys of the Phoenician coastlands (Lebanon), Baldwin of Boulogne was outnumbered and far from help. His enemies had massed around him, and in the still-warm Levantine twilight their campfires glimmered across the hillsides. He had walked straight into a trap, but he had done so knowingly because a great prize awaited him to the south: Jerusalem.

His brother Godfrey—the holy city's former ruler—was dead, and Jerusalem was Baldwin's for the taking, an opportunity that warranted the extraordinary risks he was running. Only a short while earlier, a delegation had arrived at Edessa, the newly formed county where Baldwin ruled, offering him the city. The envoys were clearly in earnest, but he was not the only contender. Others, including the recently elected Patriarch Daimbert, the most senior churchman in the holy city, and Tancred of Hauteville, a powerful Norman warrior and lord of the newly won city of Tiberias, had other candidates in mind. Tancred also had not forgiven Baldwin for their quarrels during the recent crusade. Still worse, winter was near, and the roads would soon be treacherous.

Spurred on by these thoughts, Baldwin left Edessa in haste. However, as his journey progressed, his fears that there might be another claimant receded; his main rival, Bohemond of Antioch, was now languishing in a Turkish dungeon. Indeed, when he reached the Principality of Antioch, he felt sufficiently confident to send the women and baggage ahead of him by sea, proceeding himself by land with his main force.

Baldwin's intended route was to travel from the Frankish-ruled city of Antioch, following the coast road hundreds of miles south to Jaffa—currently the only port controlled by the Franks in Jerusalem—and from there to take the pilgrim paths inland to Jerusalem itself (see map on page viii). It was a long and arduous road traversing rugged country, most of it still under Arab or Turkish control. There was a very real danger that his small force would be intercepted. Still, he had traveled on pilgrimage to Jerusalem only a few months earlier and had returned safely, so there was no particular reason to believe that this time would be any different. Most of the local Turkish and Arab rulers were far too frightened of provoking a Frankish attack to bar his passage.

Any hope of a peaceful journey was shattered at the Byzantine-held port of Latakia. News arrived that Baldwin's Turkish enemies were readying to bar his path. Duqaq, ruler of Damascus and grandson of the great Turkish sultan Alp Arslan, was assembling an army to waylay Baldwin's tiny force. This report caused such fear among Baldwin's entourage that many fled ignominiously. Others pretended to be ill. Once the backsliders had departed, Baldwin was left with a mere 160 knights and 500 infantry. By the time Baldwin's company reached Tripoli, a grave situation had worsened. The city's Arab ruler was keen to win favor with the Franks, and he informed Baldwin that Janah al-Dawla, Turkish ruler of the town of Homs, had joined his forces with those of Damascus. The combined forces were now advancing to block his path.[1]

Baldwin may have been atrociously outnumbered, but to retreat now would be a disgrace. He pressed ahead despite the gathering storm clouds of war. From Tripoli he continued on the southward road into Phoenicia, a narrow strip of land between the Lebanese mountains and the sea. This was a place of immense beauty, where deep, heavily vegetated valleys, fragrant with the scent of herbs and alive with the sound of birds, ran down from the high cedar forests on the mountains' slopes to the glistening sapphire of the Mediterranean. It was in this Eden, however, that Baldwin's enemies were awaiting him, massing their forces in a place where the road narrowed: Dog River, a few miles to the north of Beirut. This was the point of highest vulnerability on Baldwin's route. It was a place where even a handful of defenders could deny entry to an army. As Baldwin approached, his scouts reported that the road was blocked by enemy troops only a little way ahead. Battle was unavoidable.

Baldwin's first move was to launch an attack to probe his enemies' defenses. It was a complete failure. His casualties from this encounter were slight, but after a day of hard fighting, he had made no progress and was forced to make camp.

And so there he was, trapped, on the night before battle, aspiring for Jerusalem but hovering on the brink of disaster. The Turks occupied the high ground to the east, and enemy ships had disgorged more troops to the north, cutting off the road back to distant Antioch. Baldwin was blockaded in a small space without water. His men were getting thirsty and, more important, so were the horses. During the night, the Turks maintained a constant barrage of arrows into his sorry encampment. Sleep was impossible, and his chaplain Fulcher of Chartres spent the hours of darkness sitting outside his tent longing to return home to distant France.[2]

Baldwin's forces were caught between the hammer and the anvil, yet their master was far from defeated. Here was a man who had carried his sword all the way from northern France. He had fought alongside the warriors of the First Crusade in countless battles, winning on almost every occasion. The four years of war that had passed since he left his home had hardened him, giving him a veteran's eye for strategic advantage. He had become familiar with the Turks' weapons and tactics. He knew, for example, that their bows, formed from lengths of bone and horn, were bound together with glue. They were exceptionally powerful, but the glue tended to dissolve in the rain, rendering them useless. That knowledge had been decisive only a few months earlier when his knights had ripped through a Turkish raiding party near the ancient Roman city of Baalbek.[3]

On this occasion, he decided to turn the Turks' most effective tactic against them. At first light, Baldwin's troops dismantled their tents and began to force a passage back toward Tripoli, to all appearances trying to flee. He abandoned the narrows of the ravine and managed to reach an area of more level ground some way to the rear. His enemies, scenting imminent victory, clustered around

Baldwin's small force, shouting war cries and firing arrows, while more sailors disembarked from the ships lying just offshore. In their excitement, the Turks left the high ground and began to assemble on flatter terrain. This was exactly what Baldwin wanted. Suddenly, he turned and charged.

Christendom's tactics during this period were founded on one main advantage: the heavy-cavalry charge. Trained knights, armored in chain mail and mounted on big, exquisitely reared warhorses, were battle winners. They operated as shock troops, and the impact of the Christian charge could bulldoze enemy formations apart; if they could catch their enemy on open ground, they were almost unbeatable. It was precisely these tactics that had secured so many of the astonishing victories won during the First Crusade. On one occasion a group of only seven hundred Christian knights had defeated an enemy force of twelve thousand Turkish warriors; such was the power of their charge.[4] The trick was to convince an enemy to deploy their forces on flat ground suitable for such a maneuver, and this is exactly what Baldwin had achieved.

Although Baldwin was employing the same kind of attack that his peers had used during the crusade, his assault had an innovative edge. His Turkish opponents were masters of the ambush and the hit-and-run attack. Theirs was a fluid approach to war; they swooped on their enemies like a flock of birds (one chronicler compared them to a "flight of swallows")[5] and retreated just as quickly. Here, however, Baldwin was using those same tactics himself, pretending to flee before turning and unleashing an overpowering attack. The result was an astonishing victory. Despite the huge imbalance in numbers, Baldwin's warriors swept the plain clear of enemy forces before they could respond.[6]

It was an astonishing reversal of fortune and, for his enemies, a wholly unexpected defeat. The survivors from the Turkish army departed almost immediately, and the following day Baldwin returned to Dog River to find the road clear. A couple of weeks later, his battered force entered Jerusalem to a rapturous welcome. On

Christmas Day 1100, Baldwin of Boulogne was solemnly crowned Baldwin I, king of Jerusalem.

Baldwin's embattled journey to Jerusalem would soon seem like little more than a scuffle. As the newly appointed ruler of a state that had been in existence for less than two years, he would confront many far more serious challenges immediately after his arrival. Baldwin's kingdom was a shambles, and his hold as ruler was far from certain. The "kingdom" consisted merely of a motley handful of secondary towns that had been conquered in the final phases of the First Crusade and its immediate aftermath. Jerusalem itself was spiritually precious but economically poor. It controlled no major trade route. It was located in craggy hill country, far from the prosperous farmlands of the coastal plain. It had no mines, and water was scarce. Outside the walls was bandit country, and travelers were often assaulted as they braved the winding roads from the Franks' sole port at Jaffa.

To make matters worse, his army was tiny. To a pragmatic eye, his forces were insufficient even to fend off the attacks of Jerusalem's neighbors, much less to expand the kingdom's borders. His small territory was confronted by powerful enemies on all sides, most importantly the Turkish cities of Damascus and Aleppo and the Shia Muslim caliphate of Egypt, ruled by the Fatimid dynasty, each of which could deploy large field armies. In addition, Tancred of Hauteville, one of his chief noblemen, refused to acknowledge Baldwin's rule.

Baldwin's survival, like that of his kingdom, was far from certain, but his predicament was common to all the newly founded Crusader States. Baldwin's former charge, the County of Edessa to the north in the hills of Anatolia, and the Principality of Antioch in northern Syria—Christian territories founded during the First Crusade—both confronted similar problems: scarce resources, powerful enemies, and limited manpower. Yet their rulers were determined both to survive and to thrive, securing the precious gains made during the First Crusade.

The First Crusade itself began in 1095, at Clermont in France, where Pope Urban II gave a sermon that set this colossal expedition into motion. In his address, Urban berated the knights of France for their avarice, their pride, and their incessant infighting, demanding in restitution for their sins that they wield their swords in God's name. He challenged them to march east and to offer their support to the Byzantine emperor Alexius I Comnenus by defending his crumbling frontiers in eastern Anatolia. More important, he planted a further ambition that had taken root in many hearts: the reconquest of Jerusalem. In return for their service, participating knights were offered a general indulgence (specifically, a cancellation of penance for all confessed sins)—a mighty reward.[7]

The response was enormous. In the wake of the council, and as Urban toured France preaching this message, tens of thousands of warriors joined the campaign. At this early stage, few of those who had sewn crosses onto their clothes had known much either about the enemy they would face or about the lands for which they were headed. Some said they were marching against Saracens (broadly meaning Muslims); most thought they would be fighting pagans (a generic term for non-Christians). It was only when the campaign was well advanced that the name "Turks" became familiar within their ranks.[8]

As recruitment for the campaign gathered pace, hysteria swept across many parts of Christendom. It manifested itself in different ways. In some places, Jews were massacred by mobs (in defiance of church law). In others, people saw strange signs and omens. Armed and unarmed pilgrims took the long roads to the East in the thousands.

In 1096 a mighty horde assembled outside the Byzantine capital, Constantinople, led by the enigmatic preacher Peter the Hermit. But Peter's horde was hardly the disciplined contingent of knights the Byzantines had anticipated. The warriors of the "People's

Crusade" were unruly and caused continual trouble during their crossing of Byzantine territory. In practice, Emperor Alexius was appalled at their arrival and swiftly shunted them over the Bosporus (the narrow sea-lane between Constantinople and Anatolia). After that, it was only months before Peter's ragtag force was torn apart by the Turks at the Battle of Civetot.

After this early failure, the fields outside Constantinople once again began to fill with crusaders, but these were men of a rather different stamp. They were, in large part, contingents of trained troops led by senior noblemen. There were no major kings among them, but their ranks included many illustrious names: Count Stephen of Blois (husband to William the Conqueror's daughter Adela), Bohemond of Taranto (son of the famous Norman conqueror Robert Guiscard), and Tancred of Hauteville (Bohemond's nephew). There was also Duke Godfrey of Bouillon, Count Raymond of Toulouse, Count Hugh of Vermandois, and of course Baldwin of Boulogne, future king of Jerusalem. These rulers and their entourages bore a closer resemblance to the experienced troops desired by Emperor Alexius, yet there were so many of them that the emperor feared they might chance an attack on Constantinople itself.

These were the beginnings of a troubled relationship between the crusaders and the Byzantines that would characterize their relations for decades. The emperor needed the Franks' support, but he feared them as well. On the other hand, the crusaders needed Alexius's guidance and logistical support, but they also deeply resented the attacks they had suffered from Byzantine war bands during their journey and were annoyed by the Byzantines' cultivated air of sneering superiority. A particular sticking point was the emperor's demand that the crusade commanders swear an oath of allegiance to him and promise to return any formerly Byzantine cities that they might capture. Eventually most leaders were corralled, grudgingly or not, into taking the oath, but many resisted.

The young firebrand Tancred, one of Bohemond's commanders, was among the most obstinate. When pressed to take the oath, he had the insolence to state that he would only comply if, in return, the emperor would give him the great imperial tent in which Alexius was holding court, provided that it was filled with gold. Alexius was incensed at this impertinent demand and rose from his throne, contemptuously thrusting the young man away. Tancred then had the effrontery to attempt to retaliate physically against the emperor but was subdued by his uncle Bohemond, who shamed him and then forced him to take the oath.[9] Tancred submitted willingly to no one, and his stubbornness and single-mindedness were to play a major role in shaping the world of the crusader East in the years to come.

Despite this friction, enough of a bond was formed between the emperor and the crusaders for them to collaborate in the campaign's first objective: the reconquest of Nicaea, an important city that had been lost to the Turks in 1081. The Byzantines wanted it back. The siege was a success; the first contingents arrived outside its walls on May 6, 1097, and the city was under Byzantine control by June 19.

Their next target was the great Turk-held city of Antioch, which lay on Anatolia's southern margins. This city had been in Byzantine hands as recently as 1084 and represented a formidable obstacle to the crusaders' goal of reaching Jerusalem. From the crusaders' perspective, the conquest of Antioch may have been desirable but was probably not essential: it was a long way from Jerusalem, and they could have chosen simply to steer clear of its walls. For the Byzantines, however, Antioch's return would constitute a substantial advance in their reconquest of Anatolia from the Turks.

The journey to reach Antioch across Anatolia was torturous in the extreme. Many perished in the inhospitable landscape, succumbing to dehydration, starvation, or exposure. The Turks of Anatolia repeatedly attacked the crusader column, although they were soundly defeated when they risked a pitched battle outside the ruined city of Dorylaion. By the time the crusaders finally reached Antioch on October 20, their numbers were much reduced.[10]

Despite their suffering, in the final weeks of the crusaders'
advance upon Antioch they felt a growing sense of opportunism.
These lands were ripe for conquest. Both Anatolia and Syria had
been seized by the Turks only a few decades earlier, and the local Arab, Armenian, and Syriac peoples bitterly resented their rule.
With the advent of the crusade, many local leaders grasped the
chance to break into open rebellion against their Turkish masters.
The precariousness of Turkish authority was only exacerbated by rivalries between individual Turkish commanders. Their great leader,
the Turkish sultan Malik Shah, had died only a few years before,
and the Turkish sultanate was in a state of civil war.

The fragility of Turkish rule became increasingly evident as the
First Crusade crossed the Taurus Mountains and as, in city after
city, the local Armenian people threw out their Turkish overlords,
welcoming or seeking aid from the crusaders. At this stage the
Franks may not have intended to seek permanent control of these
Armenian cities. They may simply have been preparing for the siege
of Antioch by establishing a zone of friendly territory around the
city. Nevertheless, the readiness of many people in these Armenian
areas to accept Frankish control dangled the possibility of long-
term conquest.

During this phase of the campaign, two ambitious young lords
made names for themselves: Tancred of Hauteville and Baldwin of
Boulogne. These two commanders, each with a small fast-moving
contingent, were dispatched to secure various cities that lay on or
near the crusaders' line of march. Most notably, in the autumn of
1097 these adventurers managed to take the major cities of Mamistra and Tarsus, located in the fertile coastlands of Cilicia, lying to the north of Antioch. They had probably been instructed
to claim the cities in the name of the crusading army as a whole,
but they clearly saw the conquests as a route to their own personal
enrichment.[11] At both Tarsus and Mamistra, Tancred and Baldwin
quarreled over who should take control. Their disputes eventually
escalated into a bitter and bloody skirmish when it became clear

that neither would yield possession to the other. After this ugly incident, Baldwin and Tancred had little communication with one another for over three years. Their next encounter took place far to the south when Baldwin traveled to Jerusalem to claim the throne.

Soon after this incident, Baldwin broke away from the main crusader army. He had in his company an Armenian called Bagrat who had joined him at the siege of Nicaea. Presumably as a result of conversations with him, Baldwin was persuaded to venture eastward, toward the Euphrates River and further into Armenian territory, allying with local Christian nobles and driving out local Turkish garrisons. During this expedition he was approached by the bishop of Edessa, who, representing his master T'oros, the city's ruler, sought Baldwin's support against the Turks. Baldwin set out with an escort of eighty knights and was rapturously received, both in Edessa and in the neighboring towns.[12] He became ruler soon afterward, following a rebellion against T'oros, and by doing so founded the first Crusader State: the County of Edessa.[13]

While Baldwin was busy establishing himself in Edessa, the main army was occupied with the grueling siege of Antioch. After an eight-month standoff, during which the Franks beat off two Turkish relief armies, they finally took the city on June 3, 1098. The leaders' oath to Alexius obliged them to hand the city immediately back to the Byzantines, but instead, Bohemond of Taranto took it for himself.[14]

The basis for Bohemond's seizure of the city was a promise he had extracted from the crusade's leaders shortly before the city's fall. At this point the crusade had been teetering on the brink of defeat; the crusaders were weakening daily, and Antioch's impressive defenses remained fundamentally intact. To make matters worse, they had just received news that a third colossal Turkish relief army was approaching under the leadership of Karbugha, ruler of Mosul. Moreover, it was becoming increasingly clear that Emperor Alexius had abandoned them to their fate. In desperation and with nowhere else to turn, they agreed to a deal Bohemond proposed: if he could get the crusaders into the city, then he could keep it for himself.

On June 2, a windy night, Bohemond left the crusaders' camp and headed away from the city with a force of cavalry, hoping the Turkish garrison would assume that he was marching off to fight the approaching Turkish army, thus lulling the city's defenders into a false sense of security. After dark, he doubled back, returning stealthily to Antioch's walls. There, by prior arrangement, an insider lowered a bull's-hide rope ladder to let the crusaders mount the ramparts. The first warriors to climb did so reluctantly, wary of some kind of trick. But once twenty-five men had made the ascent, the remainder climbed so eagerly that the stone parapet to which the rope was attached crumbled. The ladder fell, and several unlucky climbers were impaled on a row of wooden stakes at the wall's foot. The small company gathered atop Antioch's walls quaked at the thought that the city's defenders might have been wakened by their fallen comrades' screams. Still, nothing happened; their cries had been drowned out by the sound of the wind. The rope ladder was then reattached, and when sixty fighters had assembled on the wall, they assaulted the neighboring towers and secured control of a postern gate. The crusaders were in.[15]

In the bloody aftermath of Antioch's fall a second Crusader State was born: the Principality of Antioch. Bohemond's title as ruler of the city would not go uncontested. Two days after the city fell to the crusaders, the first companies of Karbugha's Turkish army arrived outside its gates; the former Frankish besiegers were now themselves besieged. Karbugha pressed the crusaders closely, and they began to starve; after the lengthy crusader siege, the city was entirely bereft of food. Many deserted. The most famous of those to flee was Count Stephen of Blois, who returned to western Christendom in ignominy and shame. He was later persuaded by his wife to redeem himself by returning on crusade in 1101.[16] Eventually, on June 28, Bohemond led what was left of the crusader army out of Antioch's Bridge Gate. By now they had lost most of their horses, so the starving Christian army marched out on foot to confront an enemy whose forces were both more numerous and better equipped.

The Turks, who generally fought on horseback, should have been able to rain arrows on the dismounted, slow-moving crusaders without ever needing to engage in hand-to-hand combat. Nevertheless, the steely discipline imposed by Bohemond, coupled with a strong sense of religious euphoria that led some to claim that they had been assisted in battle by a company of white knights led by Saint George, Saint Demetrius, and Saint Mercurius, maintained order in the Christian ranks.[17] The crusader army also bore a mighty relic before them: the spear that had pierced Christ's side at the Crucifixion, discovered two weeks earlier beneath the floor of Saint Peter's Church in Antioch by a pilgrim named Peter Bartholomew. Not all had believed the relic to be genuine, but many had interpreted the finding of the spear as a sign of divine favor.[18]

In the Turkish camp, by contrast, Karbugha struggled to assert control over many of his lieutenants, some of whom were former enemies.[19] His forces, dispersed around the long city walls, engaged haphazardly with the crusaders, in part negating their superior numbers.[20] Most importantly, the Turks allowed themselves to be drawn into close combat and were cut to pieces by the heavily armed crusader infantry. The outcome was an astonishing victory for the crusaders, one that many believed to be miraculous.

Returning to the city in triumph, Bohemond then confronted Count Raymond of Toulouse, who challenged Bohemond on the question of who should rule Antioch. Bohemond claimed the city for himself, but other lords, including Raymond, felt that Alexius should be invited to take control. Raymond was eventually frustrated in his design, and after a bitter exchange he set out south with the remainder of the crusade, bound for Jerusalem.

Increasingly, the crusade leadership was beginning to split between those who had no intention of remaining in the East and wished only to complete their pilgrimage and return home and those who, either out of piety or opportunism or both, wanted to stay and carve out territories for themselves. From this point on, as the crusade headed south toward Jerusalem, leaders began to seize towns and cities in an attempt to assemble a nucleus of territory that could provide the basis for later growth. Raymond of Toulouse, in particular, was especially eager to acquire a foothold in the region, but he was repeatedly thwarted in this attempt.

Raymond's greatest humiliation took place at Jerusalem. It was the summer of 1099, and the crusader armies had passed south along the Levantine coast. With Jerusalem just over the horizon, their goal was almost achieved. When they had set out on crusade, the holy city had been a Turkish possession, but while they had been besieging Antioch, it had been conquered by the Fatimid caliphate of Egypt.

The crusaders harbored little enmity toward the Egyptian Fatimids. Indeed, they had been discussing an alliance with them for almost two years.[21] As they advanced upon Jerusalem, they hoped they could persuade the Fatimids to yield Jerusalem in a treaty that would maintain positive relations with this important regional power. But the negotiations collapsed, and the crusaders laid siege to the holy city soon afterward. This began a period of intense conflict that culminated on July 15, 1099, when the city fell. Jerusalem's conquest was followed by a brutal massacre of the populace—perhaps as many as three thousand people were killed.[22]

In the aftermath of the city's gruesome fall, the question arose of who should be its ruler. Raymond was an obvious candidate, given that he was a powerful and rich commander who was willing to remain in the East. Yet again he was outmaneuvered, and rule was granted instead to Duke Godfrey of Bouillon. Disgraced, Raymond was incensed and departed shortly afterward on a pilgrimage to the River Jordan. Despite his wrath and once again against a backdrop of slaughter and intrigue, a third Crusader State had been born: the crusader Kingdom of Jerusalem.

The Crusader States were now taking shape in earnest. To the north, the County of Edessa lay in the craggy regions of southern Anatolia, the only Crusader State without access to the sea. To the southwest of Edessa was the Principality of Antioch, whose territory was already being assertively expanded by its first ruler, Bohemond of Taranto. And far to the south, the Kingdom of Jerusalem lay on the edge of the desert.

The fourth and final Crusader State was founded several years later by Count Raymond of Toulouse after a series of failed attempts to establish his own state. First, he attempted to establish a lordship around the city of Latakia in northern Syria, an endeavor that angered Bohemond because Latakia was close to Antioch and formed part of its traditional hinterland. He then participated in another large crusade, launched in 1101, that sought to re-create the triumphs of the First Crusade but that met disaster while trying to cross Anatolia. Eventually, he marshaled his remaining forces and in 1103 laid siege to the city of Tripoli (in modern-day northern Lebanon). Raymond would die four years before the conquest of Tripoli in 1109. Even so, his dogged determination in the face of repeated reverses laid the foundation for the establishment of this final Christian territory: the County of Tripoli.

The challenges confronting the early rulers of the Crusader States were formidable. They suffered deficiencies in manpower and resources, and their newly established titles of "king," "prince," and "count" were mere inventions and lacked the centuries of tradition and heritage that gave such noble and royal appellations the sense of permanence and authority they required. Moreover, Jerusalem's ruler, Godfrey of Bouillon, died a year after taking power, precipitating his brother Baldwin's speedy journey south to take power.

These conquerors were also divided among themselves. After Baldwin's coronation on Christmas Day 1100, he and Tancred of Hauteville were once again at daggers drawn, just as they had been in Cilicia all those years earlier. Tancred had already made it clear that he did not recognize Baldwin as his king, and their dispute was only inflamed by persistent quarreling among the nobility over Tancred's control over the recently conquered town of Haifa.[23] The deadlock, which held the potential for civil war, was finally broken in March when a delegation arrived from Antioch. Its ruler, Bohemond I, was in Turkish captivity, and Antioch's nobles wanted Tancred to rule in his place. Tancred's promotion ended the impasse with Baldwin. Tancred was willing to yield his estates in the Kingdom of Jerusalem so that he could secure the prize of ruling the Principality of Antioch. Consequently, he and Baldwin patched up a hasty peace, and Tancred departed for the north.

In the years that followed, all four of the Crusader States faced grave military threats from their Turkish and Egyptian neighbors. The intensity of this danger compelled their rulers to work together, but it was also never lost on any of them that their Christian coreligionists were as much rivals as they were allies.

Surrounded by foreign enemies, the Franks' military policies in their early years were aggressive in the extreme. This was a strategic necessity. Their rulers were critically in need of land and cities to supply the income and manpower necessary to make their fledgling realms tenable in the face of far stronger opponents. The operative principle was clear: expand or be driven into the sea. Moreover, the astonishing victories of the First Crusade had engendered a sense of fear among the neighboring Turkish rulers, which the crusaders were eager to exploit. In the early 1100s both Antioch and Jerusalem frequently played on this fear to demand tribute from the Turks in exchange for peace.

Deliberately instilling a sense of fear in a foe was a weapon commonly used by the Normans of southern Italy—Tancred's people. One Norman chronicler describes a particularly effective instance of this practice during the Norman conquest of southern Italy from the Byzantines, several decades earlier. He recalled a moment when the Greeks were besieging a Norman castle and had sent a mounted envoy to demand the garrison's surrender. The envoy was greeted by a Norman knight called Hugh, who took the envoy's mount and began to stroke its mane. Then he suddenly punched the horse on the neck with his bare hand, killing it instantly, and the Normans threw its carcass over the castle walls. The Byzantine commanders were so appalled at this naked display of strength that they refused to tell their soldiers what had happened for fear they would be reluctant to fight in the coming battle (which they did indeed lose).[24] Fear could be a powerful weapon.

Still, fear needed to be maintained by continued conquests if it was to retain its potency. In the south, Baldwin I's primary objective was to secure as many ports as possible along the Levantine coast. These harbors were essential to his realm's survival because they opened up corridors of maritime communication with western Christendom, which could funnel reinforcements and pilgrims to the Latin East (another name for the Crusader States) and bolster their fledgling armies. Moreover, these ports would also give the Franks a stake in the lucrative commercial networks that crisscrossed the Mediterranean, creating opportunities for tax revenue and increased communications.

Christendom's leading naval powers were keen to support Baldwin in this endeavor, and the Italian city-states of Venice, Genoa, and Pisa each sent fleets to the eastern Mediterranean, seeking not only to serve God through holy war in defense of Jerusalem but also to pursue their own interests by building up their trading position in the Near East.[25] Consequently, in the early years of his reign Baldwin I maintained the momentum built up by the crusade and seized port after port, including Arsuf (1101), Caesarea (1101), Acre (1104), Beirut (1110), and Sidon (1110). He also struck inland into the fertile regions of the Hawran and southward into the Transjordan region, aggressively expanding his borders.

Conquering the Near East's Mediterranean ports was vital for the Crusader States, but the Franks' long-term survival could only be truly guaranteed by the destruction of their enemies' major centers of power: Cairo, Damascus, and Aleppo. The conquest of any one of these territories would almost certainly have paved the way for the imminent collapse of the other two (see map on page viii), and the military history of the Crusades in the years following the initial consolidation of the Franks' position in the East is essentially a tale of their repeated attempts to achieve such a goal.

Cairo (and the surrounding Nile delta) was a powerhouse in the Mediterranean. At this time, it was controlled by the Fatimids, an Arab dynasty that had taken control in 969. Technically the Fatimid state was under the leadership of a caliph, but by the mid-twelfth century effective power lay in the hands of the caliph's vizier (the leading minister), whose own authority rested squarely on the support of the army. The Fatimids were minority rulers—they were proponents of the Ismaili branch of Shia Islam, but their subjects were for the most part a mixture of Sunni Muslims, Coptic Christians, and Jews. The Fatimid army was large, but its composition was unusual, in that its core contingents were drawn from different ethnic groups, including Armenian archers; Mamluks (Turkish slave soldiers), who operated as cavalry; and infantry from Egypt's southern borders.[26] The Fatimids were also exceptionally wealthy. The fertile lands of the Nile delta produced much of the region's food, and its bustling ports of Alexandria and Damietta sat astride two long-standing commercial arteries: the gold routes from sub-Saharan Africa and the Silk Roads from the Far East. Possession of Egypt would therefore bring unimaginable wealth to its conqueror, probably sufficient—if combined with the crusaders' existing lands—to dominate the entire Middle East. The crusaders were well aware of Egypt's potential, and even before the conquest of Jerusalem the suggestion had been made that the crusaders should seize Egypt first so that its resources could underwrite the conquest of the Holy Land.[27]

Damascus, lying east of the Anti-Lebanon Mountains, was a large city under Turkish control, with a predominantly Sunni Muslim population and surrounded by dense fruit orchards.[28] It was a famous intellectual center, and its walls encompassed many libraries. By the time of the First Crusade, Damascus was still large and powerful, but its glory days were a thing of the past. Its heyday had been under the Umayyad dynasty many centuries earlier, and many of its greatest buildings, such as the Great Mosque, had been constructed at that time. Despite its reduced population and significance within the Islamic world as a whole, Damascus remained one of the linchpins of power in the Near East. If the Franks could take control, they not only would add a major city to their existing lands but would also be able to cut off all communications between Egypt and Aleppo, both of which could then be reduced separately. Again, the Franks fully recognized the importance of conquering Damascus, and they sent envoys demanding its surrender as early as 1100.[29]

Aleppo was equally vital. Surrounded by high walls punctured by seven gates and with a mighty citadel perched on a high mound at its center, it dominated the political landscape in northern Syria. The scholarly traveler al-Muqaddasi, who passed through the region in the late tenth century, spoke warmly of the inhabitants, presenting them as civilized, wealthy, and talented.[30] The city was situated close to the western banks of the Euphrates River, and Aleppo's ruler controlled many of the river crossings that linked Syria and the Holy Land to the Turks' core territories in Iraq or more distant Persia. Its fall would consequently impede the lines of communication connecting the Turks' lands in the coastal Levantine region to their lands in the east. Aleppo was also wealthy. It was a center for trade, and its markets played host to merchants from Anatolia, Egypt, Iraq, and even the distant lands of India and China. The conquest of Aleppo was a vital objective, particularly for its closest Frankish rival, the Principality of Antioch, whose rulers recognized almost immediately that Aleppo was both their greatest local rival and their most pressing military goal.[31] Godfrey of Bouillon and another crusade commander, Baldwin of Bourcq, had been discussing the city's conquest even before the conclusion of the First Crusade.[32] Bohemond of Taranto, prince of Antioch, contemplated blockading the city with siege forts—almost certainly preparatory to a direct assault—as early as 1100.[33]

The crusaders' long-term strategic objectives—Cairo, Damascus, and Aleppo—were widely understood to be overriding priorities among the leaders of the Crusader States from their earliest days in the Levant. In later years, generation after generation of Frankish rulers showed dogged consistency chasing these goals. If the crusaders were to achieve dominance across the entire region, then these vital cities had to fall. The future of the Crusader States would be decided at their gates.

Initially, all three of these cities were too powerful to risk attacking them frontally. The first crusaders made no attempt on Aleppo and purposely avoided Damascus. Throughout his reign, Baldwin I of Jerusalem occasionally raided Damascene territory, but he launched no assault upon Damascus itself; in the short term he had to concentrate on the ports. Similarly, an invasion of Egypt was simply too great an endeavor to seriously contemplate.

However, as the years passed, and as the crusaders steadily consolidated their position in northern Syria, it became increasingly clear that Aleppo was vulnerable. The city's relentless infighting and political weakness rendered it susceptible to attack, which soon came to the attention of the Frankish rulers of Antioch. The stage was set for a drawn-out war for control of the city, one that would lead to the Field of Blood.

———•———

When Tancred took up the reins of Antiochene power, he did so with an aggression worthy of his ancestors. He was a violent hawk of a man, bred for conquest. His combative nature was molded by a deep faith and a shrewd, opportunistic eye, qualities that would work to his advantage in the years to come. He was also young. Like so many knights of his time, he was to pack a great deal of living into a short life. When he took power in Antioch he was around twenty-five years old, and he did not live to see his fortieth year.

Tancred was from pedigree warrior stock. His grandfather was the great Robert Guiscard, the Norman conqueror whose family had seized control in Sicily and southern Italy only a few decades before.[34] Tancred's uncle, Bohemond, was Robert Guiscard's son. Raised in the southern Mediterranean, Tancred was well attuned to the various cultures ranged along its shores. His family were long-standing enemies of the Byzantine Empire, but there had been times when they had conducted extensive diplomacy with the imperial court in Constantinople. They were also familiar with the Muslim world; indeed, the Normans' lands in Sicily had formerly been Islamic territory, and the isle itself had a large Muslim population. Bohemond's and Tancred's forces may well have contained many who were fluent in Arabic as well as Greek.[35]

In the spring of 1101, when Tancred arrived in Antioch, the principality's future was uncertain. It had many enemies. Like his fellow crusader conquerors to the south, Tancred needed fertile land to supply him with food and revenue, and he needed ports to open up communications and trade with western Christendom. He also faced competing claims for the city, both from the Byzantine emperor—who was enraged that Antioch had not been immediately surrendered to his control—and from the neighboring Turkish ruler, Ridwan of Aleppo, who was a major regional power.

Before his captivity, Bohemond had grasped the importance of all these imperatives and had already enjoyed some success in building his position, particularly in battle against the Aleppans.[36] Tancred swiftly set to work extending his uncle's initial gains. His first strike was to the north, into the fertile plains of Cilicia. Cilicia's main towns, Mamistra, Adana, and Tarsus, fell to Tancred in swift succession. Then he bent his will upon Byzantine-held Latakia, initiating a siege in the summer of 1101 that lasted for one and a half years. The conquest of this great city, resplendent with its ancient aqueducts and fallen Roman statues, clearly stretched Tancred's meager military resources, but the gamble paid off and, with its fall, Tancred possessed an important harbor.[37]

By 1102 Tancred's power was rising so quickly that when his former rival Baldwin I of Jerusalem called for help following a crushing defeat at the hands of the Fatimid Egyptians, he was able to lead an army south to Jerusalem, hundreds of miles from Antioch's frontiers. So great was his strength that his city suffered no attack during his absence.

The Principality of Antioch had begun to consolidate itself into a more stable form, but although Tancred had substantially expanded its borders, the weaknesses of his personal position as ruler were about to be revealed. He was not Antioch's prince, merely its custodian. His tenure would end the moment his uncle Bohemond returned from captivity. Tancred was thus rather less than enthusiastic about contributing to his uncle's ransom. This reluctance was well-known to Bohemond, who (fortunately for him) had other friends who were willing to effect his release, in 1103. He regained power immediately afterward. Bohemond was understandably annoyed by his nephew's behavior, and soon after his return he stripped Tancred of most of his landholdings and resources.[38] Having tasted power, Tancred was once again merely his uncle's lieutenant.

Despite their troubled relationship, Tancred and his uncle were united by their commitment to expanding the principality, and Bohemond swiftly set about launching attack after attack on his enemies' frontiers. For the most part these lunges were successful, and by 1104 Bohemond was sufficiently secure in his power to lead his main army, supported by Tancred and the patriarch of Antioch, across the Euphrates in response to a call for assistance from the neighboring County of Edessa.

Edessan power, like Antioch's, was rising fast. When its first ruler, Baldwin of Boulogne, had set out to claim the throne of Jerusalem, he had handed the reins of governance to his kinsman

Baldwin of Bourcq. Like his predecessor, Baldwin of Bourcq proved to be an aggressive campaigner. Only the year before, he had launched a long-distance raid far to the south, attacking the Arab towns of Raqqa and Qalat Jabar.[39] Now, however, he was trying something even more ambitious.

The prominent town of Harran lay on Edessa's southern border and had recently descended into chaos. A rebel named Mohammed al-Isfahani had led a successful uprising against the town's Turkish master. Then Mohammed himself had been assassinated by his lieutenant Jawuli during a prolonged drinking bout.[40] The Franks saw this infighting as too good an opportunity to pass up, and Baldwin of Bourcq assembled Edessa's army and marched on Harran, placing it under siege while seeking support from Antioch. Tancred and Bohemond responded swiftly, motivated not merely by the prospect of securing a new conquest but also by the news that the neighboring Turkish rulers Sokman and Jokermish had united and were marching both to break the siege of Harran and, more worrisome, to assault Edessa itself. There were the makings here of a major battle.

In the event, Sokman and Jokermish outwitted the Franks. After a brief attack on Edessa, they lured the combined Frankish host away from Harran and into a pursuit that drew them far to the south, away from their own frontiers to a battlefield of the Turks' choosing. The Christian and Turkish armies were reasonably well matched with about ten thousand troops each when they met near the Balikh River. In the Christian army, Bohemond held the army's right flank, Tancred was in the center, and Baldwin of Bourcq held the left.[41] Their forces were well equipped to deal with Turkish tactics, and they arrayed themselves in a tight, armored formation, their locked shields forming a solid defense against Turkish arrows, rather like a Roman testudo.[42] The encounter was fierce, and both sides suffered many casualties. Even so, the Turks were able to split the Christian forces, and eventually Baldwin of Bourcq's line crumpled, provoking a general Christian retreat.

Part of the Christian army's problem seems to have been a lack of unity. Their leaders were squabbling among themselves, and Tancred and Baldwin especially disliked one another. This was exacerbated by discontent among their Armenian troops, who were deeply concerned about an event that had taken place during the siege of Harran. A Frankish knight had decided to play a joke on the city's defenders. He opened a loaf of bread, defecated into it, and placed the bread outside the city gates to see if any of the starving inhabitants would be hungry enough to eat it. The mischief maker probably saw this as just an unpleasant prank; the Armenians saw such defilement of bread as a deeply sinful act.[43] From this point, there seems to have been a dispiriting belief among the Armenian troops that the army was already doomed.

The crusader defeat at Harran on May 7, 1104, was a debacle. The surviving forces, far from friendly territory, had a long way to travel before reaching safety. Baldwin of Bourcq, count of Edessa, was captured during the fighting and many more men were lost in the muddy retreat. Heavy rain turned the road into slurry and the Christian forces were forced to jettison their baggage and heavier weapons to escape.

As the bedraggled survivors slunk back over the Edessan frontier, the Franks' many enemies seized the opportunity to attack both Antioch and Edessa. Antioch's Cilician lands rebelled, and a Byzantine fleet retook Latakia. The Turks were keen to press their advantage. Sokman plundered the abandoned Christian baggage train, equipping his troops with their weapons and clothing. He then led his disguised forces, marching under Frankish banners, to the Antiochene frontier, where they seized several castles.[44]

For the Franks, the Battle of Harran and its aftermath painfully underlined a series of vital strategic lessons. The first was that if the crusaders were going to survive, they were going to have to work together. Fulcher of Chartres roundly criticized the defeated Franks for their quarreling, identifying it as the central cause of the disaster.[45] Second, the battle had demonstrated the fragility of the Frankish position in Syria. A defeat on this scale could not simply be dismissed as part of the cut and thrust of frontier life. The Franks were a new presence in these lands and their population was sparse. Their Turkish enemies may have been able to whistle up new forces fairly swiftly following a defeat, drawing on the numerous Turkmen tribes that traversed the Jazira region to the east of the Euphrates, but the Franks did not have the same luxury.[46] If they lost their army, they would have to make do with their remaining soldiers until new forces could arrive either from Jerusalem or from western Europe. Moreover, they were ruling over a variety of different peoples whose loyalty or acquiescence to Frankish rule was predicated on the Frankish ability either to provide security or, for the more rebellious, to enforce control. There was a real danger that a major defeat could create a domino effect of rebellion and invasion, eventually driving the Franks into the sea.

The Franks survived, but their landholdings shrank dramatically. For Tancred, the Battle of Harran was undoubtedly a humiliation at the strategic level, but at the personal level, it created an opportunity for him to regain power. Baldwin of Bourcq was in prison. Edessa needed a leader. The populace invited Tancred to step in. Bohemond fully supported this suggestion, probably keen to rid himself of his power-hungry nephew. Tancred was to remain the acting ruler of Edessa at least until Baldwin of Bourcq should return from captivity. Soon afterward Bohemond decided that Antioch's interests would be best served by seeking reinforcements from western Christendom. Consequently, he left Antioch in Tancred's keeping and set out for the West, where, several years later, he launched an overambitious campaign against the Byzantines, an attempt that ended in failure. Bohemond died in Italy in 1111 without ever returning to Syria.[47]

Bohemond's later wars against the Greeks may have ended in disaster, but his absence enhanced Tancred's position in Antioch in two ways. Most important, Tancred was now free to rule Antioch (and temporarily Edessa) as he wished. In addition Bohemond did his nephew the great service of sending him a royal bride.

When Bohemond returned to western Christendom, he was heralded as the great victor of the First Crusade. The adulation provoked by his arrival bordered on the hysterical. He was received into the highest circles, and nobles sought him out to act as godfather to their children. Most important, he was permitted to marry Constance, the daughter of King Philip I of France.[48] He also requested that Tancred be granted the hand of Philip's other daughter, Cecilia. For Cecilia, still only a child, the prospect of being dispatched to a distant frontier to marry a grizzled crusader warlord must have been intimidating. For Tancred—little more than an adventurer and occasional caretaker ruler—this was an astonishing development. Marriage to a royal princess was a substantial honor: it raised his social status, legitimized his position as ruler, and substantially enhanced his position, given that his former dubious credentials had derived predominantly from his military competence.

With both Antioch and Edessa under his control, Tancred was free from all restraint. Even with depleted resources, he swiftly reversed Christian fortunes in northern Syria. In 1105, when Ridwan of Aleppo launched a direct assault on the principality, Tancred decisively crushed his enemies' forces before reconquering many of the towns lost in the wake of Harran. Tancred went on to push deep into Turk-held territory, posing a genuine threat even to the great city of Aleppo.

In the years that followed, Tancred continued to strengthen his position. Latakia was retaken. Cilicia was resubdued. Increasingly, Antiochene forces made headway into the mountainous region to the south dominated by the Arab-ruled towns of Apamea and Shaizar. In this atmosphere of expansion and rising supremacy, Tancred's broader objectives slowly crystallized. Militarily, perhaps the most tantalizing goal was Aleppo, the key to northern Syria. It had been riven by infighting for many years and would be a rich prize. Pressed by Edessa from the north and by Antioch from the west, and faced on the east by often-unfriendly Turkish chieftains, its conquest was becoming a realistic goal.

Steadily Tancred began to conquer the city's satellite towns. Al-Atharib fell in 1110. Zardana, a town lying in the lands between Antioch and Aleppo, was taken the following year. The inhabitants of settlements lying to the east of Aleppo (the opposite side from Antioch) were beginning to flee, fearing the Franks' advances. When he was not pummeling Aleppo's hinterlands, Tancred was demanding tribute from its rulers—a strategy that strengthened his position with minimal effort, while keeping his enemies weakened.

Tancred proved himself to be a shrewd conqueror. He recognized the need to work with local powers, whether Christian or Muslim. He was well aware that he needed local support if he was to consolidate his territorial gains in the long term. Consequently, he made sure to defend Armenian interests by seeking the liberation of those who had been taken captive by the Turks. He was so generous toward the Armenians in his lands that after his death the often-acerbic Armenian writer Matthew of Edessa remembered Tancred as a saintly man whose life was characterized by compassion and humility—a remarkable and thought-provoking verdict for so hardened a campaigner.[49]

Tancred was also careful not to alienate the Muslim farming communities in the area; he needed their cooperation, their labor, and their taxes.[50] There were even some important defections to the Christian camp; in 1107–1108 Khotlogh, governor of Azaz, rebelled against Ridwan of Aleppo and sought to hand his town over to Tancred in return for another town.[51] One group of Arab refugees is said to have come all the way from distant Basra on the Persian Gulf, seeking Tancred's protection from the Turks.[52] Antioch was in the ascendency, outcompeting its Turkish and Greek rivals. The noose was tightening around Aleppo. The battle for Syria was warming up.

Tancred's bullish exploits in the north were matched by those of the Frankish lords to the south. Christendom's interests in that region took a major step forward in 1109 with the realization of Raymond of Toulouse's long-cherished dream: the conquest of Tripoli. This was a long-awaited advance for the Crusader States, even if the unfortunate Raymond did not live to see it.

Tripoli itself lay on a promontory jutting into the Mediterranean, a location that rendered it unassailable on three sides and created a shelter for shipping. It was a center of trade, with bustling bazaars and a large population crammed into houses up to six stories high.[53] On its one landward side, the city was fortified by a great ditch and high walls. There was even an aqueduct providing fresh water. Beyond its iron gates, the land rose steadily up toward the heights of the Lebanese mountains, a range running parallel to the coast and only slightly inland. Irrigated by the plentiful rains that fell when clouds sweeping in from the sea were borne up to cross these peaks, the surrounding country was rich. Sugarcane was grown along the coastline, and the sugarcane plantations were mixed with those of oranges and lemons. Date palms and bananas grew in abundance. The ruler of Tripoli would be both wealthy and well defended.

Raymond did not wait for Tripoli's fall before founding his county. He set to work almost immediately after laying siege, conquering the surrounding towns and building an encampment outside Tripoli's walls that soon became a major settlement in its own right. Frankish forces conquered much of the coastline to the south and also pushed northward, around the shoulder of the mountains, and inland into the Homs Gap and toward the Turk-ruled cities of Hama and Shaizar. During the early years of the siege, the Tripolitans put up a staunch defense under the leadership of their *qadi* (judge) Fakhr al-Mulk and his descendants. Their main source of assistance was Fatimid Egypt. Overland resupply was impossible, given the presence of a besieging army on its landward flank, so the Egyptians reinforced the city by sea.

Despite the mounting pressure, Tripoli's populace struggled valiantly against the Frankish invaders. On several occasions they sallied out from the walls to assault the crusaders' siege works. On one occasion in 1105 they managed to penetrate the Frankish lines far enough to start a raging fire within their encampment. Among the structures consumed by the blaze was the building from which Raymond of Toulouse was surveying their attack. When it collapsed, Raymond fell into the conflagration, and he died soon afterward.[54] With his death, the struggle was continued by Raymond's cousin (once-removed) William Jordan of Cerdanya.

Even before the capture of the city itself, the Frankish County of Tripoli was fast becoming a force to be reckoned with. To the north, Tancred of Antioch was well aware of its rising power, and Tripoli's northern borders were starting to converge with Antioch's southernmost marches. To the south, Baldwin I of Jerusalem was equally keen to ensure that his interests would not be impeded by this rising power.

The siege came to a triumphant end shortly after the arrival of an army from western Christendom, led by Raymond of Toulouse's son Bertrand in early 1109. His was a significant fleet of forty ships supported by additional naval squadrons from Genoa and a large war chest donated by the Byzantine emperor; cumulatively Bertrand had enough troops and resources to decisively affect the regional balance of power.[55] His arrival should have been an opportunity for the Crusader States, but Bertrand proved to be a divisive figure, and he started to pick fights almost immediately after making landfall at Antioch's nearest harbor, Saint Symeon.

As soon as Tancred learned of Bertrand's arrival in the principality, he hurried to greet him. Large fleets of newly arrived Frankish warriors were not a common sight, and he hoped to enroll them in a campaign that would advance Antiochene interests. Bertrand, however, had other ideas. He responded to Tancred's welcome by demanding that he hand over those portions of Antioch that had briefly been held by his father, Raymond, following the city's capture during the First Crusade. Tancred's—and previously Bohemond's—possession of these sections of the city had not been contested in over ten years (an epoch in the fast-moving world of the Latin East). Nevertheless, Tancred was not ready to lose a powerful potential ally, so he declared that he was prepared to consider the request if Bertrand would help him expand his principality. Such willingness to compromise was not normal for Tancred, but despite his enthusiasm, the talks disintegrated, and the two men parted in anger. Bertrand's first act in the Levant had been to create an enemy.

Immediately afterward, events escalated into a full-blown crisis. Bertrand set sail for the south, landing at Tortosa. The town was held by William Jordan's men (Raymond's successor and the County of Tripoli's current ruler), but Bertrand summarily took control and demanded that William Jordan cede his lands to him. The implication of his demands was clear: Bertrand wanted the county for himself, and William Jordan should consider himself evicted from power. William demurred; these were his lands and he had defended the county against many perils. He too had rights to the County of Tripoli. Bertrand had made another enemy.

The upshot was that William Jordan turned to Tancred, offering to acknowledge him as his lord if he would lend his support against Bertrand. This request gave Tancred an opportunity both to expand his principality to the south (by becoming overlord to William Jordan's lands) and to cut the presumptuous Bertrand down to size—a pleasing thought. Tancred assembled his army and headed south.

Bertrand, for his part, was belatedly becoming aware of his acute need for friends in the Latin East, so, like William Jordan, he too appealed for help. He wrote to Baldwin I of Jerusalem, presenting himself as the aggrieved heir to the County of Tripoli who stood in danger of being denied his birthright. Baldwin agreed to back Bertrand's claims, and he too assembled his army and headed north. At this point, King Baldwin only inflamed the dispute further by writing to Tancred and accusing him of having stolen estates from the count of Edessa, Baldwin of Bourcq. The Edessan ruler himself was also traveling with an armed force south to the siege works outside Tripoli. All the Frankish leaders were converging on Tripoli, all were angry, and all were coming with troops.

There was the potential in the early months of 1109 for a ruinous civil war within the Latin East that would have been disastrous for the Franks. Fortunately, both Tancred and Baldwin could see the need for diplomacy. They reached a compromise that was sufficiently satisfactory to all parties to deter them from killing each other. Bertrand would receive the bulk of the County of Tripoli, but he would also accept Baldwin I of Jerusalem as his overlord. William Jordan, for his part, would retain those lands he had conquered during his time as ruler. This agreement also pleased Tancred, who became overlord to William Jordan's estates, which lay just to the south of Antiochene territory. Tancred also received some lands he had formerly held in Jerusalem, but in exchange he was required to return a group of estates he had seized from Baldwin of Bourcq.

Baldwin I of Jerusalem seems to have been the primary peacemaker here. He may have fought Tancred in Cilicia during the First Crusade (eleven years earlier), but those were the acts of his impetuous younger self; experience had weathered him into a wiser and shrewder leader. Tancred was more aggressive. He was prepared to take the field against his coreligionists if he deemed it necessary. Only the previous year, when Baldwin of Bourcq had finally been ransomed following his capture at Harran, he and Tancred had come to blows over Baldwin's restoration to power in Edessa. That violent encounter took place only a few months before their meeting at Tripoli.

Still, by the time they had assembled at the siege of Tripoli, Tancred too could see the virtue in negotiation, and he supported the proposed resolution. Viewed in hindsight, this agreement was a formative moment in the slow stabilization of the Latin East: four Frankish Crusader States were emerging from the wars, treaties, compromises, and ambitions of the post-crusade world. Even so, among these four powers, Antioch and Jerusalem remained the major players, and the question of which would achieve supremacy had yet to be decided.[56]

With this agreement in hand, the crusaders were free to turn their attention to the still-untaken city of Tripoli. Their combined armies represented a formidable force, but the Franks' land army probably was not the biggest cause of concern for the beleaguered inhabitants. The city had weathered many landward assaults, but it had often survived because it could call on Egyptian naval assistance. Now, however, a Genoese fleet completed the Frankish encirclement of the city, barring entry to the port, and adverse winds prevented the arrival of Egyptian reinforcements.

The assault could now proceed in earnest. Frankish siege tactics during this era generally centered on the use of colossal mobile siege towers. Many of the cities that fell to their armies, either during the First Crusade or in its aftermath, were captured by employing these mighty instruments of war. Siege towers typically fell into two categories. The first type was the classic wheeled construction that was rolled against an enemy's wall to disgorge a horde of fighters onto the ramparts. The second type was an elevated firing platform, generally higher than the enemy's wall, from which archers and crossbowmen could rain missiles on their enemies, sweeping the battlements of defenders in preparation for a general assault.[57] At the siege of Tripoli, the Franks employed the former type, and shortly after they trundled their towers up to the ramparts, the city's leaders capitulated, surrendering in June 1109 after years of heroic defense. The Franks then entered the city and sacked it thoroughly.

The siege of Tripoli could easily have ended in acrimony and civil war among the leaders of the Latin East. In the long run, however, it marked a substantial milestone in the continued development of the Crusader States. Against all the odds, the scattered territories conquered by the First Crusade had been translated into viable states that could now look to the future with some confidence. The majority of the coastline, with its valuable ports and fertile farmlands, was now in Frankish hands.

The history of the early Crusader States, in the years preceding the Field of Blood, is in many ways a catalog of brutal campaigns, widespread destruction, and burning cities. It is a grim tale, and the individuals who rose to prominence were generally those who displayed personal qualities that matched their environment: ruthlessness, combat effectiveness, shrewd calculation, and ambition. Men such as Tancred had such traits in abundance. Even so, it is too easy to lose sight of the other dimension of this struggle. This was also a profoundly religious war, waged in the name of God. Tancred may have used every ounce of realpolitik at his disposal to defend and expand his principality, but the mere existence of the Principality of Antioch, or indeed of the other Crusader States, speaks of their conquerors' deep faith. Understanding this spiritual dimension of their behavior is crucial to unlocking their wider worldview.

If these warriors had set out on the First Crusade in search of gold or power, they had chosen the wrong campaign. The Levant was hardly an inviting target. The region was not especially wealthy, and the Jerusalem area itself was neither rich nor conspicuously fertile. During the previous century the land had been withered by prolonged periods of drought and torn by conflict between the Fatimids and the Turkish invaders. Conquerors, like merchants, generally look for opportunities where risks are minimized and rewards maximized, but here the risks substantially outweighed the rewards. The acquisition of worldly power and money does not explain their commitment to the region's conquest.

Faith provides a better answer.[58] Certainly Christendom's knights had strong reasons for desiring the spiritual rewards promised at the campaign's outset. Their need to seek remission of their sins was rooted in the moral tensions inherent in their militant vocation. These men had been born and raised into an aristocratic society that required its members to be trained for war. Those who excelled in arms were society's heroes, held up as icons for others to emulate. Nevertheless, they had also been born into a Christian faith that offered them a radically different role model exemplified in the life of Jesus. His teaching, speaking of the need to love one's enemies and neighbors, bears little obvious relation to the bellicose noble politics of medieval Europe. The church was well aware of this tension, and in previous centuries many thinkers had advanced theological solutions to the moral problems confronting knights who wished to carry out their bloody vocation while retaining some hope of salvation.[59] Some suggested that knights should confess their sins after each battle to avoid damnation, yet it is difficult to seek forgiveness for a sin that one fully intends to commit again. Another solution was to look for inspiration in the Old Testament, with its accounts of epic wars fought by men like King David and Judas Maccabaeus against insurmountable odds. Although aspiring knights certainly called upon these ancient leaders as exemplary figures, relying on the Old Testament did little to reconcile their own actions with the teaching of Jesus. More important, even such Old Testament exemplars did not provide a justification for killing coreligionists, which was frequently demanded in the many wars that fractured western Christendom.

The medieval writer Ralph of Caen, in his account of Tancred's deeds on crusade, explained the problem very neatly. He observed that Tancred was frequently troubled by his warrior vocation, recognizing that it stood in contradiction to Christ's command to turn the other cheek to one's enemies. Moreover, Tancred was apparently concerned that, far from showing Christian charity to their fellow men, soldiers generally stripped the populace of everything they owned. These contradictions apparently caused many sleepless nights for the young Tancred, who was reluctant to abandon the martial life for which he had been raised but was equally challenged by his failure to follow the teachings of Jesus.[60]

The First Crusade helped resolve such tensions. Participation was explicitly presented by the church as an act in direct accordance with the will of God. Those who fought in its wars were joining a campaign that could save them from their former sins. This in part explains the vast response to Pope Urban's call for crusade, and the ready participation of thousands of knights underlines their collective sense of relief that they now had a route to salvation.

The crusading oath was not a license to act as they pleased. They were still required to maintain a high moral standard in all other aspects of their lives. The crusaders were not an unrestrainable barbarian horde unleashed on the Near East. Theirs was morally straightjacketed violence. They destroyed armies and remorselessly slaughtered the inhabitants of many cities, but they were not given to raping the women in the towns they captured (like so many armies throughout history).[61] Crusaders who had relations with women out of wedlock were punished severely. Crusading ideology forced their warlike tempers into narrowly defined channels.

This was the context that brought forth commanders such as Tancred and Baldwin. Men of their cadre viewed themselves—and were encouraged to view themselves—as defenders of Christendom and knights of Christ. Their role models were warrior saints like Saint George, and during the First Crusaders' battle against Karbugha, some combatants actually claimed to have received assistance from a host of mysterious warriors in white led by Saint George, Saint Demetrius, and Saint Mercurius. Later rulers of Antioch were equally admiring of these saintly heroes, and their reverence for Saint George is reflected in some of the coins issued in Antioch, which depict Saint George slaying the dragon.[62]

As shown above, Tancred did not always live up to these crusading ideals. He attacked Christian towns and sometimes fought his coreligionists. Nonetheless, the crusading ideals were the values that permeated his world, and they put moral pressure on his behavior. Perhaps for him, the conviction that he was building a new Christian land that would help protect Jerusalem was the end that justified his choice of means.

———•———

By the time Tripoli fell in 1109, with the First Crusade now far behind them, the Franks of the Crusader States were looking increasingly secure, and they had both the money and the troops to defend themselves. Now, having consolidated their territories and having achieved a degree of security, they were in a position to focus their attention toward their enemies' inland centers of power. Both Aleppo and Damascus lay only a short distance beyond their frontiers, and Aleppo in particular was ripe for conquest. The second phase of conquest could now proceed in earnest.

CHAPTER 2

RIDING THE STORM: SELJUK TURKS AND ARAB EMIRS

1111–1118

T HE ADVENT OF the First Crusade had a profound effect on the Near East's political ecosystem. The Turks especially had to confront the fact that the crusaders had inflicted the worst military reverses on their people in over a century, and the expanding Crusader States had the potential to drive them out of the Levantine region entirely. The Frankish threat to Aleppo was of special concern, because if the city should fall, Turkish authority across Syria and the Jazira could collapse entirely. For many Arab dynasties, however, as well as for many other peoples subjugated by the Turks, the rise of Frankish power was both an opportunity and a threat. Some took it as an opening to try to throw off their Turkish overlords; others found themselves trapped between two rival conquering powers.

Looking back from the year 1111, the conquest of Tripoli two years previously had been a major blow for the Arab emir of Shaizar, Sultan ibn Ali ibn Munqidh.[1] Strengthened by Tripoli's revenues and emboldened by their success, the Franks had substantially enhanced their position. This had immediate consequences for the Munqidh dynasty's small territory, lying just south of the Antiochene border. Soon after Tripoli's fall, Tancred had advanced assertively to the south, seizing the nearby towns of Banyas and Jabala. Antiochene troops had then begun to curve round Shaizar's southern flank, conquering the castle of Hisn al-Akrad (known as "Krak des Chevaliers"). The Franks from Tripoli were also in a position to advance north toward Shaizar, and their forces attacked the town of Rafaniya, lying to the east of Hisn al-Akrad, in late 1109. Their attack failed, but for the Munqidhs the possibility of being squeezed between two major Frankish powers was ominously real. Such was their reach that the Franks could even draw revenue from Eastern Christian farmers living near the Munqidhs' lands.[2] Shaizar was starting to resemble a sand castle surrounded by an incoming tide.

Other neighboring Arab elites had recently sought accommodation with their Frankish conquerors, acknowledging the reality of their rising power. Jabala's governor Fakhr al-Mulk (a former ruler of Tripoli) had recently agreed to hold his town in Tancred's name, although he himself had traveled to join the Munqidhs at Shaizar soon afterward.[3] For Sultan ibn Munqidh in 1111, the Franks were easily the closest threat to his small emirate.

This had not always been the case. In previous decades the Turks had nearly always been the greatest danger. When they burst into the region in the 1070s, creating widespread havoc and destruction, many Arab Muslim dynasties had been swept away by their relentless advance. The Turks had seized control across the land, setting up regional centers of power in formerly Arab cities. It was during that turbulent period that Sultan ibn Munqidh's family had acquired Shaizar, becoming rulers of the town and its immediate hinterland in 1080. Shortly afterward, they too had been compelled to submit to Turkish authority, and in 1086 Sultan ibn Munqidh's brother Nasr had preserved the family's independence only by ceding vast swaths of territory to the Turkish sultan. The cost of this treaty had been colossal, but, unlike so many Arab dynasties in northern Syria, the Munqidhs had survived.[4]

In Arab eyes, the Turks were an object of both fear and scorn. Historically they had been viewed with the contempt that settled agricultural civilizations commonly held for their nomadic steppe neighbors. Turks were often depicted as barbaric, stupid, uncouth, and drunken. One irreverent story circulating at this time, one that seems to have been well-beloved among the Munqidhs, concerned the Turkish sultan Alp Arslan during his brief stint in Aleppo. It describes him drinking himself into a stupor one evening and then calling for the execution of the city's Arab governor. An adviser tries to persuade him to relent but ends up being injured when his master hits him with a washbasin. The sultan's wife then arrives and orders her husband to bed; the following morning she berates him for his conduct on the previous evening. The sultan supposedly denies all knowledge of the execution he had ordered.[5] This derisive story, presenting the sultan as a gullible, brutal fool, is a stereotyped anecdote designed to poke fun at the Turks, even if it also tacitly accepts that the Turks were in charge.

The background to this tale was one of rising Turkish domination. The despised nomads from the steppe were now in power over the very people who used to sneer at them. Whereas previously the Arabs could deride the Turks overtly, now they mocked them covertly. However, there was another, shrewder, response to Turkish rule practiced by many subjugated Muslims during this time. Arab politicians, theologians, and courtiers endeavored to immerse their Turkish conquerors in their own religion and culture, encouraging them to embrace Islam and aspire toward Muslim role models. This approach will be explained in greater detail later, but it represented a strategy that was subtler than straightforward name-calling: if you can't beat them, make them join you.

———·———

No sooner had the Arabs started to come to terms with their Turkish conquerors than the First Crusaders came bursting out of Anatolia, advancing into Syria in their countless legions. This was a delicate moment for the Munqidhs. Shaizar lay directly on the crusaders' line of march, and the Franks posed a clear threat. Even so, the Munqidhs also recognized the inherent opportunity in the crusaders' onslaught. By the conclusion of the siege of Antioch, the crusaders had demonstrated their ability to destroy the Turks' main regional field armies, having beaten off four big forces in a little over a year, an unprecedented achievement. The Turks had suffered battlefield defeats before, most notably at the hands of the Fatimids, but never with such consistency. Emboldened, many subjugated peoples of the Near East saw an opportunity to resist their Turkish masters. Consequently, while the Franks were besieging Antioch, Sultan ibn Munqidh seized the moment and began to plot against Ridwan of Aleppo (the most powerful Turkish ruler in the region), giving refuge to Ridwan's vizier, who had fallen out with his master.[6]

The Munqidhs were not the only Arab dynasty to take advantage of the sudden Turkish reverses during the First Crusade. Following the crusaders' defeat of the Aleppan army during the siege of Antioch, the Arab Banu Kilab tribe (rulers of Aleppo before the Turks' arrival) had risen up and plundered the Aleppan region, further weakening Turkish control.[7] For a moment there had been a real chance that with the relentless cycle of crusader victories over the Turks, followed by a groundswell of rebellions instigated by Armenians, Arabs, and other groups against their former masters, Turkish dominance in northern Syria would be rolled back once and for all. Even distant Georgia—hundreds of miles to the northeast—felt the ripples created by this radical shift in the balance of power; the Turkish attacks, formerly an annual scourge, ceased abruptly and King David the Builder of Georgia felt able to halt his tribute payments.[8]

For these reasons, when the First Crusade reached the gates of Shaizar, the Munqidhs, like most of the Arab rulers in the region, had little interest in barring their passage. Shaizar was too small in any case to resist so large a force. Instead, their respective leaders met and agreed not to fight one another. Sultan ibn Munqidh also supplied the crusaders with food and gave them the opportunity to purchase fresh horses.[9] This was a prudent strategy, one that ensured Shaizar's survival without hampering the crusaders in their efforts to overthrow the Turks.

Although they were cautiously friendly toward the Franks, the Munqidhs and the region's other leading Arab Muslim dynasties seem to have viewed them with little more favor than they viewed the Turks. In former centuries, western Europe had been a backwater in comparison to the Islamic caliphate and had generated little curiosity among its elites. Some emirs in North Africa or distant al-Andalus (Islamic Iberia) had pillaged the coastline of southern Europe, and slaves had been transported in large numbers across the Mediterranean to work the great estates of North Africa, but Christendom had been too poor and weak to arouse much attention. The Franks and their fellows were generally considered—when they were considered at all—with slight curiosity or supercilious disdain. The advent of the Crusades, however, forced these peoples into closer contact, and the Arabs would come to learn a great deal more about the Franks (and vice versa) in the years to come.[10]

Rather as they had with the Turks, the Munqidhs responded to the Franks' arrival by creating "funny" stories about their supposed foibles. The stories are generally contemptuous in tone, although they always acknowledge that the Franks were formidable opponents on the battlefield. A particular source of incredulity was the Franks' willingness to permit their women—both those who had come to the East on crusade and those who had traveled from western Christendom to settle in the region—substantial personal freedoms. For example, it was noted with astonishment that if a Frankish married couple were walking along the road and another man came to speak to the wife, the husband would simply leave his wife to complete her conversation without a chaperone. The crudeness of Frankish medicine also horrified them.[11]

Although the Franks were often presented as stupid and ill-mannered by Arab Muslim authors, various surviving tales do also contain some indications of cross-cultural respect. Sultan ibn Munqidh's nephew Usama ibn Munqidh portrays some individual Franks quite favorably, even as friends—particularly those who were more acclimatized to life in the Near East. Usama also described how he had once approached the king of Jerusalem demanding justice for an infraction he had suffered at the hands of a Frankish nobleman. After deliberation, the Christian court decided in Usama's favor, and therefore against one of their own cadre, and concluded that he should receive reparation. This tale speaks of Usama's confidence that a Frankish court would treat his case evenhandedly.[12]

———

Noninterference and negotiation had offered sensible ways for many Arab rulers to manage the passing of the First Crusade, but by 1111 the geopolitical situation had developed substantially. The Turks no longer posed the same level of threat to the Munqidhs in Shaizar, but now the Franks were hovering on the frontier. Admittedly, Ridwan, the Turkish ruler of nearby Aleppo, remained an ongoing source of danger, not least because of his strange friendship with the much-feared Assassins.

The name "Assassins" was a hostile term applied to a feared religious group known as the Nizaris.[13] The Nizaris were the adherents of an Ismaili sect of Shia Islam, which had emerged only a short time before in Egypt and had many followers across northern Syria. They were famous for their use of murder as a political tool, and they were loathed by the Turks, whose leaders persecuted them. Ridwan of Aleppo was an exception to this rule. The vulnerabilities of his position in Aleppo—where he faced both Frankish attack and internal dissent—compelled him to work with the Assassins. In return, they were prepared to murder his enemies; Ridwan was rumored to have instigated at least one assassination of a nearby Arab ruler.[14]

Ridwan was a continual source of concern for the Munqidhs, but in 1111 the Franks were the greater menace. The recent fighting between Arabs and Turks had worked in the Franks' favor. It had kept the Turks occupied while the Franks were vulnerable in the early years of the Crusader States. Now the Franks were firmly entrenched in the Levant and were expanding confidently. They had already launched a raid on Shaizar in 1108. More worryingly, two years earlier, the Arab ruler Khalaf ibn Mulaib, master of the neighboring town of Apamea, had been murdered by the Assassins, and his son had voluntarily offered the town to the Principality of Antioch. Tancred had responded swiftly, taking control and subsequently treating Khalaf's sons with high honor, granting them lands and status within his principality.[15]

The basic dilemma that had confronted the surviving members of Khalaf's family in 1106 was essentially the same as that facing the Munqidhs in 1111. They were trapped between two rival powers, the Franks and the Turks, and did not view either of them particularly favorably. In Apamea, events had forced the surviving members of the ruling family to take sides, and they had chosen the Franks. The Munqidhs, however, were determined to preserve their independence. This meant monitoring events closely, playing a weak hand with cunning, and judiciously deploying a mix of diplomacy, intrigue, and force to ensure that they were never caught on the losing side. This created a strange relationship between the Munqidhs and the Franks of Antioch, one that mixed moments of peace, courtesy, and friendship with times of intercultural misunderstanding, brutality, and slaughter.

Usama ibn Munqidh, Sultan's nephew, captured this environment well in his account of a small encounter between the men of Shaizar and the men of Antioch. After the fighting Tancred and Sultan ibn Munqidh agreed to make peace, and, in the spirit of revived friendship, Tancred sent word to Sultan that he greatly admired one of the emir's horses (whose performance he had presumably noted during their skirmish). Sultan courteously sent the horse as a gift to Tancred along with his representative, a young Kurd named Hasanun. Having arrived at the Franks' court, Tancred chivalrously arranged some horse races against his own Frankish riders and Hasanun performed very well, winning the races. Tancred was so impressed by Hasanun's horsemanship that he showered him with gifts. Hasanun responded by refusing the gifts, asking only for Tancred's assurance that he would be spared if he was captured in battle. Sometime later, once fighting had resumed, Hasanun's horse was wounded by a Frankish spear thrust. The animal bolted, throwing Hasanun, who was captured by the Franks. Tancred ordered that before he was ransomed, his right eye was to be gouged out to impede his fighting abilities. Hasanun, once a friendly emissary, was now a mutilated prisoner of war.

Had Tancred broken his promise of safe conduct? Usama thought possibly not. He noted that when Tancred had made his original arrangement with Hasanun, neither had fully understood the other's language, and consequently their agreement may have been misinterpreted by both sides.[16] This was a world where gifts and horse racing operated side by side with death and mutilation.

Now, however, in 1111, Shaizar's future was balancing on a knife edge. In the spring Tancred arrived with his army and began to build a fortress in Shaizar's immediate vicinity. His intention was plain. Using this newly constructed fortification as a base, he would cut off all supplies to the town and place it under blockade. This was a typical invasion strategy that the Franks had been using since the First Crusade. The construction of such a fort allowed an attacker to entrench himself at the very gates of an enemy stronghold and essentially strangle it into submission. Fortunately for Sultan ibn Munqidh, a new power had arrived in the region, one powerful enough to save them from this threat.[17]

The Munqidhs' hopes of a rescue were founded on a major geopolitical shift that was shaping the political landscape across Syria: the Franks were closing in on Aleppo and its conquest seemed imminent. Though at first glance the prospect of the city's overthrow might have offered little comfort to the Arab dynasties of the region, they soon realized that the Turkish sultan in Iraq was starting to take the prospect of losing Aleppo seriously. This created an opportunity for an alliance. A few months earlier a group of clerics and merchants from Aleppo had traveled to the Turkish sultan Mohammed's court in Baghdad seeking aid. To make their point, they had approached the Turkish sultan while he was in his mosque. Weeping, they had disrupted Friday prayers,[18] and refused to be silent until Mohammed promised to send them aid.[19] The sultan responded assertively, raising an army for Aleppo's defense under the command of his lieutenant Mawdud of Mosul. Mawdud was an effective commander who was experienced at fighting the Franks. He had attacked Edessa only the year before on the sultan's orders.

In 1111 Mawdud gathered a major force and set out for northern Syria. Learning of the army's approach, Sultan ibn Munqidh seized his chance and wrote to Mawdud seeking aid against their common enemy. Initially his appeal seems to have been ignored. Instead, the great Turkish army launched its assault far to the north, briefly attacking Edessan territory before moving to Aleppo (as had been requested).

At this point, Mawdud probably expected Ridwan of Aleppo to march out and join him, but Ridwan refused to help. Nervous that Mawdud's army would treat him like an enemy because of his alliance with the hated Assassins, and not wanting to violate a peace treaty he had with the Franks, Ridwan barred the gates. Ridwan's actions set him at odds with a large chunk of the populace (including those who had made the appeal), so he closed the city and even decapitated one of his citizens whom he caught whistling on the city's walls. In retribution for this betrayal, Mawdud's army ravaged Aleppan territory, sacking the very lands they had come to assist.[20]

After this inglorious beginning to his campaign, some of Mawdud's commanders began to return to their homelands, but Mawdud was still determined to attack the Franks. One Turkish commander suggested that Mawdud attempt to recapture Tripoli. This would have been a major blow against the emerging Frankish power, and it fitted well with Mawdud's larger strategy.

However, shortly after he began his march toward the Tripolitan border, Sultan ibn Munqidh approached Mawdud and begged him for a second time to assist beleaguered Shaizar. Mawdud this time agreed and diverted his forces toward the besieged city.[21] This was a huge relief for the Munqidhs, who were obsequious both in showing their gratitude and in cultivating Mawdud's goodwill. They took pains to ensure that his troops were well provisioned, and their family members personally waited on the leading Turkish commanders.[22]

Outside Shaizar, the situation had deteriorated still further by this time. Tancred had joined his forces with those of his rival, Baldwin of Jerusalem. Tripoli and Edessa had also sent soldiers. The combined armies then moved out toward Shaizar. Fortunately for the Munqidhs, with the arrival of Mawdud's army, the two camps quickly became locked in a stalemate across the Orontes River, which flowed past Shaizar's walls. On one bank were the Turks and the Munqidhs, and on the other were the Franks. The Turks' strategy was to play to their main military strength: mobility. Their numerous companies of light horsemen circled the Christian encampment, depriving it of supplies, and their bowmen prevented the Franks from collecting water from the river. Eventually, their harassment paid off, and, much to the Munqidhs' delight, Tancred and Baldwin were compelled to retreat after days spent enduring a depressing standoff. Shaizar was safe.

Now, with the Franks returning to their own lands, there was a chance for the combined Arab-Turkish force to strike a blow against the Frankish army, perhaps converting its retreat into a rout. Historically, tactical withdrawals have always been difficult maneuvers, testing even the most experienced commanders. Tancred's strategy was to break camp during the night and march under the cover of darkness. This was a sensible choice.[23] The darkness prevented the Turks' archers from using their bows effectively, compelling them either to permit the Christians to leave or to engage in hand-to-hand combat (which the Franks usually won). However, the Turks were clearly buoyed up by their initial successes, so they set out in pursuit and harried the Frankish army when Tancred tried to make a new camp further downstream. For a second time, Tancred had to abandon his camp and order another night march. This time the Turks were so confident that they attacked the Franks' marching column, despite the darkness. The crusaders were clearly on the verge of a major defeat, but disaster was averted by an individual act of heroism. A single Frankish knight charged out of the Christian ranks and assaulted the entire Turkish army. The knight's horse was killed almost immediately, but the man himself managed to fight his way on foot back to his own comrades while deterring the Turks from advancing any further.

This astonishing act of courage has an interesting sequel. Some months later, this same knight traveled to Shaizar, bearing both his wounds and a letter of introduction from Tancred. He explained that he had come to visit them and to observe their warriors in training, and he was welcomed by his Arab enemies. This incredible meeting again captures the spirit of the age. Warriors might fight bitterly on the battlefield and their leaders might perform all manner of brutal acts to secure their own political advantage, but this was not a head-to-head confrontation between either religions or ethnicities.[24] There was always room for admiration, knightly deeds, and even friendship across the cultural barrier.

After their notable victory, Sultan ibn Munqidh of Shaizar bade farewell to Mawdud and his departing Turkish troops. Sultan had achieved a great personal success, narrowly averting a major crisis while strengthening his own position. He was really the only winner in the campaigning season of 1111. For the Franks it was a disappointment; they had failed to take Shaizar and had been driven back. For Mawdud, the campaign must have been an embarrassment. He now had the task of explaining to Sultan Mohammed why he had achieved virtually nothing with his colossal army except to ravage lands belonging to the very people who had originally appealed to the sultan for help. The army may have been raised to offer support to Aleppo, but in the end it had left the city even more vulnerable than before.

———•———

The Munqidhs had won this round in their family's long game of survival, but their security would not last forever. The Arab position across the Near East was in long-term decline. The Turks were steadily driving most Arab dynasties, particularly those whose lands lay further to the east, out of the handful of towns that remained under their control. Shaizar itself would eventually be claimed by the Turks after an earthquake in 1157.

The First Crusaders had arrived in a world where Turkish supremacy was in the process of entrenching itself across the region and native rulers had, for the most part, already submitted or been crushed. The Christian victories of 1097–1099 disrupted that dominance, creating a window of opportunity for those who wished to resist the Turks, and it was several decades before the Turks fully regained their grip. During this time, the remaining Arab emirs were still very much in play in the bitter arena of the Near East, and their leaders would help shape the events of the following years.

For the Turkish leaders of northern Syria, the 1111 campaign was something of a nonevent. Yet Ridwan's refusal to cooperate with Mawdud's forces underlined the distrust and dissension that plagued the Turkish sultanate. There had always been some in-fighting within their ranks, but prior to the First Crusade it had rarely prevented the Seljuk Turks from expanding their authority across the Near East. Now, however, far from advancing, the Turks were struggling even to hold on to their existing lands. The Frank-ish threat to Aleppo was especially hazardous. The next few years would be decisive in determining whether the Turks would resume their former position of supremacy or be driven back. Their domi-nance across the Near East was deceptively frail. Like the crusaders, they were conquerors who had arrived in the region only recently, and their supremacy was not fully entrenched.

The Turks' earliest incursions into the Muslim world had be-gun in the years before the turn of the first millennium, far to the east. At this time, tens of thousands of nomadic warriors and their families had suddenly poured out of the steppe country of central Asia and into the cultivated agricultural lands of the Islamic world to the south. Exactly why this migration took place is unclear. One suggestion is that they were driven south by climate change: cool-ing temperatures forced these nomadic tribes south into warmer climates. Another hypothesis is that the movement was driven by the implosion of several tribal confederations.[25] Whatever the un-derlying cause, multiple Turkic peoples along with other nomadic groups penetrated the Islamic world's frontiers and swiftly took control across Persia (modern-day Iran) before moving west into Iraq. Their arrival caused widespread devastation as Turkish com-manders battled against their rivals, and nomadic Turkmen tribes spread out to pillage the landscape.

The Turks' main leaders were the descendants of a mighty war-rior named Seljuk (d. 1002). During the wars for the Islamic world, the Seljuk family managed to secure a position of supremacy over both their native Arab and Kurdish opponents and their Turkish rivals, and, following their capture of Baghdad in 1055, Seljuk's grandson Tughril took the title of Seljuk sultan. In the following years, the Seljuks conquered province after province, drawing them into their newly founded empire. Some local Arab and Kurdish rulers submitted to Turkish rule, others managed to negotiate a form of quasi-independence, and still others chose to resist and were destroyed. Either way, Seljuk power grew steadily during this time and much of southern and central Asia and the Near East came under their control. By the 1060s their territories spanned from the Himalayas to the marches of Anatolia.

During the 1070s and 1080s, the Turkish advance across Syria and Anatolia was almost uninterrupted. In 1071 the great sultan Alp Arslan moved into Syria, forcing Aleppo's Arab ruler Mahmud to acknowledge him as overlord, before continuing on into Byzantine lands. At the Battle of Manzikert, he crushed the main Byzantine field army, led by Emperor Romanus IV Diogenes, breaking open the Greeks' frontier defenses and allowing the nomadic Turkmen tribes to spread far into Anatolia, causing havoc. Alp Arslan had already laid waste to Christian Georgia only a few years previously. To the south, in Syria, the Turkmen commander Atsiz conquered Jerusalem in 1073 and Damascus in 1075. With these towns in his grasp, he was able to advance on Egypt, and it was only with the greatest difficulty that the Fatimids drove him out of the Nile delta.

The Turkish sultan's authority reached its apogee in the 1080s under the leadership of Sultan Malik Shah and his great vizier Nizam al-Mulk. This high point did not last. Malik Shah's death in 1092 caused a ruinous civil war that fragmented Seljuk power across much of their empire and ultimately opened the door to external invaders, including the crusaders. At the heart of the infighting was a major struggle over the sultanate in Iraq between Malik Shah's sons Berkyaruq and Mohammed. This war, coupled with a slew of rebellions and invasions that broke out across the empire, kept the eyes of the Turkish world focused squarely on its central territories until Berkyaruq's death in 1105.

The arrival of the First Crusade on the empire's western margins was initially not a priority for the combatants waging war over the sultanate. The coastal regions of Syria and the Holy Land were peripheral to the empire and had never been satisfactorily brought under Seljuk control. Karbugha, Berkyaruq's commander in Mosul, did set out to engage the First Crusaders in battle, but this was an isolated case. There were far more pressing concerns for the contenders for the sultanate—in fact, some Arabic historians of the Seljuk dynasty recorded the events of this period without even mentioning the Franks.

Viewed from the sultanate's perspective, the Syrian region was of secondary importance, merely one among a large number of frontier provinces. After Malik Shah's death, rule in the area was claimed by his brother Tutush. He too had pretentions to become the new sultan but in 1095—on the eve of the crusade—he led his army against Berkyaruq, only to be defeated and killed at the Battle of Dashlu. Tutush's power was split between his young sons, with Ridwan receiving Aleppo and Duqaq taking power in Damascus. Overall, Turkish authority in Syria on the eve of the First Crusade was in chaos. The civil war engulfing the central lands of the sultanate to the east drew the bulk of their attention (and troops). To make matters more complicated, Ridwan and Duqaq immediately began to fight one another and continued to do so even as the crusaders advanced from the north.

As the crusade progressed, the Turkish position crumbled still further. Both Ridwan and Duqaq suffered major defeats at the crusaders' hands in their separate attempts to break the siege of Antioch, and these losses encouraged dissent and rebellions from the region's native Arabs and Armenians. The Fatimids also scented blood and took advantage of the chaos to invade from the south, retaking Jerusalem in 1098 (the year before the crusaders conquered the city). It was for these reasons that Turkish resistance to the Franks was so limited in the years following the First Crusade. Their authority was tenuous, and the Franks were merely one enemy among many.

———

Confronting such hazardous regional politics, Ridwan of Aleppo had often judged it wiser to pay tribute to the Franks than to risk facing them in battle. He had tried to wage campaigns against them in 1097, 1100, and 1105 but had been defeated on each occasion. The city itself was riddled with dissent and imperiled by raiding from the local Arab tribes. Even some of his own Turkish officers had defected to the Franks. Moreover, the ongoing civil war for control over the sultanate both threatened his position and occupied warriors who might otherwise have marched to his aid.

The events of 1106–1107 provide a classic example of the kind of political knots that entangled the competing Turkish warlords of the region and prevented them from offering serious resistance to the Franks. In 1106, the Seljuk sultan sent a commander named Jawuli to Syria to assert the sultan's authority and to fight the Franks. Jawuli was promised control of the town of Rahba to serve as his base. He proceeded to Mosul to seek military support for this venture from its ruler. The ruler of Mosul, no doubt concerned about maintaining his own power, was reluctant to render aid, so Jawuli first raided his lands and then soundly defeated Mosul's army in battle. The ruler of Mosul's sons then appealed to the Turks of Anatolia, who came to their assistance against Jawuli but were also beaten off. Jawuli then traveled to Rahba, which he tried to seize, only to find himself vigorously resisted by the inhabitants (members of the Arab Banu Shayban tribe) and their overlord, the Turkish ruler of Damascus. At this point Jawuli summoned Ridwan of Aleppo and some Turkmen forces to his side. With their help, he captured Rahba, only to be almost immediately confronted again by the Anatolian Turks, who had arrived in force. He was forced to defeat this new challenger before heading east to take his revenge against Mosul, which he captured soon afterward. During this eastward journey to Mosul he alienated his former allies, Ridwan and the Turkmen.[26]

This rather unedifying series of events played into Frankish hands. Jawuli may have been dispatched with the intention of striking a blow against the Crusader States, but his actions had the reverse effect. Rather than facing a new enemy, Frankish forces from Jerusalem, Edessa, and Antioch were all free to expand their territories, safe in the knowledge that the Turks were warring among themselves. The fractured political landscape of the Turkish world meant that suspicion, treachery, and conflicted loyalties prevented the many Turkish warlords in the region from forming a united front against any enemy, and the Syrian Turks distrusted forces led by the sultan's commanders, fearing that they might try to force them to submit.

All these problems manifested themselves in a new campaign instigated by the Turkish sultan in 1115. Two years earlier, Ridwan of Aleppo had died of illness, and Aleppo became engulfed in factional infighting. Ridwan's eldest son and heir, Alp Arslan, attempted to take control, but he was assassinated by one of his eunuchs, a man named Lou Lou, in 1114. Lou Lou then called on the Turkish sultan Mohammed for aid, offering him the city in exchange for his protection. Sultan Mohammed saw an opportunity to solidify his power and launched another major campaign to the north. The resulting campaign revealed, yet again, the fracture lines in the Turkish world.[27]

The army set out in February 1115 under the command of Bursuq of Hamadhan. It mustered additional forces in the Jazira and then marched west, crossing the Euphrates at Raqqa. As Bursuq approached Aleppo he asked Lou Lou to fulfill his promise to yield control of Aleppo, proffering letters from the sultan to confirm his authority. Lou Lou seems to have panicked and to have decided that it was too dangerous to give up power. Consequently, he called on the Damascenes (under their current ruler Tughtakin; Duqaq had died some years before) and the Turkmen commander Ilghazi to rescue him from this predicament.[28]

This request placed Tughtakin and Ilghazi, two leading Turkish warlords in Syria and the Jazira, respectively, in a dangerous position. On the one hand, if they defied the sultan's army, they were *in effect* declaring themselves to be rebels. This was not necessarily a major problem because both Tughtakin and Ilghazi were out of favor at this time anyway (and allied to the Franks), though purposely obstructing the sultan's army would be an unnecessarily overt statement of their defiance. On the other hand, if they simply allowed Sultan Mohammed to acquire a strong foothold in Syria by taking Aleppo, it would only be a matter of time before all the local rulers were brought to heel—themselves included. The region's Turkish chieftains might have been prepared to acknowledge the sultan's theoretical supremacy, but that authority was generally far away, and the chieftains prized their independence. Eventually both men made their choice: they converged to defend Aleppo, in direct opposition to the sultan's army.

With armies massing to the east, the Antiochenes, under their new ruler Roger of Salerno (Tancred having died in 1112), grew alarmed at these troop movements and feared that the Turks were uniting to attack Antioch. So they too assembled their army, at their frontier stronghold of al-Atharib. They do not seem to have immediately appreciated the deep divisions hindering the Turkish army, but the fracture lines soon became apparent when Ilghazi and Tughtakin made contact with the Franks, offering to make common cause with them against the sultan's army. The Franks accepted their offer and sought further aid from their allies in Tripoli and Jerusalem, who set out for the principality shortly afterward.

These cascading events must have both surprised and alarmed Bursuq. He had been told to expect the willing compliance of the Aleppan leaders but was instead confronted by a major alliance of Syrian Turks and Franks. He was more enraged with his fellow

Turks than with the Franks because, after taking a brief swipe at Edessa, he moved south to punish the Damascene ruler Tughtakin by attacking his town of Hama. This siege was swiftly and successfully concluded, and Bursuq moved on to Shaizar to confront the Frankish and Damascene armies, which were then encamped outside the Antiochene town of Apamea.

For the Munqidhs in Shaizar, these events created yet another awkward dilemma: Should they support the sultan's army as they had in 1111 (and risk angering all their neighbors, both Frankish and Turkish)? Or should they jettison the sultan's goodwill and treat his approaching army as an invading force? In the event, they sided with the sultan. Unfortunately, this time they made a bad choice. The sultan's army, under Bursuq, remained inactive outside Shaizar's walls, and rumors abounded that the Turks were drinking heavily. It was only when news came that Baldwin I's army would soon arrive to join forces with the existing Frankish-Turkish coalition that Bursuq's forces stirred themselves to action.[29]

Bursuq launched a frontal assault on the Antiochene camp before it could join forces with Baldwin I's army but he achieved nothing. Roger of Salerno was a capable warrior who understood that the Turks' strengths lay in their archers and in their mobility. Consequently, he formed his army into a tight array and harshly ordered his men to remain in line. He marched along their ranks, sword unsheathed, instructing them that under no circumstances were they to charge against the Turks. This was frustrating to many impetuous knights—eager for a chance at glory—but it was also sensible.[30] The Turks wanted to provoke a reaction. If the Christians could be stung into making an ill-timed charge, the Turks would simply veer away and stay out of reach until the Christians exhausted their horses. Then the Turks could descend upon them. Roger understood this danger. He was also determined to wait for Baldwin's arrival before he risked battle.

Bursuq, seeing that the usual strategy would not work, adopted a different approach. He pretended to withdraw, giving the impression that he had accepted defeat. His enemies fell for the deception and split up their forces, assuming the threat had passed. Tughtakin and Ilghazi returned to their homelands, Roger headed back to Antioch, and the other Frankish forces returned to Tripoli and Jerusalem. Once the main army had disbanded, Bursuq suddenly wheeled around and, in early September 1115, launched a new and vicious assault on the Antiochene frontier at Kafartab.[31]

The siege of Kafartab was executed with the utmost speed. Whereas Frankish lords tended to carry out slow, grinding sieges supported by towers and catapults, seeking to climb over or destroy enemy walls, Turkish commanders preferred to tunnel under them. They employed specialists to carry out this dangerous work, most famously miners from the region of Khurasan, far to the east. Starting in Kafartab's dry moat, the miners excavated under the walls. This was skilled work. First they cleared a large space under the ramparts, propping up the walls' foundations with large wooden beams so the masonry would not fall on the diggers. When they had burrowed far enough under the wall, they filled the whole space with firewood and set it alight. The fire burned the supporting beams, causing the wall to collapse and creating a breach that the troops could assault.[32]

Learning of the attack, Roger hurriedly regathered his troops, marshaling them, along with supporting Edessan contingents, at Rugia in preparation for meeting the sultan's army. By this time, having taken Kafartab, Bursuq was besieging Zardana (another frontier stronghold).

As Roger's army moved against the Turks, his scouts reported that the enemy was unaware of their approach; Roger had the element of surprise. With this advantage, early on the morning of September 14, he led his army against the sultan's forces. The Frankish horsemen were divided into different squadrons, and each formation was instructed to attack the enemy army at a different point with their lances couched (held under the arm, rather than raised above the head like a javelin). The cavalry launched themselves at

their enemy, breaking their lances on first impact and then drawing their swords to engage in hand-to-hand combat. The Turks did
not have time to form into squadrons and consequently were stam-
peded by the oncoming cavalry. The Turkish army panicked, and
Bursuq himself only managed to survive his army's rout by climb-
ing a hill with his bodyguard, from which he was able to escape.[33]

This battle, which came to be known as the Battle of Tell
Danith, was a classic cavalry victory, of the kind that had made the
Christian knights so feared during the First Crusade. Their strategy
was to ensure that the full energy of their charge broke directly on
an enemy formation, without giving enemy troops any opportunity to take evasive action. The knights could then plow through
their foes, producing shock and disorder that would spread virally
throughout the enemy ranks and rout any resistance before the
opposing army could swamp the Franks with their overwhelming
numbers.

For the Franks, the Tell Danith campaign was a major victory,
and their army returned to Antioch laden with their enemy's riches;
they were met at the city's gates by a triumphal procession led by
the patriarch. For Bursuq, it was a humiliation, and he felt deeply
shamed by his defeat. He died the following year. For Syria's Turkish warlords—Tughtakin and Ilghazi—the campaign had forced
them to show their true colors. They had made it clear that they
would side with the Franks if the sultan attempted to take control
in Syria. The Turkish world was as divided as ever, and as Bursuq's
remaining forces fled back east, Tughtakin's own troops harried the
survivors.

For Tughtakin of Damascus, this campaign had been a triumph of sorts, yet his opposition to the sultan had been too visible,
and he worried about how his Turkish peers would respond. Rumors reached him that he had made many enemies in the sultan's
court, so in 1116 he set out for Iraq, sending magnificent gifts in
advance of his arrival, and seeking to be reconciled to Sultan Mohammed. In the event, Mohammed proved tractable to Tughtakin's

overtures. Perhaps the Turkish sultan concluded that Syria was too distant and too complex to be subdued and that it was better to accept Tughtakin's shallow display of loyalty than to reject him and drive him into permanent opposition.

———·———

The 1115 campaign had been a disaster for the sultan's army in many respects, and it had failed to take control in Aleppo. This was the second time the sultan had dispatched forces to support the city, and his armies had met resistance from the city's rulers on both occasions.

With the defeat of Bursuq's army, the eunuch Lou Lou's power in Aleppo grew steadily. He had already murdered Ridwan's heir Alp Arslan and declared himself to be the *atabeg* (guardian of the prince) for another of Ridwan's sons, the six-year-old Sultan Shah.[34] By 1116 Lou Lou grew bold enough to leave his eyrie in the city's citadel and begin to exercise power more publicly. This proved to be his undoing. One day Lou Lou set out to hold talks with the Banu Uqayl, a neighboring Arab dynasty that ruled the town of Qalat Jabar on the banks of the Euphrates. En route he paused, apparently to relieve himself, and was shot by his own troops.[35]

With Lou Lou's death, Aleppo imploded. His rule may not have been a showcase of moral rectitude, but he had nonetheless provided some semblance of order. In the months that followed, power slipped from hand to hand as internal factions squabbled among themselves. The city's political fault lines were plain for all to see, and the major neighboring rulers began to ponder the idea of taking control for themselves. The first to try was the Turkish ruler of Rahba named Aqsunqur, a commander loyal to the Turkish sultan. Rumor had it that he had been responsible for Lou Lou's murder, and certainly he advanced aggressively toward the city immediately afterward. His approach divided the populace. Some of Aleppo's soldiers were keen to welcome him; others resisted his candidacy. These dissenters were not prepared to receive a ruler so closely connected to the sultan.

In the event, the city shut its gates on Aqsunqur, but they now had to find a way to drive him away. Anxious about Aqsunqur's imminent arrival, the Aleppans appealed first to the Turkmen leader Ilghazi, who did not immediately arrive, and then to the Franks, who briskly launched a massive raid into Aleppo's eastern provinces and forced Aqsunqur to retire. Having been saved from the threat, the city made a treaty with the Franks in about 1117 granting them substantial rights to levy taxes on the city's trade.

The agreement might have stabilized matters except that soon afterward, in the summer of 1117, Ilghazi arrived outside the city's gates, following up on his invitation. He was permitted to enter the city but found that the citadel's garrison was prepared to resist him. He departed soon afterward, declaring that the city was unmanageable. By this stage there seems to have been a faction within Aleppo that strongly supported the idea of a Frankish takeover because soon after Ilghazi's departure a joint Aleppan-Frankish force attacked Ilghazi's town of Bales, to the east of Aleppo, in an attempt to drive him away.

The contest for rulership of Aleppo was becoming a free-for-all, and soon another force arrived outside its walls, under the command of Tughtakin, ruler of Damascus. He hoped that the citizens would voluntarily admit him, given that he had fought alongside their warriors in the past. But the gates remained shut, perhaps because Aqsunqur was among Tughtakin's entourage and the citizens may have feared that he would be imposed upon them as their new ruler. Instead, Aleppo again appealed to the Franks for military protection. Tughtakin departed soon afterward upon learning that the Kingdom of Jerusalem had invaded Damascene territory.

By 1118 Aleppo was passing swiftly under Frankish hegemony. The city's civic leaders regularly looked to Antioch for protection against the neighboring Turks, and they had already granted a large chunk of the city's revenues to the Christian principality. As for the Franks, they were within a hair's breadth of achieving a long-standing goal: control of Aleppo. Antioch's position was now so strong that in the summer of 1118 Roger could lead a large force to support the Kingdom of Jerusalem against a Fatimid invasion, and remain near Ascalon for almost three months at the height of the campaigning season, with no fear that his enemies would take advantage of his absence. Even the Byzantines, their long-standing opponents, were changing their tactics in response to Antioch's ever-increasing power. The principality was now too formidable for them to stage an armed overthrow, so instead they began to seek a marriage alliance, hoping to win Antioch by diplomatic means.[36]

With his military strength, Roger's forces could now range freely around Aleppo's lands, striking far to the east of the city with impunity. The city was at their mercy, and the Franks were positioned to force its submission, transforming a protectorate into a possession. This would be a decisive event. Aleppo was the key to Syria. Financially, Aleppo's ruler could call on its vast revenues, drawn from the city's markets and the surrounding farmland. Strategically, the city and its satellite towns controlled many of the major crossings of the northern Euphrates, including most of the roads connecting the Levantine coast to the sultanate in Iraq. Militarily, possession of Aleppo and its hinterland would help isolate Damascus to the south, surrounding it on three sides with Frankish territory. At this point, with Aleppo so very nearly under Frankish control, a bookmaker would probably have offered favorable odds that the Franks would soon rule the entire region.

In reflecting on this history of wars, treaties, friendships, and betrayals, it is striking how little the events of the early twelfth century resemble the commonly held view of the Crusades. This was no war of Christianity versus Islam, East versus West, Europe versus the Middle East. The reality was far more complex—and more interesting. In practice, the wars of this time were a conflagration of many different factions, with each group advancing agendas in which their leaders' personal ambitions merged with the broader objectives of their kinsmen. The battle lines were rarely simple. The campaigns of the First Crusade and the wars of the early twelfth century include examples of Turks fighting Turks, Christians fighting Christians, Christians and Turks fighting other Christians and Turks, Christians and Turks fighting Arabs and Turks, and the list goes on. For many commanders, yesterday's enemy might be today's friend and might become tomorrow's rival. If nothing else, this political world was no straightforward battle of "us" against "them."

Perhaps the most misleading interpretation of the crusades is the notion that it was a war between two rival religions, Christianity and Islam. There was, without doubt, a religious element to the conflict, yet the surviving sources from the period rapidly break down such a simplistic model. To begin, there were the Franks, newly arrived after their crusade to the East. The First Crusade was not a deliberately staged war against Islam. Most of the participants had set out knowing only that their opponents would be non-Christians of some kind, and even those who believed they were marching to fight "Saracens" knew virtually nothing about the Islamic religion. The crusaders' overriding objective was to restore Jerusalem to Christian control, and to achieve that end, they had no objection to allying with the non-Christian powers of that region.

This is not to say that they viewed Islam favorably or perceived Muslims to be their spiritual equals. They considered Islam to be a serious religious error.[37] Nonetheless, their conviction that Islam was a false religion did not lead them to cut off all relations or to indiscriminately identify all Muslims as targets. Medieval Christianity imposed no such obligation (indeed, it stressed the need to reach out to nonbelievers to bring about their conversion), and Frankish rulers were not so foolish as to alienate a large proportion of their population, who represented a sizable chunk of their tax base. Consequently, they were fully prepared to work with their Muslim neighbors and subjects. However, the First Crusaders and their descendants were indeed intent on conquering the region in the name of Christendom. They did not intend to forcibly convert, kill, or expel all of its non-Christian inhabitants, but nonetheless they were determined to impose Christian rule. To this extent, there was a religious agenda.

In addition, there were other Christian groups in the region, including the Armenians and Byzantines. The Byzantine Greeks in particular had a troubled relationship with the Franks, which occasionally broke into open conflict, particularly in their dealings with the Principality of Antioch. When Sultan Mohammed began to launch campaigns against the Franks in the 1110s, Muslim sources tell us that he received encouragement from the Christian emperor Alexius I Comnenus; the Franks were their common enemy, and religion was not the issue.[38]

Identifying a distinctively "Muslim" side to this conflict is even more problematic. The Turks were the most powerful non-Christian force in the Near East, having conquered the area a few years previously. Yet their spiritual identity was in transition. Before their violent migrations into the Islamic caliphate during the eleventh century, the majority of these Turkish tribesmen would have been shamanistic in their core spirituality. Their beliefs might have incorporated some influences from Judaism, Christianity, or Islam, but these would then have formed hybrids with their traditional convictions. There seem to have been rather more adherents to Islam among those communities that were in close proximity to the Muslim world, but even here the picture was mixed.

Later, once they had crossed into Islamic territory, the Turks do seem to have generally started to acquire Islamic beliefs and cultural practices (the classic tale of military conquerors being culturally conquered by the people they had subjugated). Even so, this was a long process. By the early twelfth century, the Turks were only midway through this transition, and many of their original shamanistic beliefs persisted for decades.

These mixed religious allegiances were noted by the First Crusaders as they marched into Turk-controlled territory. Some observers commented that the Turks tended to grow beards and that they responded to the call to prayer in the towns under their control, both indications of a movement toward Islam. They also noticed that the Church of Saint Peter in Antioch had been turned into a mosque by its Turkish conquerors, who had then covered the statues with cement (reflecting the prohibition in Islam of depicting the human form in religious buildings).[39]

These accounts of distinctively Islamic practices, however, were mixed with rather different reports. Some crusaders observed that the Turks buried their dead with valuable grave goods, including gold, clothing, and weapons.[40] This practice was not Islamic and reflects the traditional beliefs of their former steppe way of life. Many writers, from multiple cultures, describe the Turks' love of alcohol (prohibited by Islam), which also recalls their former nomadic lifestyle, in which fermented mare's milk (*qumiz*) formed part of their staple diet.[41] There are also reports of the Turks' respect for astrology, again potentially a continuation from their former way of life, although such practices were popular in the Muslim world too, despite the attempts made by Islamic religious leaders to stamp them out.[42]

Overall, the surviving clues to the Turks' religious beliefs during this period are mixed and reflect a culture in transition. The Islamic, the Arabic, and the Persian were merging with the shamanistic and the Turkic and with the world of the steppe. The Turks themselves, having acquired dominion over much of the Islamic world, probably drew on whichever customs inspired or attracted them while rejecting those that conflicted with their basic cultural identity. As victors, it was for them to pick and choose.

Such conquerors—like others before them—probably deemed it prudent to acculturate themselves to their subjects. The Turks were minority rulers governing a broad populace, and local support would be more forthcoming if they presented themselves as coreligionists. This pragmatic approach to spirituality is much in evidence during this period. Before the arrival of the First Crusade, while Ridwan (technically Sunni) was fighting his brother Duqaq, he courted aid from the Fatimids (Shia). In return for Fatimid assistance, Ridwan allowed the *khutbah* (the Friday sermon given in mosques) across much of his territory to name the Fatimid caliph, an important sign of submission.[43] And there are reports that later, during the First Crusade, certain unnamed Turkish commanders (possibly including Ridwan) offered to adopt Shia Islam in return for Fatimid assistance.[44] Overall, there is every indication that many Turks of this period carried their beliefs lightly and were perfectly happy to adjust their religious affiliation for political expediency. With this in mind, the Franks' wars against the Turks cannot easily be reduced to a simple battle between Christianity and Islam. The reality was much more complex.

In addition, other Muslim groups participated in the events of this time: Assassins, Fatimids, Arab emirs, and Bedouin tribesmen. These communities, too, were far from uniform in their beliefs and culture, adhering to a variety of Islamic sects and relating to each other in different ways. Many groups feared the Assassins, and some were naturally aligned with the Fatimids.

Ultimately, the Near East in the early twelfth century was an arena that drew in many different peoples. The groups discussed so far were the major players, but there were also many other communities, including Jews, Druze, Samaritans, Zoroastrians, and Coptic Christians. Each group had its own objectives.

At times the conflict was fought along religious lines; much of the time it was not. More frequently, conflict was driven by political divisions. The sultan's attempts to reassert control in northern Syria fall comfortably into this latter category; so, too, do the Byzantines' efforts to reconquer Antioch. There were also instances of ethnic violence, with the Arabs and the Armenians seeking to rid themselves of the Turks. The mixing of these competing agendas and the chaos they created underpins the dramatic events of this time, creating a whirlpool of clashing interests that both drove some into conflict and created many extraordinary partnerships.[45] As a contemporary Islamic author once lamented: "Today the world has been turned upside down; there is concord with the Franks and dispute with the Muslims."[46]

———•———

Quite apart from the clash of war, the period of the Crusades also saw some fascinating moments of intercultural interaction. In the centuries before the First Crusade, there had been some trade and correspondence between western Christendom and the peoples of the Near East, but the advent of the Crusader States brought these cultures into far closer proximity. The Italian cities substantially increased their commercial stake in the eastern Mediterranean, trading with both the Crusader States and the Byzantines. Their representatives also built on existing links with the Egyptians through ports in the Nile delta, particularly Alexandria. Likewise, returning crusaders and pilgrims carried back to their native soil both news of strange places and curios from these distant lands. Muslim pilgrims and travelers found themselves journeying through the Crusader States, and there were many Muslim communities under Frankish governance. Interactions across cultural boundaries became increasingly common, and different groups came into more direct contact—willingly or not.

The outcomes of such encounters were varied, and certainly they created some bizarre dilemmas for the spiritual and secular leaders of the communities involved. In 1126, for example, the religious authorities in Alexandria were asked to determine whether Islamic law was contravened by the import of cheese from Christian territory.[47] On the other side of the Mediterranean, it seems that so many returning crusaders traveled home wearing Turkish hats that there were attempts to ban them.[48] Palm branches and devotional items were also common souvenirs carried home by pious travelers from the Holy Land. A rather more ambitious case was the attempt by one Frankish knight to transport a tame lion back to France. He seems to have formed a strong bond with the beast during his time in the Holy Land, but he was unable to find a shipmaster

willing to convey such a ferocious passenger. When the knight reluctantly took ship for the West and abandoned his "pet," the lonely
lion apparently swam some way out to sea following his master's
vessel.[49]

The era of the Crusades and the many encounters it provoked
across cultural or religious boundaries also led some to borrow
ideas or imitate techniques that they had observed in other cultures. Frankish arms and armor were popular among Arabic and
Turkish warriors and were either seized eagerly from the bodies of
the fallen or acquired by trade. This traffic in arms was so great that
it worried the papacy, which tried hard (but to no avail) to prevent the sale of arms to Muslim ports. Likewise, Frankish symbols
and devices began to infiltrate the Levantine culture and art. The
fleur-de-lis seems to have captured many artists' imaginations, and
examples survive to this day of artistic work produced by Armenian and Muslim craftsmen during this period including it in their
work.[50] In their turn, the Franks drew inspiration from eastern
models. Some Franks, for example, began to construct or inhabit
homes that drew upon Muslim models. Typical Islamic houses for
this period were based around a central courtyard, often with high
windowless exterior walls, stressing the need for privacy.[51] There
also seems to have been a growing trend among the Franks in the
Levant for visiting bathhouses, also uncommon in the West.

The Franks borrowed from the other Christian societies of
the Near East, drawing on eastern influences in their art, coinage
(many coins had inscriptions in Greek or Arabic), and clothing.
It is also evident in many of the buildings constructed during the
crusader period, such as the Church of the Holy Sepulchre. This
church, the focal point for Christian spirituality in Jerusalem, en-
compasses the sites where Christ's crucifixion, burial, and resurrec-
tion are thought to have taken place. During the Franks' time in
the city they augmented the building, perhaps most noticeably by
constructing its main two-story facade. It is a striking feature of

their embellishments that they drew upon both their own customs and those of Eastern Christians, particularly Armenians.[52]

The merging of western and eastern Christian architectural styles is also indicative of a wider mixing at a social level, and from the outset of the crusader settlement in the East, there were examples of intercultural marriages. Both Baldwin I and Baldwin II wedded Armenian brides, and many future rulers married Armenian or Byzantine noblewomen.[53] Marriage represented an important medium for the sharing of ideas and customs. For example, Melisende, daughter of Baldwin II, and therefore Armenian on her mother's side, is thought to have been responsible for several major building works that took place in Jerusalem in the mid-twelfth century, including the Holy Sepulchre, and these incorporated many distinctively Armenian features. Intermarriage may have represented a bridge between different Christian societies, but it also reflected the boundaries of social interaction because, although it was common for Christians to intermarry, marrying outside one's faith was forbidden.

Another form of intercultural mixing took place on the dietary level. Many newly arrived pilgrims, settlers, or crusaders would have been entirely unaccustomed to the local cuisine and climate. Some clearly immersed themselves in their new surroundings, as can be seen in a tale written by Usama ibn Munqidh. He tells of an old Frankish knight in Antioch who invited a Muslim acquaintance for a meal. The guest arrived, possibly appearing a little nervous, and was immediately told by his Christian host that he never ate Frankish food and that his meals were prepared by an Egyptian cook. Pork was forbidden in the house. This seems to have reassured the guest, who ate, albeit sparingly.[54] In this case at least, this knight's acculturation was pronounced.

In other cases, settlers sought to remold their surroundings to re-create the cultural norms of their homeland, and pig farming and viniculture became increasingly widespread in Frankish lands, reflecting preferences for pork and wine.[55] The Middle Eastern diet also exposed the newly landed crusaders' digestive systems to a new set of parasites, for which they were ill-prepared. Recent bio-archaeological studies of medieval feces, found in ancient cesspits, have demonstrated that the crusaders in return inadvertently introduced new parasites to the Near East, such as the dysentery-causing *Entamoeba histolytica.*[56]

On an intellectual level, the information carried home by returning crusaders provoked a series of debates in western Europe. One particular source of fascination was the Turks, who had hitherto been largely unknown. Their sudden appearance raised the scholarly challenge of identifying their origins and ethnic roots. Intellectuals responded to this dilemma by delving into their archives for inspiration, with various results. Some suggested that they were the descendants of the Parthians of the classical era, who had shown a similar proclivity for the use of mounted archers in war. Others called up an old legend that claimed that following the fall of Troy, a group of refugees had fled the city and, after long wandering, divided into two groups, thereby establishing the Frankish and Turkish peoples.[57] Astonishingly, the Turks themselves may also have believed that they were related to the Franks, but for different reasons. They seem to have understood that both peoples had similar origins in their descent from Gomer, grandson of the biblical Noah.[58]

From an Islamic perspective, the Franks also attracted attention and generated some thought-provoking questions for scholars. Several of these challenges are manifested in a Persian work produced in Aleppo named *The Sea of Precious Virtues,* essentially a book of advice and counsel to a young Turkish nobleman, written in Syria in the mid-twelfth century. This work demonstrates considerable theological hostility toward elements of the Christian faith, yet the author had clearly been impressed by some aspects of Frankish religious culture. He praised the reverence shown by Franks for their

priests and suggested that his fellow Muslims emulate this respect-
ful behavior in their relationships with Islamic religious leaders.[59]

The author of *The Sea of Precious Virtues* also seems to have been
troubled by the speed and frequency of Frankish battlefield victories. He recorded a debate that took place in Baghdad in which a
questioner asked why, in the early years of Islam, a mere handful of
Muslims were able to defeat huge numbers of infidels, whereas now
a small number of infidels were able to triumph over vastly superior
Islamic armies. The answer given was that the people of Islam had
fallen into vice in recent years and that the virtues of their early
years were now possessed by their enemies.[60]

These are mere excerpts from the broader encounter of various
cultures at the time of the Crusades. The variety and complexity
of these interactions are what make them so fascinating. When different civilizations come face-to-face, all those involved are forced
to consider the stance they will adopt in that meeting. They need
to ask themselves in which zones of life they are prepared to share,
and in which they are not; in which areas they are ready to learn,
and in which they are only prepared to instruct; in which ways they
are prepared to be easygoing, and in which they can only be hard-
line; which ideas they can consider open-mindedly, and which they
must reject out of hand. This complex posture is almost always a
product of a mixing of various ingredients, including individuals'
cultural and religious norms, their genders and social statuses, the
nature of the meeting—on the battlefield, in the bathhouse, at the
market, in the marriage bed—and their characters and personal
dispositions. It is particularly fascinating to observe those occasions
when, for whatever reason, a society feels challenged or threatened
by its encounter with another culture, when it realizes that issues
or questions have been posed for which it does not have answers
within its existing traditions.

It is not difficult to imagine that the events of the 1110s
would have raised many such questions for the people of Aleppo.
Theirs was a perilous position that necessitated some hard decision

making. In recent decades their city had been fought over time and again and was now consumed by internal unrest, and their farmlands had been repeatedly wasted by external enemies. Arabs, Turks, Armenians, Franks—their region had become an arena for the aspirations of many peoples. Now in 1118 it seemed as though the Franks had the upper hand. Could they accept their status as a Frankish protectorate? Was the prospect of a Turkmen takeover any more appealing? Was there any way that they could maintain their independence? Certainly, they lay at the eye of the storm, and the next few years would be decisive.

CHAPTER 3

THE BATTLE

1119

B Y 1118, ALEPPO was steadily coming under Frankish control. Antioch held many of the surrounding strongholds and
was increasingly acting as the city's overlord. Antioch's commanders were well aware that the city's final overthrow would ensure
their regional dominance and that its possession would substantially strengthen the Crusader States to the south. The Turkmen
rulers of the Jazira were equally aware of the city's drift into the
Christian fold, and they recognized the threat this would pose to
their own lands. From their perspective, this Frankish expansion
had to be resisted. The struggle for the Near East was now on the
verge of a major turning point. The stage was set for a major confrontation between these rival conquerors.

———•———

During 1118–1119 the wars of the Near East raged unceasingly.
In the south, King Baldwin I had launched an expedition into
Egypt, but he became seriously ill soon after his forces reached
the Nile delta. Reportedly, while he was swimming in the Nile, an

old wound reopened, which refused to heal. Realizing that he was nearing death, he tried to return to Jerusalem, carried in a litter, but he died en route on April 2, 1118. He was succeeded by the count of Edessa, Baldwin of Bourcq, who became King Baldwin II.

Controversially, Baldwin of Bourcq had not been the late king's named heir. Baldwin I had hoped to pass the throne on to his brother Eustace III of Boulogne, but Eustace was far away in western Christendom, and the kingdom was in immediate need of a new defender. Baldwin of Bourcq was in the right place at the right time. He had reached Jerusalem on pilgrimage only a little while before news arrived of the king's death, so, following strenuous arguments made by the patriarch on his behalf, he was chosen to be the late king's successor. He was anointed as King Baldwin II of Jerusalem on Easter 1118 and crowned on Christmas Day 1119. Eustace and his supporters had been supplanted, and having already set out for the East, he was forced to return home.[1]

Soon afterward, in the arid summer of 1118, the Kingdom of Jerusalem suffered simultaneous invasions from the Damascenes in the northeast and the Egyptians in the south. This pincer attack placed the new king in a perilous position, so Baldwin II called upon the Franks of Antioch and Tripoli for aid. Soon afterward, Tughtakin joined forces with the Fatimids at Ascalon, massing their forces in the south. However, the Egyptian-Damascene invasion came to nothing, resulting in little more than a prolonged standoff. Neither side had the armed might to attempt an attack on the other.

The Kingdom of Jerusalem's forces took the offensive soon afterward on their northeastern flank, launching a series of raids into Damascene territory. Such forays were regular occurrences in medieval warfare, utilized by Franks and Turks alike. Raiding was an effective, if brutal, instrument of war because its object was to destroy the enemy's rural infrastructure. The basic principle was to carry off anything of value—money, people, animals—and then to burn or destroy anything left. It was economic warfare, strengthening one's own position while weakening one's enemies by stripping them of their resources. The great advantage of this kind of attack was that it could normally be carried out without risking a full battlefield encounter. Raiders could conduct their cruel work and then escape back over their own frontier before enemy relief forces could arrive. Jerusalem's main frontier stronghold and raiding base facing Damascus at that time was the town of Tiberias, on the western shore of the Sea of Galilee. Its lord, Joscelin of Courtenay, was a capable soldier, and in 1118 his forces ranged widely into Turkish territory, scoring a series of small victories.

Eventually, Joscelin's incursions stung Tughtakin into responding, and he sent an army under his son Taj al-Mulk Buri's command to hunt down Joscelin's war band of 130 knights. Fortunately for the Damascenes, Joscelin had made a serious error in judgment. Joscelin's raiding party had moved to the north of Damascus, seeking out the fertile lands around Homs, and was hundreds of miles from the kingdom's borders. They were in an exposed position, and the Turks pounced upon the company, trapping it on a small hilltop. With the Frankish knights in his grasp, Tughtakin arrived in person and ringed the hill with his army, seeking initially only to contain them. He was an experienced commander, and he knew that a frontal confrontation with even such a small number of Christian heavy cavalry was ill-advised. It made more sense to wear them down before chancing a direct confrontation.[2]

The problem was that Tughtakin's son did not share his father's sense of caution. He was impetuous and opted to attack directly uphill into the teeth of a Christian charge. The result was disastrous. The Franks fought all the more fiercely because they were cornered, and put the entire Damascene force to flight.

The fortunes of war in the south set the scene for the far more important confrontation over Aleppo that was brewing in the north. Tughtakin was now unexpectedly weakened, and the Damascene borders needed shoring up. Consequently, he set out toward Aleppo and the Jazira to seek help from Ilghazi. Ironically, as Tughtakin journeyed into northern Syria, he encountered a deputation from

Aleppo that had been dispatched hoping to solicit *his* aid against the Franks.

Aleppo's position had deteriorated still further. The Aleppans had been looking to Antioch for protection, but the Franks had proven to be untrustworthy guardians. Recently their troops had started to waylay merchants traveling through the Aleppan region, enslaving them and seizing their goods. The citizens of Aleppo had made representations to them, asking them not to break their agreement. Initially, the Franks had yielded and had returned the stolen goods, but soon afterward, they decisively broke the treaty, raiding the Aleppan countryside and conquering the town of Azaz.[3] They felt their position was now so strong that they no longer required any kind of agreement with the citizens and could move to take full control. The conquest of Azaz, lying just to the north of Aleppo and dominating a broad expanse of fertile farmland, was a major blow, tightening the Frankish encirclement around the city.[4] Aleppo's fall seemed imminent.

In a panic, the people of Aleppo resumed their earlier search for a new defender. Tughtakin was their preferred choice. He had long experience ruling Damascus and was known to be a capable commander. However, he had just been defeated by Joscelin's forces. Far from being in a position to render help, he was himself asking for assistance. Consequently, the Aleppans approached the ruler of distant Mosul for support, but he was unable to send aid. Finally, and with nowhere left to turn, they opened the gates to the Turkmen commander Ilghazi. He was a deeply unpopular choice, known to be aggressive and politically controversial. The citizens wavered in their resolve as his army approached the city, and they shut the gates in his face. Then they wavered again and allowed him to enter.[5]

Ilghazi's ascension to power was as bad as the citizens had feared it would be; his first actions fully justified their vacillation. He purged the city's elites and brutally took control. His message was clear: he was here to stay; he was in charge; he was going to make the rules. His next move was to purchase a ruinously expensive peace from the Franks. This was no alliance of the kind he had negotiated back in 1115, when he and the Antiochenes had joined forces against Bursuq. It was merely an agreement designed to give him breathing space to raise the largest army possible. If Ilghazi was going to hold Aleppo, the Franks would have to be driven back. A major confrontation over the city's future governance—and therefore over the future direction of Syria as a whole—was now looming.

———•———

In 1119 Ilghazi began to assemble his full might. He also allied with Tughtakin, who was equally concerned to see the Franks driven back. Their goal was to secure Ilghazi's control of Aleppo in the face of recent Frankish advances. They were both seasoned campaigners whose sheer ability is revealed by the plain fact that they had survived for so long in the complex—and often murderous—world of Seljuk politics.

Tughtakin had been part of the Turkish conquest of Syria from the beginning. He had served under Sultan Alp Arslan during the Seljuk invasions of the 1070s, and he later supported the sultan's son Tutush. Tughtakin had prospered in the service of his Seljuk masters, and they in turn had recognized and rewarded his abilities. Shortly before the arrival of the First Crusaders, he had been permitted to marry Tutush's divorced wife Safwat al-Mulk, a notable honor.[6] This union also made him stepfather to Tutush's son Duqaq, who became ruler in Damascus after his father's death in 1095. Duqaq had been too young to take up the reins of power himself, so Tughtakin had ruled in his stead as *atabeg*. Since then, Tughtakin had governed the city, initially in Duqaq's name, and then after his death, briefly in the name of his siblings. In 1104 Tughtakin became sole ruler.

As lord of Damascus, Tughtakin was in a powerful position. The city's population was wealthy, numerous, and literate (by the standards of the day).[7] Tughtakin seems to have been well regarded by the populace as an able ruler, and contemporary authors praised him for his many virtues.[8] His main objective was to survive, and ideally to thrive, in the muddied politics of the Near East. In this ambition he was confronted by three main challenges. The biggest danger was almost certainly the threat of overthrow from the Turkish sultanate to the east. The arrival of several large armies from the sultanate, particularly after the conclusion of the civil war between Berkyaruq and Sultan Mohammed, raised the much-feared specter of the sultan's enforcing dominion over the entire region, thereby destroying Tughtakin's independence. This concern was so potent that Tughtakin was prepared to side with the Franks (as he had in 1115) if it would block the sultan's ambitions.

The other major threat was from the Franks. Tughtakin had been among the first Turkish warriors to encounter this new foe, and he and his young master Duqaq had led the Damascene force that had attempted to break the siege of Antioch during the First Crusade.[9] Their defeat in that endeavor seems to have taught Tughtakin to be wary of confronting the Franks. He made no serious attempt to dislodge them from the coast for almost a decade after the conquest of Jerusalem, and he was generally content to assume a defensive stance: fending off invading forces, pushing out their raiding parties, and rendering aid to the besieged coastal cities.

This should not imply that Tughtakin was averse to the idea of conquering new territory. He was a veteran campaigner who had cut his teeth in the midst of the Seljuk overthrow of northern Syria. However, rather than engaging the militarily skillful Franks, Tughtakin instead directed much of his energy into the enforcement of his and his master's interests in the Jazira to the northeast. In 1099, shortly after the fall of Jerusalem to the Franks, the Damascene army set out in the opposite direction, seeking to subdue the distant town of Mayyafariqin.[10] In 1103 and 1104 Damascus launched two expeditions to capture and hold the town of Rahba, far to the east along the line of the Euphrates.[11] These ventures to secure Rahba are indicative of Tughtakin's and Duqaq's strategic priorities. Rahba sits on a key route that leads from Damascus to Iraq. Control of Rahba would have given Damascus a listening post and an advanced position facing the regions being contested during the Turkish civil war over the sultanate.

Tughtakin's preoccupation with Rahba also bears upon his third major external threat. Like Ridwan and the other Turkish rulers of the region, he ruled over a large populace that was by no means reconciled to Turkish rule. The people of Damascus seem to have been largely quiescent under Tughtakin's leadership (unlike the population of Aleppo under Ridwan's), but this was not universally the case in his wider territories. In 1101 the *qadi* of Jabala asked the Damascenes to take control of the port of Jabala, but Tughtakin's deputy and his Turkish warriors were soon thrown out by an angry populace.[12] By 1107 the Arab Banu Shayban had rebelled in Rahba, rejecting Damascene overlordship.[13] Even Frankish authors recognized the Arabs' hatred for their Turkish overlords, and a writer named Albert of Aachen reported that in 1100 Damascene forces were compelled to abandon a proposed night attack on a Frankish army because of fears that they might be attacked by their own Arab auxiliaries.[14] To make matters worse, the Arab Bedouin tribes on the southern margins of Tughtakin's territory often worked in concert with the Franks to seize the heavily armed caravans that set out from Damascus toward Egypt.[15]

Juggling these problems, Tughtakin was generally keen either to ignore or to pay off the Franks where possible. In the past, there had generally been greater challenges to his survival in the east and much more enticing opportunities for expansion in the war-torn Jazira. He clearly had no intention of confronting the much-feared Frankish heavy cavalry if he could possibly avoid it.

This seems to have been his general policy for many years. Yet times were changing, and not for the better. The Franks' territories were expanding steadily, and their warlords had begun to raid more deeply both into Tughtakin's lands and into those of his neighbors. On his eastern flank, facing Iraq, the civil war was over, and the new sultan was showing a worrying enthusiasm for interventions into Syria. Still, Tughtakin was a skillful diplomat, and by 1119 he had already demonstrated that he could play the two sides off against one another. When the sultan had dispatched Mawdud of Mosul to fight the Franks in 1113, Tughtakin had joined their army and waged a punishing campaign against the Kingdom of Jerusalem, savaging their frontier positions around Tiberias. In 1115, in contrast, he had sided with the Franks to throw out the sultan's armies under Bursuq. He had proved himself capable of benefiting from supporting either side when it was in his interests. In 1118, however, the balance of power was changing rapidly. The Franks were advancing along the full length of their frontier. If Tughtakin's rule over Damascus was to be maintained, they had to be held back.

———•———

Ilghazi's strategic situation was comparable to that of Tughtakin. They were in a similar predicament, both attempting to defend their territories against a range of threats. Like Tughtakin, Ilghazi was a born survivor weathered by years of experience on campaign. His family, the Artuqids, originally came to prominence under the patronage of the Seljuk ruler Tutush, and in 1085–1086 his father had been granted Jerusalem as his *iqta* (a grant of land). Following their father's death, Ilghazi and his brother Sokman inherited the territories, although it was not long before they were driven out of Jerusalem by the Fatimids in 1098. Sokman returned to his family's other lands in the Jazira; Ilghazi set out for Iraq, hoping to make a career for himself in the civil war raging over the sultanate.[16]

Ilghazi prospered in Iraq and rose to the eminent office of *shihna* (governor) of Baghdad. His prominence may have been due in part to the long-standing support he received from a group of Turkmen tribes that remained in his service throughout his life and represented a large proportion of his armed following. During his time as governor, he came to be deeply disliked by the people of Baghdad, and his behavior eventually led to civil unrest. The people's resentment apparently boiled over after a group of Ilghazi's men shot a boatman for being too slow in bringing his boat to their side of the river. This was the last straw; the enraged populace seized the perpetrator and threw stones at Ilghazi when he tried to effect his release. Ilghazi's reaction to the simmering discontent was to sack the Cotton Merchants' district in the city.[17]

This inglorious phase in his career came to a close with the end of the civil war between Mohammed and Berkyaruq for the Turkish sultanate. Ilghazi had supported Berkyaruq, so when Mohammed emerged victorious in 1105, he wanted Ilghazi replaced. Ilghazi left Baghdad and took the long road to the Jazira to take control of his late brother's lands around Hisn Kayfa and the town of Mardin. Having put as much space as possible between himself and Mohammed, he began to plot against the sultan and formed alliances with his enemies. This troublemaking created problems for Ilghazi when the sultan began to send armies into Syria and the Jazira between 1110 and 1115, and Ilghazi initially deemed it prudent to make some show of support. He participated in the first indecisive campaign launched by Mawdud against Edessa in 1110, but he refused to take part in the second (1111), sending his son Ayaz in his place. Nor did he join the later campaigns launched by Mawdud against the Franks in 1112 and 1113, although he sent Ayaz with some troops in 1113.

In 1114, the sultan sent yet another army against the Franks under Aqsunqur (the man who later attempted to seize Aleppo). The main target on this occasion was Edessa, but Aqsunqur was instructed to bring Ilghazi to heel en route. Consequently, the two warriors engaged in sporadic fighting, which concluded with a decisive defeat for Aqsunqur. Ilghazi was victorious, but he was also now politically isolated. He made overtures to the Franks in 1114, and the following year he worked with the Franks to fend off the sultan's army. The 1115 campaign, led by the sultan's commander

Bursuq, was significant for another, sadder reason. Following the defeat of the sultan's army at Tell Danith by the knights of Antioch, Bursuq's soldiers executed Ilghazi's son Ayaz, whom they had been holding hostage.[18]

By 1118, Ilghazi's career had been characterized by moments of opportunism mixed with a surly resistance to the sultan's authority. Nevertheless, his priorities were changing. Aleppo's progressive enfeeblement was both a source of concern and a spur to ambition. On the one hand, a Frankish victory—which by 1117–1118 seemed imminent—would strengthen their position incalculably, raising the possibility that the Franks would advance in strength into the Jazira. On the other hand, if Ilghazi could get hold of the city, his own position would be substantially enhanced. Another important development was the death of Sultan Mohammed in 1118. This changed the political game, raising the possibility that Ilghazi might rebuild his relations with the sultanate. Consequently, he sent messengers to Baghdad both to seek aid against the Franks and to make contact with the new sultan, Mahmud II.[19] Change was in the air and Aleppo sat squarely in the center of many leaders' ambitions.

———·———

By 1119, both Tughtakin and Ilghazi were rallying their full strength for a major aggressive war against the Franks. This was not a familiar situation for either of them. One of the most significant features about the careers of both Ilghazi and Tughtakin prior to 1119 is that neither had previously manifested any real commitment to fighting the Franks. Tughtakin had been slightly more combative toward the Franks, and he could claim to have landed a heavy blow against the Kingdom of Jerusalem in 1113. Nevertheless, his campaigning had generally been defensive, and he had certainly shown little enthusiasm for driving the Franks out of Jerusalem. Ilghazi, despite an impressive military career, had scarcely ever taken the field in person against a Christian army.

Later Islamic authors, reflecting on the exploits of these capable leaders, would garland their deeds with praise, presenting them as the great heroes of Islam. Their lives were set up as models of righteous conduct (more Tughtakin, less Ilghazi) and vigorous war against the Franks (more Ilghazi, less Tughtakin). This was how they wanted them to be remembered.

In reality, these Turkish leaders' commitment to jihad, rather like their commitment to Islam itself (at least at this point in history), seems to have been opportunistic at best. There is little in their conduct before 1119 to suggest an ongoing devotion to holy war against the Franks, and the Turks had little familiarity with jihad. Before their early incursions into the Islamic world, the shamanistic Turks were more accustomed to being on the receiving end of such holy wars than to taking part in them. In later years, as the Turks slowly adopted Islam and began to adopt a Muslim way of life, there seems to have been a slight engagement with such ideas. There were jihad volunteers in Karbugha's army at the Battle of Antioch in 1098, and the Muslim caliph made some efforts to find warriors to fight alongside the Turks during his attempts to block the First Crusade, but the response appears to have been very limited.[20] The Turks had other problems.

A few years after the First Crusade, a Damascene scholar named al-Sulami tried to stir the Turkish sultan into a jihad against the Franks, pointing out, quite rightly, how few they were and how far they were from help. However, his passionate cries for holy war provoked very little reaction, either from the sultan or from his immediate ruler, Tughtakin. It must have been very frustrating for him to watch the Franks steadily building in numbers and landholdings without sparking any significant response from his own Turkish masters.[21]

In practice, men like Ilghazi and Tughtakin probably felt little excitement at the thought of jihad. They, like their fellow Turks, had only partially absorbed Islamic culture and beliefs at this stage, and they continued to observe much of their steppe culture and spirituality. Both Tughtakin and Ilghazi were known for their love of lengthy drinking binges. Alcohol is prohibited in Islamic law, and its continued use among the Turks reflected the long-standing customs of the steppe, where a ruler displayed his authority by organizing titanic bouts of inebriation. Other rather un-Islamic traits include Tughtakin's penchant for turning the skulls of his fallen enemies into drinking vessels.[22] He also liked to execute captives by tying them to posts and shooting them with arrows.[23] Symbolic acts involving bows and arrows were at the heart of Turkish elite ritual, and bows and arrows were also used as symbols on Seljuk coinage.[24] There are also reports that Tughtakin scalped captives.[25] These are all characteristically steppe practices. Ilghazi is also described as frequently seeking astrological guidance in his decision making, also a common fascination among the Turks.[26]

In the final analysis, despite the idealized portraits offered by some later writers, both Tughtakin and Ilghazi emerge as transitional figures whose customs and practices reflect a merging of different cultures and beliefs. They had some adherence to Islam, and, to take one example, they are known to have encouraged Frankish prisoners to become Muslims.[27] Still, their newly acquired faith was clearly spliced with the traditions of their forefathers.

———•———

Roger of Salerno, ruler of Antioch, first learned that Ilghazi had crossed the Euphrates and was heading straight for Christian territory in June 1119. There was no mistaking the Turks' intentions. This was a full-scale invasion, designed to drive the Franks back and assert Ilghazi's control over Aleppo. It had been a long time since Antioch had been tackled with a frontal assault, and most Turkish attackers had become bogged down by their internal disputes long before they reached the Christian frontier. Still, Roger was willing to march out and meet Ilghazi, so he immediately set about raising his army.

Roger had taken power in Antioch in 1113. His predecessor, Tancred, had had no heir, so on his deathbed in 1112 he had ordered that Roger of Salerno, his relative, should take power.[28] This was a pragmatic choice. The other obvious contender had been Bohemond's son, Bohemond II, but he had still been a child. Antioch had needed a ruler immediately, so Roger swiftly assumed control. His ascension to the principality had not been entirely unproblematic. Some had claimed that he should rule only until Bohemond II could take his place. Others were less concerned about Bohemond's rights as heir. The debate on the succession was bitter enough to attract even the attention of Muslim writers, who reported this incident.[29] In the event, however, matters were smoothed out by the church, and Roger soon felt sufficiently well established to march south to offer military support to the Kingdom of Jerusalem.

Roger himself has received mixed reviews for his time as ruler of Antioch. He was widely acknowledged to be brave, valiant, and handsome.[30] He was also clearly a capable field commander, and he scored several important victories, most notably at Tell Danith in 1115. He was feared by his enemies, one of whom described him as a "real devil."[31] He was also well attuned to the complex political world of the Near East. His strong grasp of the region and its politics reflects his ties to Tancred and his family's long service in Antioch. His father Richard was one of Tancred's most trusted lieutenants.[32] Like Tancred, Roger understood the importance of maintaining positive relations with neighboring Arab and Turkish powers, when the need arose, just as he grasped the political value of extracting tribute payments from vulnerable neighbors. He further strengthened his position by marrying his sister to the nobleman Joscelin of Courtenay.

Roger also had his vices. He was widely accused of avarice and was apparently miserly even when paying his own soldiers' wages.[33] More worryingly, he was a famous adulterer. Like other rulers, he married politically, and Roger chose to wed the sister of Baldwin of Bourcq (count of Edessa and later king of Jerusalem). Despite his spouse's royal connections, it was well-known that he was not a faithful husband.[34] This was a serious matter for the principality as a whole because contemporaries believed that the sinfulness of the ruler cast a spiritual shadow over his realm and its people, depriving them of God's support. The Antiochene forces, as they mustered in June 1119, were well aware that they needed God's blessing for the coming battle.

Roger's persistent adultery was not the only spiritual problem hanging over the army during its muster in June 1119. The army began to gather at Artah, a strong position, lying on the edge of a fertile plain to the northeast of Antioch, and messengers were sent to Baldwin II in Jerusalem, requesting his assistance. The patriarch of Antioch, Bernard of Valence, joined them soon afterward and counseled Roger to wait for Baldwin's arrival before seeking battle. It was sensible advice, and it should have rung especially true for Roger. In 1113 Roger had advanced to support the Kingdom of Jerusalem against a Damascene attack only to find that Baldwin I had rashly engaged Tughtakin's forces without waiting for his support. Baldwin's subsequent defeat had enraged Roger. He had been furious that Baldwin had been unable to wait for his reinforcements. He knew the value of combining forces.[35]

Still, the memory of that disappointment seems to have faded because in this case, in the early summer of 1119, Roger decided to advance, unsupported, against Ilghazi. The patriarch was not the only person to try to stop him: even the frontier lords, whose lands were most imperiled by Ilghazi's advance, agreed that he should wait. Nonetheless, he would not be dissuaded.[36] Battle was imminent.

Choosing whether or not to give battle was a difficult decision for any medieval commander, but it was an especially fraught question for the rulers of the Crusader States.[37] On the one hand, Roger may have felt that he had no choice but to give battle without waiting for his allies. He would have been aware of the sheer scale of his enemies' forces and the speed with which they could overcome his frontier defenses. If he chose to wait for reinforcements before giving battle, he might have to permit his enemies to ravage a sizable chunk of his principality before he was in a position to face them.

Such a decision would dent his credibility as a ruler, revealing him to be negligent in his responsibility to protect his people. The subsequent reconstruction work would take time and money, curbing his own expansionist ambitions. On these grounds, he could not afford to wait. By extension, if he could win a victory, unaided, against Ilghazi at this stage, his position would be substantially strengthened, stressing his credentials as a great Christian warrior.

On the other hand, Roger would have been aware that battle was a very dangerous business, and most Frankish rulers in the Crusader States tried to avoid large-scale encounters. The Antiochene army may have been an elite force, but it was also small and could not easily replace heavy casualties, either in men or horses. Even a hard-won victory could leave him in a worse position than his opponents. His manpower reserves were extremely limited, whereas his Turkish enemies would have no difficulty finding new Turkmen tribesmen to fill their ranks. Thus, the consequences of victory were potentially dire, but a defeat could be catastrophic. The Battle of Harran in 1104 had demonstrated how much could be lost following a major defeat, raising the specter of long-term damage to the principality and its territorial integrity.

Roger chose to fight. Perhaps he reminded himself of his earlier victory over the Turks at Tell Danith in 1115. Perhaps he realized the value of maintaining a healthy sense of fear and respect among the Turks, a feeling that would be dispelled if he refused battle. Perhaps he hoped that victory over Ilghazi would pave the way for the subsequent conquest of Aleppo. Certainly, the city's future hung on the outcome of this battle between its two aggressive suitors. Either way, his decision to advance was highly controversial and was made against the express wishes of many of his closest advisers.

Realizing that Roger was determined, the patriarch challenged him to confess his sins so that he might go into battle unstained by the crimes of his past. Roger was impressed by this chastisement and, in his main tent, he unburdened himself of his misdemeanors and received absolution from the group of clerics assembled there.

The army then made camp at Sarmada, a place that would become known as the *Ager Sanguinis*–the Field of Blood. The Franks fortified their encampment but soon came to realize that the location was poorly provided with food and water. It was at this point that the first enemy scouts arrived, masquerading as bird sellers. They took the lay of the land, and worked out the best paths and lines of approach to the Christian position.

Soon afterward, news arrived that Ilghazi had made his first attack. He had assaulted the Christian frontier fortress of al-Atharib, a strategically important staging post for attacks on Aleppo.[38] If al-Atharib were to fall, it would give Ilghazi a strong base close to Roger's camp.

Strongholds such as al-Atharib were vital to Antioch's defense. The maintenance of the principality's borderlands hinged on possession of strongly fortified towns and castles such as Zardana, Apamea, Artah, Kafartab, and Azaz. This was not the case in all the Crusader States. Some regions, such as the Kingdom of Jerusalem's Damascus-facing frontier, were only rarely challenged in these years, so they maintained few fortifications.[39] But the intensity of the fighting in northern Syria required Antioch to maintain a heavily fortified frontier facing Aleppo. A serried rank of large fortresses provided the strongpoints that could absorb an enemy attack until the Antiochene field army could assemble and march out to their relief. They also helped amplify the deterrent effect of Antioch's main field army. Enemy commanders did not like fighting battles with a Frankish army that had a castle in the immediate vicinity because such strongholds could both supply the Franks with information and resources and provide them with a place of refuge. There was also a danger that the garrison would sally out from the gates midbattle and attack from an unexpected quarter. This combination of castles and field armies enabled the Franks to stave off far larger forces than might otherwise have been deterred by their meager companies of cavalry and infantry.

The Turks could always choose to avoid the fortresses when staging an attack, simply advancing past them and into the Frankish heartlands beyond. In practice, however, both in 1119 and on other occasions, they rarely selected this option. Leaving a well-garrisoned enemy fortress to one's rear, along the line of retreat, was a dangerous business: If an attack went badly, the Turkish commander would have nowhere to run. Even if an attack went well, the garrison could still cause trouble on the Turks' return journey because they would be burdened with plunder, captives, and stolen cattle. Consequently, Turkish attackers preferred to cut a hole in Antioch's fortified frontiers before pressing on into the lands beyond.

Building a castle was expensive and time-consuming, and for the most part the early Frankish rulers, like their Turkish counterparts, preferred to augment existing structures rather than create new fortresses from scratch. This was a cheaper alternative, and building materials, often stripped from ancient Greek or Roman remains, could be easily reconstructed into fortifications. Among the most striking examples of such reused classical sites is the fortress of Bosra in the Hawran region, where, during the twelfth and thirteenth centuries, a series of Turkish rulers transformed a Roman amphitheater into a fort.[40] Many other strongholds were constructed around ancient forts, often Byzantine in origin. Very few were newly built. Even the cost of maintaining and strengthening existing fortified towns such as al-Atharib, Zardana, and Azaz must have been considerable. Many took a pounding when they were originally captured, and al-Atharib in particular was heavily damaged during Tancred's long siege in 1110. In addition, in 1114 there was a major region-wide earthquake, which caused significant damage to all three towns. Nevertheless, the Franks invested heavily in these strongpoints and rebuilt them as swiftly as possible. These towns were strongly fortified, and several had two lines of walls so the costs of repair—particularly given that the Franks must have rebuilt or refortified them at speed and under threat of attack—must have been very high. Fortunately for the Antiochenes, their revenue during this period seems to have been equally impressive, and both their prolific coinage and their ability to raise armies year after year testify to their substantial financial resources.[41]

Castles were not solely intended for frontier defense. They could be constructed for a range of purposes, including as a base for staging attacks. In 1111 Tancred had started to build a fort near Shaizar, from which the Franks could launch attacks and throttle the town by relentless raiding. This was a common tactic, and, further south, Baldwin I used the same strategy in 1117, building the fort of Scandalion to isolate the city of Tyre.[42]

Away from the frontier, in the principality's heartlands, Antioch's barons established castles that provided places of refuge in time of attack, centers for Frankish settlement in rural areas, and visible symbols of Frankish dominance. One particularly impressive example of such strongholds is Saone (now referred to in Syria as "Saladin's Castle"), owned by the Mazoir family. As with other castles, it had formerly been a Byzantine site, but when the Mazoirs took control in about 1108 they substantially augmented its fortifications.[43] As with many crusader castles, the Franks took full advantage of its natural defenses. This castle is situated on a valley spur with steep slopes dropping down to the valley floor on three sides. The remaining side, which connects the spur to the surrounding hills, was fortified with a massive ditch, twenty yards wide and twenty-eight yards deep (eighteen meters by twenty-six meters), cut into the solid rock.[44]

Castles served various purposes across the Crusader States. It must have been very disconcerting to be so far from western Christendom, so few in number and with nowhere to retreat except the sea. Castles helped address the ongoing manpower deficit that was a continual military weakness for the Crusader States, while at the same time also helping establish a network of secure locations from which the Franks could enforce their control and settle the land with their own people. Perhaps these ramparts, towers, and ditches also helped them look beyond the inherent insecurity of their position while affirming their hope that their frail grip on the coastline could have a future. Whatever their motives, the rate of building was exceptionally rapid in all the Crusader States, and in the Principality of Antioch, "[the] steep slopes and narrow valleys must have rung almost unceasingly with the sound of masons' hammers."[45]

In 1119 Roger of Salerno had been prepared for Ilghazi's assault upon the castle of al-Atharib and had already sent additional men to support the garrison. When the Turks arrived, they mounted a frontal attack on the fortress and then started to withdraw. The Turkish plan seems to have been to feign flight in order to draw the Christian defenders into a trap. However, they bungled the maneuver and were soundly beaten off by the castle's troops, led by Robert of Vieux-Pont. The men of Antioch had won the first round.[46]

News of the repulsed attack against al-Atharib heartened the Antiochene army, and Roger sought to build on this early victory by making plans to march on the fortress, presumably in an attempt to force his enemy to withdraw. The journey would be reasonably safe, given that, except for one low range of rocky hills, it would be on flat terrain. It was in this spirit of rising confidence that plans were made to dispatch scouts and prepare for their advance.

This confidence, however, did not last long. Just as the assembled commanders were concluding their council of war, a strange woman entered the tent where they were assembled. She harangued them, foretelling that they would all be killed on the following day. This unexpected and alarming event seems to have unnerved many of the Frankish barons and to have struck a jarring note against their former enthusiasm. A morning service held the following day by the archbishop of Apamea seems to have somewhat rebuilt the army's shaky morale, and they prepared to put their plans into action.[47] But it was too late. Scouts had returned to the Christian army in great haste, their horses suffering from many arrow wounds. The Turks had moved first and were advancing against the Frankish camp along three separate trajectories. Battle was upon them.

—————•—————

Ilghazi had taken the Franks by surprise. They had not anticipated that he would move so soon, particularly following his failed attack on al-Atharib. Roger still had time to prepare his army for the coming encounter, but even so Ilghazi had picked the battlefield.

Ilghazi had spent the months prior to his invasion of Antioch traveling around the Jazira, gathering his forces and using his family's lands at Mardin as his base. He knew that he would need an overwhelming force to confront the Franks and that such an army could only be raised from among the Turkmen tribes who traversed the region. Fortunately for him, he arrived in the Jazira to find these tribes seething with rage and spoiling for a fight. The Turkmen had just suffered a major raid by the Edessan Franks, who had seized hundreds of their people and thousands of their livestock and carried them back to their own lands. The Turkmen fighters were willing to accompany Ilghazi, and they offered him hostages as a tender of their good faith.[48]

By the time Ilghazi recrossed the Euphrates, he had assembled a great army. Medieval authors are notorious for their poor guesswork when reporting army sizes, and estimates for this force by Arabic authors range from twenty thousand to eighty thousand troops.[49] The real number was probably toward the lower end of this range, but writers from almost every culture underline the fact that the army was far larger than most armies of this period.

It was probably his army's overwhelming might, and its large contingent of Turkmen warriors, that led Ilghazi to attack without waiting for Tughtakin. Despite his defeat the previous year at the hands of Joscelin of Courtenay, Tughtakin was hurrying north with his own army, but Ilghazi's chieftains were not inclined to delay. Turkmen cavalry were enthusiastic raiders, but they were not regular troops; they required a steady stream of plunder and incentives if they were to remain with the army. The Muslim writer Ibn al-Athir commented about such tribal fighters that "each one of them would arrive with a bag of wheat and a sheep and would count the hours until he could take some quick booty and then go home."[50] Ilghazi may have been held in high regard by these tribes, but their impatience may have forced an immediate attack.

On the day of the battle itself, as Ilghazi's army prepared to attack, the Aleppan *qadi* Ibn al-Khashshab addressed the troops, encouraging them to fight bravely in a holy war against the Franks. This speech provides an important indicator of the Turks' engagement with notions of jihad, or lack thereof.[51] On the one hand, that he addressed them at all, even if he himself was Shia whereas the Turkmen were, at least nominally, under Sunni leadership, shows their receptiveness to such ideas. On the other hand, the Turks' response reveals their rather mixed religiosity: apparently the *qadi* was heckled by a Turkmen warrior, who asked his fellows whether they had traveled all the way from their own land only to take instruction from a man in a turban (by implication, an Islamic cleric).[52] The tribesman clearly felt that the *qadi* had no business claiming authority over them, and the Turkmen tribes may have considered him as little more than the defeated representative of a city that their master now controlled. For his part, Ibn al-Khashshab, apparently ignoring the impolite jibe, delivered such an inspirational speech—presumably in Turkish—that he brought his listeners to tears. He had won them over, but it is striking that the soldiers had not automatically understood or accepted his presence within their ranks. They were clearly not accustomed to receiving instruction in jihad.

The mainstay of Ilghazi's army, thus, were Turkmen warriors. They were capable fighters whose war craft and command structure still largely reflected their former life on the central Asian steppe. In that culture almost all children were raised to ride and shoot from an early age, so almost all adult males (and some females) had skills suitable for the battlefield. This was very different from the structure of agricultural societies (such as in Europe or the Islamic world), where only a small proportion of the male population was raised for war and the majority were destined for a life working the land.[53] Practicing their skills of archery and horsemanship on a daily basis, the Turks were extremely adept warriors, and Muslim travelers to the central Asian steppe had formerly remarked on the Turks' proficiency. One Arab envoy, Ibn Fadlan, sent to those regions from Baghdad in 922, noted that one archer had managed to shoot a goose from the sky while riding a galloping horse.[54]

Turkish arms, armor, and horses also reflected their nomadic background. Theirs was typically a life spent in the saddle, and the vast majority of the Turkmen forces would have been mounted. Their horses were hardy but were often rather small. Turks kept their horses in herds, and there were no fences or enclosures to let them selectively breed for size and strength. On these smaller horses, it was impractical for the Turks to wear the kind of heavy armor worn by crusader knights, although Frankish chain mail was highly prized. Turkish armor was probably mostly made of leather derived from their flocks and herds. The Turks' main weapon was the bow. Turkish composite recurved bows were powerful weapons and were manufactured from lengths of bone and horn taken from their livestock.

Confronting an army almost entirely made up of archers had initially been a shock for the First Crusaders. In western Europe archers were generally only one contingent within a broader army, and they were rarely mounted. On campaign, the Turks adopted an approach to warfare very different from that of their Arab, Byzantine, or Frankish enemies, prizing the bow and depending on fluidity of movement and command. For their agricultural enemies, warfare was a business of supply trains, logistics, and structured formations of infantry mixed with cavalry squadrons. It required money, encampments, and clearly defined command structures. War was generally fought to secure or weaken specific towns, cities, or strongholds.

The nomadic Turkmen had a rather different approach. Their war craft was characterized by movement and fluidity, and their goals were to control areas of grazing and to seize plunder and, only to a lesser degree, strongpoints. Nomadic armies did not require the same supply chains as did the armies of sedentary peoples because they brought their herds with them, a major advantage. Nor did campaigning incur the same costs because warfare was conducted within a tribal culture that did not require regular wages and taxation in quite the same way, and because weapons were sourced from their own herds and were the responsibility of the individual warrior.

In battle, Turkmen tactics similarly reflected this fluidity. They fought in tribal groupings under their various chieftains. Typically, these contingents did not form a steady battle line; rather, they fanned out, surrounded an enemy, raced in to shoot a few volleys of arrows when the opportunity arose, and then withdrew to await a new chance. They took their time, and a battle could be spread over several days. These tactics were not predicated on a decisive hand-to-hand duel in the center of a predetermined battlefield, like the classic encounter anticipated by their enemies, but consisted of grinding their enemy down in a relentless cycle of attacks that steadily reduced the enemy's numbers and morale. Turkmen acted rather like lions, circling herds of prey, picking off stragglers, and lunging into their ranks only when the time was right.

This approach to war could be extremely intimidating, spreading fear and panic. The Turks sought to amplify this effect by shouting war cries, beating war drums, and blowing great trumpets to unnerve their enemies. As a later Muslim author once commented, "Let the [emir] terrify the hearts of the enemy by displaying banners, beating *kusat* (small drums) and sounding *buqat* (trumpets), along with the noise of *tubul* (large drums) and *naqqarat* (kettle-drums)."[55]

These maneuvers sought to maximize the Turks' strengths (mobility and skillful archers) while minimizing their weaknesses (light armor and vulnerability in hand-to-hand combat). Their objective was to rout large, structured enemy formations, breaking them into smaller, poorly coordinated groups that could then be picked off singly.

The efficacy of these steppe tactics was demonstrated by the sheer scope of the Seljuk conquests in the eleventh century. Their approach to war proved adaptable to a range of military encounters with a host of different civilizations, proving its worth against enemies as diverse as war elephants in Persia and Viking mercenaries in Anatolia. By the end of the First Crusade, only the Egyptians and the Franks had shown any consistent ability to face them in battle (at least in the Near Eastern theater).

The Turks' approach to war, like their broader culture, had not remained static during their incursions into the Muslim world, and by the time they faced Roger of Antioch in 1119, many decades separated them from their former lives on the steppe. In the intervening period they had conquered much of the Islamic world, and it is likely that many among them would have picked up better weapons or armor, either as plunder or from local craftsmen or traders. Their leaders may also have acquired stronger mounts through purchase, tribute, or conquest. The Turks used an array of weapons to supplement their consistent use of the bow, including lances and swords. They tended to favor either narrow, straight-bladed swords, on the pattern of the early Islamic weapons, or very slightly curved sabers,[56] and they preferred blades manufactured in China, India, or western Europe.

The Turks were also learning to adapt themselves to Frankish tactics. The Franks had already demonstrated on several occasions that if the Turks could be caught unawares, or if they allowed their forces to cluster, they were vulnerable to the Frankish heavy cavalry, which would swiftly overpower their light cavalry in hand-to-hand combat. The Turks' goal, then, was to provoke the Frankish knights into a charge that could easily be evaded and would exhaust their horses. The Turks could then close in on the tired soldiers and pick them off. The Turks also increasingly made use of maces in combat, bludgeoning weapons that shattered flesh and bone on impact. Maces were not intended to cut through chain mail; rather, they sent shock waves through metal armor, thus circumventing the Franks' considerable defensive advantage.

—————•—————

Opposing Ilghazi was a substantially smaller Antiochene army. Later Muslim authors suggested that Roger had mustered twelve thousand to twenty thousand troops, and an Armenian author estimated about eleven thousand (including six hundred heavy cavalry).[57] Antioch's chancellor, Walter, who was present at the battle, said that there were seven hundred cavalry and three thousand infantry, along with auxiliary forces.[58] The figure of seven thousand to eleven thousand, with a core contingent of perhaps four thousand Frankish troops, feels reasonable and tallies well with the armies the Antiochene Franks had deployed in previous encounters. Additional troops would have been made up of mercenaries, as well as a large troop of Armenian allies.

The most important contingent within any Frankish army in the Crusader States was their heavy cavalry. These troops, despite their small numbers, were the fighters who really mattered. A successful charge by these armored cavalrymen could scatter vastly superior forces, as they had done at Tell Danith four years before. This tactical reality was fully understood by all sides in the Near East, and one Muslim writer acknowledged it freely: "A thousand [Turkish] horsemen will not [ordinarily] withstand the charge of three hundred Frankish knights."[59]

The great strength of these heavy-cavalry formations was their horses. Medieval warhorses were specifically raised for battle on stud farms where stallions and mares were selectively bred and reared to be powerful weapons. Stud farms had been used since the Roman era, and the warhorses they produced, known as "destriers" or "coursers," were extremely valuable, prized possessions. In the melee, such mounts were trained to barge into, bite, and kick their enemies, smashing enemy battle lines apart. They were trained to charge in close formation so that a squadron of knights would break upon an enemy formation as a solid block.

Medieval knights were equally well trained, often having been raised from childhood to handle both horses and arms. They were almost always heavily armored, generally wearing a long chain-mail jacket known as a "hauberk," which was essentially a shirt made up of thousands of interlinked metal rings (full plate armor was not common until the early fourteenth century). Chain mail had been used since the Roman era and had the advantages of being tough and flexible. It also covered all parts of the torso equally, leaving no weak points. Hauberks were usually worn over padded clothing, which was designed to reduce the impact of an enemy's blow. The hauberk could be supplemented by other chain-mail garments, such as the "coif" (essentially a chain-mail balaclava), which protected the head, neck, and upper chest. Chain-mail armor was extremely effective; Usama ibn Munqidh tells the story of his cousin Hittan, who had once been surrounded by Frankish knights, all hacking at him, but survived thanks to his chain-mail armor.[60] For additional protection, knights wore helmets, which were often conical in shape and supplemented with a nose guard. Shields would also have commonly been used, often so-called kite shields, which look like an inverted teardrop and whose long tail covers a rider's leg.

A knight's close-combat weapons were generally a lance, a sword, and a dagger, but other arms could also be employed. Lances were carried to enhance the shock effect of the cavalry charge, with the momentum of the charging horse and rider lending it force. They could be held above the arm, like a javelin, or couched under the arm. The latter style became more common over time. Swords were generally double-edged and broad-bladed, designed to impact heavily on armored enemies.

An infantryman's arms were less sophisticated than those carried by a knight. This was a time when a warrior's role in battle was determined by his wealth and social status, so foot soldiers necessarily possessed less expensive equipment. In battle, they provided protection for the cavalry squadrons, which could shelter their unarmored horses from enemy arrows behind the infantry's locked shields until the time came for them to unleash the full force of their charge. Infantrymen could wear chain mail and/or padded jackets, and they would often bear spears designed to fend off enemy horsemen.

Some might also carry missile weapons, and during the Crusades there was a growing awareness that such weapons were essential when tackling mounted Turkish archers. These would have been either bows or crossbows. The crossbow was more powerful, but it also took far longer to reload. It was not a medieval invention, having been used by the ancient Greeks, Romans, and Chinese, but it did not become a common weapon in medieval Europe until the eleventh century. Crossbows were used throughout the Crusades, and they were feared for their power. They typically had a range of about 220 yards (about 200 meters) and could pierce a piece of wood to a depth of almost three inches (seven centimeters).[61] They provoked such fear that in 1139 the Second Lateran Council banned their use against Christians.[62]

When Ilghazi's Turks arrived on the field of battle, Roger's Frankish army was already in full array. His infantry forces were formed up to provide a perimeter against enemy attacks, screening the cavalry. Banners flew above the Christian army, and the sound of trumpets resounded off the neighboring hills. At the army's center was its great cross, a mighty standard that contained a sacred relic, a piece of the True Cross of the Crucifixion. Messengers darted back and forth among the Christian contingents, relaying Roger's instructions. The army's cavalry was divided into individual commands, each under the control of a senior nobleman. These leaders had been instructed to charge sequentially directly into the enemy ranks, the idea being to hit their foes in percussive succession, like waves beating on the shore. The first wave was led by the elite battle line of Saint Peter, and this cohort was succeeded by companies under the command of Geoffrey the Monk, Guy Fresnel, and Robert of Saint Lo, and finally by the Turcopoles, warriors, often of Turkish, Eastern Christian, or mixed descent, who fought alongside the Franks as light cavalry.

After the opening maneuvers, Roger unleashed his cavalry on his Turkish foes, who were initially scattered by the Christian charge. This was a promising start, but during the charge the knightly companies lost cohesion and started to hamper one another. The fleeing Turks regrouped and joined a second wave of Turkish horsemen who countercharged the Frankish cavalry, both shooting at them with their bows and engaging in hand-to-hand combat. Confronted with this renewed onslaught, the left wing of the Christian line, composed of Robert of Saint Lo's contingent and the Turcopoles, began to buckle. Soon the Turks routed the entire wing, and the fleeing horsemen impeded the contingents led by Roger of Salerno.

The battlefield degenerated into a general melee of struggling men. In the midst of this churning bloodbath, a strong wind picked up the dry soil that had been kicked up by the horses' hooves, filling the air with thick dust that got into the warriors' eyes and limited their vision (1118 had been a very dry year and the ground was parched).

While the main battle was raging, another cavalry column under Rainald Mazoir engaged one of the Turks' advancing columns and put it to flight. With this success he should have been able to double back and rejoin the main army, but he was badly wounded in the fighting, and he and his forces had to take refuge in a nearby tower.[63]

As the battle wore on, the Christians began to falter. They had played their strongest card, the cavalry charge, and it had failed. Their enemies had been temporarily driven back, but neither their ranks nor their morale had been broken. With the heavy cavalry now locked in a bitter melee and on the defensive, it was only a matter of time before the Turks' vast numerical superiority asserted itself. Slowly the knights were ground down until they were locked in a defensive huddle surrounded by enemies. Roger was knocked from his horse, and soon afterward, the great standard of the cross toppled. The enemy surged forward, sensing their advantage, although the Antiochene author Walter the Chancellor—who may have been in that small huddle—tells us that several Turks were struck down as soon as they reached out to grasp the cross, crushed by divine power.[64]

Soon it became clear that Roger was dead; a sword thrust had caught him on the nose and pierced his skull.[65] A later legend states that Roger was initially captured, not killed. He was surrounded by Turks, who stripped him of his chain-mail armor and attempted to wrest his sword from his grip. He resisted these efforts to disarm him, saying he would only yield his sword to an enemy commander. His Turkish captors accepted his statement and sought out an emir. This Turkish leader duly arrived and, taking off his helmet, demanded the Antiochene ruler's sword. Roger responded defiantly by slicing off the emir's head and was cut down immediately by his bodyguard.[66] Whatever really happened, Roger was dead.

With the collapse of the knightly companies, the survivors and the remaining foot soldiers tried to make a last stand on a nearby hill, seeking to muster sufficient numbers to deter attack and to negotiate their escape. This was a vain hope, and they were torn apart. Very few from their ranks—or indeed, from the Frankish army as a whole—escaped. Many prisoners were taken, including an envoy from the Byzantine emperor who had come to negotiate a marriage alliance with Antioch. The envoy was later ransomed for fifteen thousand bezants and traveled south to discuss another marriage agreement with Baldwin II of Jerusalem.[67] The captives (about five hundred) were tightly bound; the wounded were beaten to death with rods and scalped (a steppe custom).[68]

The Field of Blood was a brutal encounter in which the Turks realized the full advantage of their substantial numbers, while employing their maneuverability to outflank and surround their enemies. Their decision to attack in waves, with the first provoking and absorbing the Christian charge, helped them absorb the impact of the Frankish heavy cavalry, and their archers exacted a grim toll among the Frankish horses. A later Arabic author commented that after the battle, the Franks' fallen steeds were so riddled with arrows that they looked like hedgehogs.[69] There was nothing especially new about such tactics. They were the cultural norm for Turkish light-cavalry commanders, but they had been used to devastating effect. The Turks seemed to have worked well in concert, executing a simple but effective strategy, and this reflects well on Ilghazi's ability to communicate a clear battle plan to a large mixed force of tribal Turkmen warriors.

From the Christian perspective, the initial cavalry charge was clearly a disaster. The knights allowed themselves to be drawn too far away from the relative security of their infantry lines. As they did in most battles, they relied on their mounted shock troops to negate their enemies' substantial numerical advantage, but this time the horsemen failed to inflict sufficient trauma on their enemies to create a cascade reaction of panic.

With the almost complete annihilation of the Antiochene army, the principality was wide open. The Turkmen crisscrossed its hinterlands, pillaging everything within range and reaching as far as Antioch itself and even beyond to the Amanus range, where they killed a group of monks in the Black Mountain region.[70] While Antioch's estates were being systematically plundered, its strongholds along the Aleppan frontier were falling. Artah surrendered almost immediately. Al-Atharib's citadel was taken, and its garrison, including some refugees from Aleppo, capitulated. Zardana also fell. Antioch's crisis only deepened when Tughtakin arrived with his Damascene army, supplementing Ilghazi's horde.[71]

Reflecting on this catalog of victories, the Muslim author Ibn al-Qalanisi expressed his exasperation that Ilghazi did not immediately attempt to conquer Antioch itself, ending the Frankish principality once and for all.[72] The thought must surely have occurred to him, but the goal was probably out of his reach. He may have brought together a large company of Turkmen, but they were raiders. Many had simply drifted off after the battle to pillage the surrounding countryside. Moreover, the Turkmen existed in a world defined by movement and the search for pastureland, not by the geopolitics of agricultural societies. They may not have attached much importance to the capture and retention of a major urban center, lying so far from their homelands, nor would they necessarily have been keen to engage in a difficult siege, for which they were ill-suited. As for Ilghazi, he had only recently taken control in Aleppo, and his tenure in that city was far from secure. Acquiring a second major city, simmering with resentment and rebellion, would probably have seemed both overambitious and unappealing. Better to give the Turkmen the plunder they wanted and focus on securing Aleppo's frontiers. Whatever his motives, Ilghazi did not move to besiege Antioch.

Another warning light appearing in Ilghazi's strategic planning would have been the rapid advance of the king of Jerusalem from the south. Baldwin had responded quickly to Roger's summons for help and had set out briskly along the coast road toward Antioch. En route he collected Pons, count of Tripoli, and their combined force arrived in Antioch in early August 1119, defeating a Turkmen raiding party during the final stages of their journey. He arrived in Antioch to find its people in a state of high alert. The patriarch had temporarily taken charge of the city and prepared its defenses for an attack. Baldwin relieved him of command and immediately began to lay plans that would ensure Antioch's survival.

Baldwin's first move was to hold a council to arrange for the succession. Bohemond's son Bohemond II was the natural choice, but he was only a boy of eleven years, and so it was decided that Baldwin himself would govern Antioch until Bohemond II reached adulthood. The council also agreed that Bohemond II would marry one of Baldwin's daughters, cementing ties between their states.[73]

The king of Jerusalem then summoned Antioch's remaining fighting strength, ordering the principality's surviving warriors to gather at the capital. Messengers were also sent to the Edessans commanding them to dispatch their forces as soon as possible. Baldwin II of Jerusalem was still technically count of Edessa, having only recently become king, so he could issue this order directly. Once he had assembled this hastily formed army, Baldwin set out eastward to seek battle with Ilghazi. He made camp at Tell Danith, where Roger had triumphed back in 1115.

Ilghazi was well aware of this new threat, and he set out to meet Baldwin. At the crack of dawn on August 14, Baldwin deployed his army. It was not a large force. A Muslim chronicler suggests that it included only four hundred knights and additional infantry; a Christian author suggests a knightly contingent of seven hundred.[74] Either way, they were substantially outnumbered, and the odds facing Baldwin were probably greater than those Roger had confronted at the Field of Blood. Ilghazi's own position was exceptionally strong. Not only would his men have been ebullient in the wake of their earlier victory, but his ranks were supplemented by Tughtakin's army and by several large contingents of Arab warriors; seemingly news of Antioch's weakness had spread far and wide, and many had been drawn to the prospect of feasting on its bones.[75]

In the early hours of the morning the two forces converged. The Frankish infantry was arrayed in the rear, providing a place of retreat for the Frankish horsemen. Baldwin's vanguard consisted of three waves of cavalry, with a further six cavalry squadrons deployed in the army's center. On the right were the men of Tripoli, and on the left were Antioch's barons.

Ilghazi's strategy was standard. His troops had taken stations all around the Christian force, a noose around the Franks' necks. This deployment denied his enemy any line of retreat and was intended to instill a sense of fear. The feeling of entrapment was only amplified by the incessant drumming that the Turks began all around the Frankish force at first light. As the summer sun began to rise, the Turks launched their first assault on the Christian army. These lunges were not attacks pressed home in earnest; rather, small companies rode up to the Frankish lines, fired a few volleys of arrows or threw javelins, and then wheeled away. At this early stage, the Turks focused their attention specifically on the Franks' infantry rear guard, seeking to deny the knights a place to retreat. Their objective was to utterly annihilate the small Christian army.

The attacks continued until it became clear that the infantry was not going to break ranks, at which point the Turks attempted to use their overwhelming numbers in one colossal onrush intended to submerge and smother their foe. Their decision to seek close combat—not typically a Turkish strength—at such an early stage in the battle reflects their confidence that the Christians would simply be overwhelmed by the sheer mass of their army.

The Turkish charge almost worked. The infantry took heavy casualties, and three waves of knights were overwhelmed. Viewing the rising disorder, the archbishop of Caesarea, standing next to Jerusalem's great standard, the cross of the Crucifixion, proclaimed God's vengeance upon the Turks.[76]

The day was warming up. August temperatures in northern Syria would have been in the mid-nineties (mid-thirties centigrade), but the day of the battle is said to have been especially scorching. Knights fighting in layers of padding and armor, mounted on hot, sweating horses, were extremely vulnerable to heat exhaustion and dehydration, and many of their Turkish enemies are said to have collapsed during the fighting.[77]

It was only when the bulk of the Turkish army had engaged the infantry that Baldwin charged. He seems to have waited almost until the point of complete disaster before making a move, but his patience bore fruit. He wanted to be sure that the greater part of the enemy army had immobilized itself in the press of fighting men and could not scatter or flee from his charge. Then he struck, bulldozing through the enemy lines from vanguard to rear guard. The

Turkish army was put to flight, and Baldwin soon found himself in possession of the battlefield.

The Second Battle of Tell Danith was not much of a victory, and most writers describe it as a bloody draw.[78] The Christians took heavy casualties, and they suffered badly in several smaller skirmishes fought on the margins of the battlefield between scattered Frankish formations and retreating Turks. Even so, the Turks had been driven off, and Baldwin's men now stood uncontested on the field of battle. This in itself was an exceptional achievement, especially given the extreme imbalance in numbers. Baldwin could now go back to Antioch to a rapturous reception. The city was safe, for the present, even if its ambition to seize Aleppo was in tatters.

In the wake of the battle, it was time for both sides to count the cost. For Ilghazi, the battle at Tell Danith took the shine off his earlier victory at the Field of Blood. He had not exactly been defeated, but despite the size of his army, he had not decisively crushed the principality either. He returned to Aleppo to find that the citizens had received mixed reports concerning the recent battle, some claiming the Turks had been routed, others proclaiming victory.[79] To add to his troubles, there was murmuring that some of the city's elites, who had suffered during Ilghazi's ascension to power, were starting to plot against him.

To quiet such voices, Ilghazi immediately announced, less than truthfully, that he had won a second great victory, and to stress the point, he had his prisoners tortured and presented to the populace. The nobleman Robert Fitz-Fulk was decapitated by Tughtakin of Damascus, a former friend. His head was carried around Aleppo's streets and presented at the houses of the rich, who were expected to show their appreciation by making gifts. Robert's skull was later turned into a drinking vessel. Other prisoners had all their limbs cut off, and their torsos were thrown into public spaces. These were brutal acts of torture and death, but they had a clear political purpose. They sent an unmistakable message to the Aleppan people about Ilghazi's strength, power, and ruthlessness. Through these events, Ilghazi and Tughtakin had been drinking heavily in their tents, which had been erected outside the city walls.[80]

Ilghazi's actions unnerved some of the Islamic elites in his entourage. Both his conduct in war and some of the distinctive tortures he inflicted on his captives were characteristic of the central Asian steppe and would have seemed alien to a local religious leader. A later report by one of the Frankish prisoners is suggestive: Ilghazi had offered a *qadi* the opportunity to execute Arnulf, seneschal of Marash, but he had refused, seemingly troubled by what was going on, and had handed the blade to a nearby emir.[81]

Ilghazi's acts may have worried those religious leaders who had accompanied the army, but to rulers and authorities in more distant parts of the sultanate, he was a hero. He had struck a decisive blow against the Franks, and his deeds in battle were celebrated (generally with the Field of Blood played up and the Second Battle of Tell Danith played down). Verses were created to commemorate his achievements, stressing that they should be understood as acts of holy war carried out by a devout holy warrior against the followers of Christianity:

> *The Koran rejoiced when you brought it victory.*
> *The Gospel wept for the loss of its followers.*[82]

Such ideas hardly bring Ilghazi's actions and objectives into focus. He had scarcely fought the Franks before 1119, despite his long career, and he had even marched alongside them. He was formerly known among Armenians as being "very intimate friends" with Roger of Salerno.[83] But after the Field of Blood, that did not matter. What mattered was that Ilghazi had just stepped into the halls of legend. Irrespective of his deeds in life, his memory would now be a potent symbol encapsulating the notion of defending Islam against the Franks, a symbol that could be used by Muslim scholars and courtiers to guide their partially converted Turkish masters to fully embrace and internalize an Islamic identity. As for Ilghazi himself, he had supplied the Aleppan people with some very explicit reasons to remain loyal to his cause.

———◆———

On the other side of the border, the Franks were rediscovering their fighting spirit. Baldwin launched repeated raids to reassert Antioch's position along its eastern margins, and he sent further forces to attack the Munqidhs, who had sided with Ilghazi immediately after the battle and had seized some neighboring towns.[84] Baldwin also called upon his cousin Joscelin, lord of Tiberias, to take charge in Edessa. This combative nobleman swiftly assumed power and then launched a series of punishing raids on Aleppan territory, seeking to reassert Frankish dominance on its hinterland. Through his prompt action and gutsy conduct both at Tell Danith and during the following weeks, Baldwin II partially mitigated several of the deep injuries inflicted on the principality following the Field of Blood.[85]

These would have been comforting thoughts to Antioch's remaining defenders, but they would not have obscured the severity of the Field of Blood's impact. Antioch's power was much reduced, and its former ambitions now had to be savagely curtailed. The Franks had formerly possessed a formidable army, made even more intimidating by its fearsome reputation. It had been a force strong enough to seriously contemplate the conquest (or, more probably, the political annexation) of Aleppo. But the Frankish tide that for many years had seemed likely to sweep across the entire region, carrying all before it, had been brought to an abrupt halt. Now Antioch's army was shattered, and the agricultural estates that supplied the principality with the bulk of its resources had been thoroughly pillaged. Antioch's war of conquest in the north was over. If the Frankish struggle for Aleppo was to continue, it could now only be carried out by King Baldwin II of Jerusalem. This too was

a crucial change for the region. Before the battle, Antioch and Jerusalem had challenged one another for predominance; now that
contest was finished. Jerusalem was in charge.[86]

In addition to its strategic consequences, the Battle of the Field
of Blood dented Frankish self-confidence across the Latin East.
In recent years, the rulers of the Crusader States seem to have felt
comfortably self-sufficient, surviving on their own resources along
with the seasonal influx of pilgrims and settlers. They rarely wrote
to western Christendom seeking aid and were generally content to
wage war without actively seeking additional reinforcements. After
the battle, however, they began to write to western Europe in earnest urgently asking for help.[87] The realization had clearly dawned
on them that the momentum of their conquests was stalling and
that their broader position was now vulnerable.

The Field of Blood also provoked an intense period of spiritual
soul searching across Frankish lands. Victory and defeat on the battlefield were perceived not simply as a question of cavalry maneuvers and companies of spearmen; they were the will of God. What
had the people of Antioch done to deserve such a catastrophe?

To answer that question, the Franks had to look to themselves,
to their moral conduct. It was their vice that had raised the barriers
between themselves and God, isolating them in the face of their
enemies. Victory required righteous conduct, and it was common
knowledge that the armies of the First Crusade had triumphed
solely because their moral behavior had found favor in the eyes of
God. In the aftermath of the Field of Blood, the Franks examined
their recent actions and found them wanting. Their sins were numerous. They had turned away from abstinence and fasting to in-
dulge in gluttony, allowing their stomachs to dictate to their heads.
Some were known to have visited brothels and to have indulged
in sexual sin. Others had handed themselves over to the love of
money and had become entrapped in avaricious pursuits. Women
in particular were thought to have shamed their people with their
lustfulness, seeking to ornament their bodies rather than to work

for the salvation of their souls. To make matters worse, God had warned his people of his rising displeasure, sending a plague of locusts to the region some time before, but no one had paid attention. The people of Antioch had paid more attention to another sign, an earthquake that had rippled through the region, but seemingly not enough. Antioch had sinned, and its people were well aware that only a fool ignores the will of God.[88]

Further south, in the Kingdom of Jerusalem, Baldwin II reached a similar conclusion, and in January 1120, soon after his return to his southern kingdom, he convened a council at the town of Nablus.[89] Here the assembled nobles debated the fortunes of war, the plague of locusts, and the recent destruction of a large party of Frankish pilgrims as they visited the holy places. Clearly something needed to change if they were to regain favor in God's sight. Consequently, they instituted a series of strict laws, borrowing from Byzantine models, that were specifically designed to improve the Frankish people's moral behavior. These regulations specified tough penalties for adultery, sodomy, rape, and all sexual relations with Muslims. More remarkably, the council also permitted clerics to use weapons in their own defense (a major break with tradition).[90] Another outcome of the council—and in part, therefore, of the Field of Blood—was the agreement by the assembled elites that a small band of dusty knights who served as pilgrim escorts should be given formal institutional recognition. This group would in time rise to become one of Christendom's most powerful religious institutions: the Knights Templar.[91]

As the storms of war settled following the campaigns of 1119, several realities began to set in. Most obviously, Antioch had been crippled and would need sustained assistance in the coming years if it was to survive. This in itself was a major shock to the geopolitics of the Near East, whose rulers were accustomed to a bullish and expansionist Antioch. Now, suddenly and for the first time in more than a decade and a half of steady expansion, Antioch's policies had been brought to an abrupt halt. The principality was at a dead stop and needed assistance. This support could only realistically be rendered by the Kingdom of Jerusalem, so it was fortunate for Antioch that Baldwin II was willing to focus his efforts on the principality's needs.

Jerusalem had the resources and the manpower to sustain its northern cousin; its revenues and settler population had been growing steadily in recent years. Its major enemy, Fatimid Egypt, was in steep decline, and Baldwin II either ruled or could influence all four Crusader States: Jerusalem (his kingdom), Antioch (now under his protection), Edessa (his former territory whose ruler he had recently appointed), and Tripoli (subordinate to Jerusalem). He was determined to resume the struggle for northern Syria and regain the forward momentum that had been lost at the Field of Blood. Meanwhile, on the other side of the border, Aleppo may have found a strong, if brutal, defender, but Ilghazi had not taken up permanent residence in the city. He had returned home to Mardin. The city remained vulnerable. It would not be long before the fields of Syria would run with blood once again.

CHAPTER 4

FIELDS OF BLOOD

1120–1128

THE BATTLE OF the Field of Blood had been a major defeat for the Antiochene Franks, and the Christian advance across northern Syria was stalling. Antioch no longer possessed the resources to maintain its own frontiers, much less to keep up a war of expansion. Even so, the struggle for Aleppo was not over. Baldwin II of Jerusalem was bullish in his determination to seize the city, and he pursued this goal energetically in the years following the Field of Blood. His ambition was to regain the momentum of Antioch's earlier rulers and push the frontier east. The fight would go on, but the obstacles barring the road to Aleppo were far greater than they had been. Before the Field of Blood, the city had almost been within their grasp, but now Aleppo had a powerful defender, and Baldwin would have to carry out his campaigns far from his own kingdom while simultaneously reconstructing the Principality of Antioch.

<hr />

By August it was becoming clear that 1121 was going to be a bad year for Ilghazi. A few months earlier, he had received a cry for help from his Turkish peers to the north. The Georgians had been pushing into their territory, led by King David the Builder, and were threatening the city of Tbilisi. Although this frontier lay far from Ilghazi's core lands in the Jazira, he had responded to their appeal and mustered his own forces to join the campaign. He had stomached enough inconclusive campaigning against the Franks in recent years and was looking for more promising prospects. Only the previous year he had launched an assault on Frankish Edessa and Antioch, but he had not achieved much. The Georgian campaign, on the other hand, raised new opportunities to score a major victory while loading his Turkmen's saddlebags with Georgian loot. However, the campaign proved to be nothing but an embarrassment. The Turkish force engaged the Georgians in battle, but after initially forcing their opponent to retreat, they were soundly defeated. Thousands were killed, and later writers describe a landscape strewn with Turkish dead.[1] Many more were captured, and Ilghazi was compelled to retire in disgrace.

The Georgian campaign had been bad enough, but it was only the start of Ilghazi's nightmare year. On his return journey, news reached him that his son Shams al-Dawla, governor of Aleppo, had rebelled and executed Ilghazi's lieutenants in the city. To make matters worse, even before Ilghazi had set out for Georgia, King Baldwin II had started to put Aleppo under renewed pressure. His attacks in the spring of 1121 had begun with a series of assaults on the frontier strongholds of al-Atharib and Zardana (both of which had been lost after the Field of Blood).[2] Neither assault had been successful, but they had been sufficient to force Ilghazi to the negotiating table. To secure peace, so that he could depart for the Georgian border, he had made major concessions, allowing the Franks to claim taxes from Aleppan territory, even from suburbs just outside the city's walls. He had also promised to grant them control over several strongholds, including al-Atharib. Frustratingly, his garrison at al-Atharib had refused to hand over their fortress, jeopardizing the treaty. Then, in the summer, while Ilghazi was far away fighting the Georgians and his son Shams al-Dawla was in rebellion, Baldwin had attacked again, raiding across the land, re-occupying Zardana, seizing towns, and destroying crops. No one had been able to restrain him, and when Baldwin's army appeared outside Aleppo's gates, the Franks had defeated the small force that had sallied out from the city to drive him away.[3]

As Ilghazi returned to his homeland, his authority was hanging in the balance. Despite all that he had won in 1119, Aleppo was once again on the verge of slipping from his grasp. These were dangerous times, but he still had the advantage of a fearsome reputation, and his son was clearly worried by his father's imminent reappearance. As Ilghazi's surviving forces reached the Euphrates at Qalat Jabar and were preparing to set out on the final leg of their journey to Aleppo, Shams al-Dawla lost his nerve and attempted to make peace with his father. Ilghazi declared he was ready for this reconciliation, so when he reached Aleppo in November 1121, he found the gates standing open and his son ready to receive him. He could not leave the matter there. Ilghazi was clearly worried about the effect this family feud might have had upon the Aleppan people's always-questionable loyalties, because he staged his arrival with great pomp, reminding them of his greatness.

He also slashed the city's taxes for the second time since 1120 in an attempt to win the people's support.[4] At some point during this period he also began to establish favorable relations with the Assassins, just as his predecessor Ridwan had done, even though they were loathed by his Turkish counterparts. They were too powerful a faction to ignore. Then he punished the plotters surrounding his son, and the tortures he inflicted on their leaders were every bit as gory as the torments he had meted out to the captured Antiochene nobles after the Second Battle of Tell Danith. He tore out one conspirator's tongue and gouged out his eyes. He blinded another and cut off his hands and feet. Other rebels had their eyes burned out and their hamstrings cut. These brutal disfigurements sent a message to future rebels. His son received far more lenient treatment. He was spared any physical punishment, although he fled to Damascus as soon as possible.[5]

Having firmly asserted himself against his son, Ilghazi turned to the Franks. In June 1122 he set out to reconquer Zardana supported by his nephew and Turkmen ally Balak and by Tughtakin of Damascus. At that moment Baldwin was at Tripoli, but he hurried north on receiving news that Ilghazi's troops, equipped with catapults, were besieging this vital frontier town.

The resulting encounter was an impasse. Baldwin adopted a shadowing strategy, occupying defensible locations that were close to the Turkish foes but too strong to be attacked, while refusing to give battle. This ploy prevented his enemies from making incursions into Christian territory without risking the uncertainties of a full-scale engagement. Baldwin's approach succeeded, and having achieved nothing, Ilghazi's conglomeration of forces withdrew and dispersed.[6] This was another inglorious operation for Ilghazi, and it was also his last. He became ill during the campaign and died soon afterward in November 1122.

With Ilghazi's passing, a power vacuum emerged in northern Syria. Ilghazi had long been a dominant voice, both in the Jazira and further afield, and the Turkmen tribes respected his authority. Now the field was open to new contenders. The first to exploit this opportunity, predictably, were the Franks. They attacked immediately, pushing far to the east of Aleppo toward Bales until they were bought off in April 1123 with the concession of the much-coveted al-Atharib. They were not strong enough to attack the city directly, so they concentrated on strengthening their hold on the hinterland.

————

Ilghazi's death proved to be a major boon for the Franks, but—as Baldwin would soon discover to his cost—the Turkmen tribes of northern Syria did not have to wait long for a new champion. Their new leader was Balak, Ilghazi's nephew and an experienced commander. Like his uncle, Balak had been operating in northern Syria for decades, and had enjoyed a lively career, waging war against multiple enemies with the support of loyal Turkmen tribesmen.

Balak had first encountered the Franks during the First Crusade. At the time he had been ruling the town of Saruj (modern-day Suruç) in the name of another uncle named Sokman. Saruj was a wealthy and prosperous town lying to the southwest of Edessa. It had only been in Turkish hands since 1095, when it was wrested from the Arab Banu Uqayl tribe. By 1098 Balak was struggling to maintain control over the populace, and when he learned that Baldwin of Boulogne (future Baldwin I of Jerusalem) had become the ruler of Edessa, he sought his aid against the local Muslim populace, who were refusing to render tribute payments. Baldwin set out for Balak's lands, but the proposed alliance swiftly broke down in acrimony (a Frankish writer claimed that Balak had been conspiring secretly against Baldwin with the support of another Turkish warrior in Frankish service).[7] Whatever the cause of their disagreement, the result was that Baldwin marched on Saruj with a train of siege engines. The people had no especial loyalty to Balak, so they yielded the city to the Franks and forced their former ruler to leave. Sokman was unable to retake the town a few years later, even after a prolonged struggle.[8]

This early encounter set the tone for Balak's subsequent dealings with the Franks. Like the region's other Turkish rulers, he harbored no distinctively anti-Frankish agenda, and he was prepared to fight them or ally with them depending on his evolving interests. In 1101 he joined forces with a group of Turkish rulers to attack a crusading army that was seeking to cross Anatolia, but by October 1103 he was in northern Iraq, where he besieged the Arab town of Ana on the banks of the Euphrates.[9] He seems to have been looking for a new base of operations, but his attack failed in the face of staunch resistance from the local Arab tribes.

He next appeared serving with his uncle Ilghazi during his sojourn as governor of Baghdad. Balak's role in his uncle's service was to prevent the various Turkmen tribes in the region from attacking the merchant caravans transporting their wares to Baghdad from the Far East. He performed this task well, and he later supported Ilghazi in the Jazira, fighting against local Turkish rulers and, in 1114, resisting the sultan's attempts to draw the region under his control.[10]

During this time, in about 1113, Balak acquired the town and fortress of Kharput in central Anatolia, and he used this base to launch a devastatingly effective raid on the Byzantines in the early 1120s. By this point, it had been many years since Balak had last taken the field against a Frankish army, yet in 1122 he thrust himself decisively back into the fray by supporting Ilghazi in his attack on the Principality of Antioch, joining him with a large force of Turkmen.[11] The expedition was indecisive, but it seems to have whetted Balak's appetite for war with the Franks. Soon afterward, in September 1122, he launched a raid into Edessan territory toward his former stronghold of Saruj. The incursion was an act of opportunism, seemingly intended merely as a glancing blow on his return to his fortress of Kharput, but it proved to be a spectacular and unexpected success.

Soon after Balak entered Edessan territory, the Edessan ruler, Count Joscelin of Courtenay, set out to track him down with a company of one hundred knights. Balak had eight times that number of horsemen at his disposal, so despite the Frankish cavalry's formidable reputation, he was prepared to meet Joscelin in battle. More importantly, he had an innovative ploy to defeat the Christian cavalry charge. He picked his battlefield carefully, leading the Franks on a long chase ending in an area of low ground near a river. Joscelin's cavalry arrived soon after Balak, already exhausted by their long pursuit. The Turks then incited the Christian knights to launch their charge across marshy terrain. The horses, carrying heavily armored knights, sank into the mud and were immobilized. It was then easy work for the Turks to shower the Franks with arrows until their leaders capitulated. This was a minor skirmish, but it won Balak a valuable prize: Count Joscelin was now his prisoner.

Initially he hoped to capitalize on his high-value captive by demanding that he surrender Edessa, but Joscelin flatly refused. As a result, Joscelin was ignominiously sewn inside a camel skin and transported to Balak's stronghold of Kharput.[12]

This encounter was a notable success for a Turkish chieftain who had previously been virtually unknown, and it is striking that contemporaneous writers from multiple cultures now started to take a closer interest in Balak. For Balak, this was a great victory, and his power only grew when, following Ilghazi's death, he received many of his uncle's former territories. Armed with this might, he launched attack after attack on Frankish and Armenian territory.

His first move was to besiege the Frank-controlled town of Gargar. Baldwin II hurried north to its relief in April 1123, but Balak set a successful ambush for the king, who was riding ahead of his army with only a light escort. Baldwin was taken prisoner and placed in Kharput along with Joscelin.[13] With this second unexpected victory, Balak now had two of the most important Frankish rulers in his custody, rendering Jerusalem, Antioch, and Edessa leaderless. Such heavy and sudden blows against the Franks fully committed Balak to the struggle with the Franks.

Balak's next move was equally ambitious. Like so many other successful warlords in northern Syria—Frankish or Turkish—he set out to secure the greatest prize of all: Aleppo. Balak wanted to assert himself as Ilghazi's successor and disenfranchise any other claimants. Control of Aleppo would give him the resources to aspire to region-wide dominance, and he pursued this goal with the utmost ruthlessness. In May 1123 he began his approach on the city by seizing the town of Harran, to the northeast of Aleppo and on the eastern banks of the Euphrates. In late May he reached Aleppo's hinterlands, where he burned the crops (apparently his signature tactic) and blockaded the city, provoking a famine. He raided the surrounding villages and enslaved the populace. By late June 1123, the city's defenders had suffered enough. They opened the gates and admitted Balak as their new ruler.[14]

Like Ilghazi's before him, Balak's ascension to power was brutal. Interestingly, however, Balak was more moderate as governor than he was as conqueror. His methods for seizing strongholds may have been ruthless, but once installed he could see the value of more restrained policies. Eastern Christian authors speak favorably of his virtues, observing that Balak was a stern protector of his subjects' rights and was even prepared to execute fellow Turks if he caught them stealing.[15] His Frankish opponents also fully recognized his abilities.[16]

By June 1123 Balak had been campaigning, scarcely without pause, for almost a year, yet his thirst for war was unsated. No sooner had he conquered Aleppo than he flung himself on the Principality of Antioch, conquering the town of Apamea. By this stage, his relentless attacks, both against Franks and against fellow Turks, were as unremitting as they were successful. A new power had risen, and the leaderless Franks were at a disadvantage. Under repeated attack and with Baldwin and Joscelin in prison, Aleppo was steadily receding as an achievable goal, and Antioch's own frontiers were under threat.

Yet in August 1123 Balak's gaze was suddenly drawn away from the frontier by an act that was as daring as it was unexpected. Baldwin, Joscelin, and the other prisoners at Kharput had received covert assistance from a group of Armenian fighters, overthrown their Turkish guards, and conquered their fortress prison.

———————

By the time of the First Crusade, the Armenians had been long accustomed to invaders. Since the time of Christ they had often found themselves on the frontier between competing enemies—Romans against Persians, Arabs against Byzantines—and more recently they had been in the path of the Turkish onslaught. Their communities had lived for centuries in the much-contested lands that stretched between the mountains of the Caucasus and the headwaters of the Tigris and Euphrates, but in the tenth century large numbers of Armenians had also begun to travel west into the coastal regions of Cilicia and the Amanus mountain range. The catalyst for this movement had been the Byzantine Empire's sustained effort to push its border south into Syria and toward the Holy Land. In these wars, the coastal regions of northern Syria and southern Anatolia were retaken and settled by large numbers of Armenian soldiers serving in the Byzantine army. It was these western Armenian communities that first encountered the crusaders, and both the Principality of Antioch and the County of Edessa possessed a substantial Armenian population.

The Armenians were a Christian people of long standing; in 314, King Tiridates III had been the first Armenian ruler to accept the faith. Since then Christianity had spread rapidly among their number, and they formed their own distinctive Armenian Church.[17]

In the decades directly preceding the First Crusade, the Armenians had been deeply affected by the Turkish invasions. The Turks had swept across Byzantium's borders (from about 1029), scoring a series of victories against the imperial armies. As Byzantine authority began to recede, many Armenian communities, which had formerly been within the empire's borders, found themselves caught on the front line of the fighting. In later years, as the Turks pushed further west toward Constantinople, these same lands degenerated into a chaotic melee of competing local rulers, whether Turkmen, Armenian, or Byzantine, each vying for control. Even before the crusade, there were Frankish mercenaries who joined the contest, seizing the chance to carve out their own states.

The arrival of the First Crusaders shortly afterward represented a potential opportunity for the subjugated Armenians. Some among their number at first saw the crusaders' arrival as the long-awaited fulfillment of apocalyptic prophecies made by the Armenian hermit Yovhannes Kozern, who had foretold that the Franks would arrive, conquer Jerusalem, and usher in the end-times.[18] But many Armenian leaders seem to have sought to gain the greatest advantage and security possible from the arrival of this unexpected army. Some appealed to the Franks for protection, including the people of Edessa, who asked Baldwin of Boulogne to become their ruler. Others saw an opportunity in the catalog of Turkish defeats to throw off their Seljuk and Turkmen rulers and assert their independence.

The Franks, for their part, were not gentle in imposing their control on Armenian areas as the Crusader States steadily took shape, and the relationship between the two could be tense. Ultimately, the crusaders were conquerors in a politically fragmented land, and when they sided with one Armenian warlord, they often found themselves at odds with others. Also, clear differences separated the Franks from their Armenian subjects. Both groups were Christian, but they were divided by culture, language, religious denomination, and the many hundreds of miles separating their homelands.

Nonetheless, in the years that followed, there were attempts to narrow the cultural divide where possible, stressing their common Christianity while trying to overlook their theological differences. In perhaps the greatest markers of cross-cultural integration, Franks and Armenians intermarried freely and marched side by side into battle. Many Armenian warriors became knights in the Crusader States (an elite social rank), and the Frankish counts of Edessa likewise adapted themselves to their Armenian subjects, observing local customs, marrying Armenian noblewomen, and showing respect for the Armenian Church (and indeed for the other Eastern Christian churches in the area).[19] Still, for all these efforts, their worldviews were only ever in partial alignment, and though Armenians could rise to high office in Frankish service, there was never any doubt about who was fundamentally in charge. Both groups wanted to cooperate, yet neither quite saw the other as being "one of us."

The Franks and the Armenians may have had their moments of friction, but generally relations were sufficiently positive to instill a deep sense of loyalty to the Franks among at least some of the Armenian populace. One particularly devoted group of fifteen

Armenian warriors respected Baldwin and Joscelin enough to attempt to rescue them from Balak's stronghold of Kharput with an exceptionally daring plan.

Upon learning of their masters' captivity, this band set out to Kharput and started to reconnoiter their surroundings. They quickly discovered that the stronghold's guards were lazy and could be duped. More importantly, the Turkish commander was currently holding a banquet and was already drunk. They approached the gates pretending to be peasants involved in a local dispute and seeking a resolution from the Turkish authorities. They demanded to speak to the commander and were taken to the guardroom to wait while a message was sent to the banqueting hall requesting the commander's presence. When the guards were distracted, the Armenians seized their weapons and cut their way into the fortress. They freed the imprisoned captives and took control of the castle. The rescue was incredibly bold, but it placed the former Frankish captives and their Armenian saviors in a new predicament. The castle was far from help, and Balak's local forces swiftly gathered around Kharput's walls, preventing all egress. Meanwhile, fast messengers were dispatched to Balak, requesting his immediate return. He was in Aleppan territory at the time, but he hurtled back to Kharput upon hearing the news.[20]

It took Balak fifteen days to make the journey, and by the time he arrived, events were far advanced. Joscelin had managed to slip out through the ring of besieging forces and set out for Christian territory, skillfully evading Turkish patrols and crossing the Euphrates at night with the help of two inflated bags (he could not swim).[21] En route he received assistance from a farmer, who helped disguise him as a peasant by traveling with him, giving him an ass to ride, and putting a young daughter before him on the saddle to create the impression that this was simply a family group. When Joscelin reached Turbessel, he quickly put together a relief force. He had promised Baldwin that he would come to his aid as soon as possible.[22]

Nevertheless, Balak reached Kharput long before Joscelin. He tore down the walls with siege engines and miners, forced the defenders to surrender, and flayed the Armenians alive. Only the senior prisoners were spared.[23] Learning that he was too late, Joscelin traveled through the Crusader States, assembled a great force, and staged a series of vicious attacks on Balak's lands. Enraged, he plundered Aleppan territory mercilessly, destroying tombs, mosques, orchards—anything in his way. He beat off every Aleppan attempt to drive him away. Joscelin's bitter incursions provoked an equally furious reaction from the citizens of Aleppo, who demolished several Christian churches in the city and converted others into mosques. Only two churches remained. The Orthodox bishop was forced to take refuge with the Arab Banu Uqayl in Qalat Jabar.[24]

Joscelin's rampage, however, was far from over. He crossed the Euphrates and plundered the Turkmen tribes and seized their cattle. He waylaid trading caravans and used fire to drive refugees out of caves where they were hiding. His anger was terrible, and his men inflicted untold suffering, but it did little to help the imprisoned king of Jerusalem.

———

Meanwhile Balak had learned of Joscelin's attacks to the south, so he hurried back to Aleppo. Balak's presence initially compelled his adversary to withdraw, but before long the conflict escalated still further. Two other Turkish commanders—Aqsunqur and Tughtakin—were moving north to assist Balak's forces against the Franks. This powerful conglomeration assembled in January 1124 and staged an attack on the Antiochene border at Azaz.[25] The siege was unsuccessful, but there was some bitter fighting before the Turks decided to retreat.

No sooner had Balak left Azaz than he set out on a new campaign, this time against a rebellious emir called Hassan who ruled the town of Manbij to the northeast of Aleppo. Joscelin, who had been observing his movements closely, saw this new Turkish expedition as a chance to finally meet Balak on the battlefield. Joscelin had clearly been craving a head-to-head confrontation with Balak for some time, and he got his chance on May 5, 1124. Hassan had solicited Joscelin's support, giving him an additional advantage. Nevertheless, after some fierce fighting, Balak finally gained the upper hand and drove Joscelin from the battlefield.[26]

Balak was the victor, but his achievement seems to have made him overconfident. After executing all the Frankish prisoners, he set out to organize the placement of his siege catapults against the walls of Manbij's citadel. He was not wearing his armor, and one of the town's defenders shot him in the left shoulder with an arrow. He died soon afterward. The Armenians seem to have had mixed feelings at his passing. They were well aware that his death was a source of profound relief for the Franks. Yet later Armenians would remember Balak with a degree of fondness. He had ruled over many Armenian subjects and was regarded as having been a just and compassionate master.[27]

Later Muslim authors saw Balak as a great hero of jihad, just as his uncle had been before him, and he was remembered as the "sword of those who fight holy war."[28] Such a memorial scarcely captures the career of a man who had only shown a commitment to fighting the Franks—alongside other campaigns against rival Turks—in the last two years of his long career, a man who, moreover, had responded to the advent of the First Crusade with an offer of joint enterprise. But that was not the point. Those agitating for jihad needed heroes, and Balak had provided them with sufficient raw material to let them rework his deeds into an inspiring role model for holy warriors yet to come.

When news arrived in Frankish territory of Balak's death it must have seemed almost incredible that his campaigns against the Crusader States had only begun two years before. He had crammed a great deal of fighting into that time, and the fortunes of war had shifted repeatedly from one side to the other. Hatred and enmity had been stirred up on all sides to an almost unprecedented degree, and Franks and Turks alike had committed atrocities that at least equaled those of their forebears. As this storm passed, it became clear that the future of Aleppo—which had long been at the epicenter of the conflict—was once again uncertain. After all these years of war, the contest for the city was still not settled. There was one last hand to play in this cruel game.

———◦———

Following Balak's death, Ilghazi's son Timurtash took power in Aleppo, and on July 25, 1124, he agreed to a treaty with Joscelin of Edessa designed to bring about Baldwin's release. The stipulations, brokered by the Banu Munqidh, were stringent. In return for his liberty, Baldwin agreed to pay eighty thousand dinars, deliver several high-ranking hostages (including one of his daughters), and hand over al-Atharib, Zardana, and Azaz along with several lesser towns. In essence, Timurtash wanted Antioch to strip off its armor plating by handing over its main frontier strongholds. Baldwin accepted these terms and was released into the keeping of the Banu Munqidh in Shaizar. Once he had arrived, Baldwin was treated with high honor, and he returned the Munqidhs' hospitality by suspending their annual tribute payments.[29] Baldwin left Shaizar a free man on August 29 and returned to Antioch, where he gathered his leading nobles to discuss how they might pay his ransom.

The council finally agreed that the Franks would have to break their promise. They could not afford to yield either such vast sums of money or the frontier castles that guaranteed their safety. Instead, they took the opposite course of action, deciding to launch a frontal assault on Aleppo itself. In making this decision, they reneged on one further important clause in their agreement: a promise to support Timurtash against a new and dangerous foe named Dubays ibn Sadaqa, "king of the Arabs" and leader of the Banu Mazyad. Dubays had only just arrived in the Syrian region, but his

arrival and his prominent position as a leading Arab emir threatened to destabilize Timurtash's tenuous grip on Aleppo.

———•———

Dubays ibn Sadaqa's family (the Banu Mazyad) was the last Arab
dynasty in the Near East to retain substantial resources in what was
becoming an increasingly Turk-dominated region. They were a Shia
Muslim family who ruled the region around al-Hilla in northwest
Iraq, and unlike so many of their Arab counterparts, they had survived the Turkish conquest. In the 1050s they had joined a Fatimid-
led coalition against the Turks, but that alliance had collapsed and
they had been forced to change tactics and ingratiate themselves
with their conquerors.[30] In the chaos of the late eleventh century,
Dubays's father Sadaqa had steered his family safely through the
civil war between Berkyaruq and Mohammed that had divided
the Turkish world. He initially supported Berkyaruq, but, fortu-
itously, he switched sides to Mohammed in 1101. From then on he
remained loyal to Mohammed, serving him in his struggle for the
sultanate. Following this victory, Sultan Mohammed recognized
how much he had relied on Sadaqa during the civil war and, seemingly intent on maintaining his loyalty, had showered his family
with lands and gifts.[31]

Sadaqa understood that the best way to guarantee his family's
lands and safety was to teach a powerful Turkish patron to depend
on his assistance. Still, Mohammed's need for Sadaqa's support did
not last forever. In 1107, within a few years of Berkyaruq's death,
rumors began to spread in the sultan's court that Sadaqa was a
Nizari (a member of the Assassins). The Seljuks hated the Nizaris,
making this a particularly damaging allegation, even though it was
false. Other voices drew Mohammed's attention to Sadaqa's considerable power and resources, citing the potential threat this posed
to the sultan's authority.[32] The conspirators succeeded in driving
a wedge between Sadaqa and the sultan, and, with some reluctance, the two men found their relationship deteriorating. It finally

became an all-out war in 1108. Sadaqa discovered that he was not without allies in the conflict, and Ilghazi and other Turkish rebels from the Jazira—Mohammed's detractors—were prepared to offer their support.

The war began with a series of major confrontations in northern Iraq between the Banu Mazyad and the Turkish sultan. Initially Sadaqa had the upper hand. He could raise tens of thousands of troops, and his armies could compete with even the largest Turkish hosts. Nevertheless, the tide turned on March 4, 1108, when the Arab and Turkish forces came together at the village of Matar near the banks of the Tigris. Sadaqa picked a good spot from which to give battle. He aligned his forces carefully, taking advantage of the strong wind sweeping the battlefield, ensuring that it would blow directly into the faces of the oncoming Turks. This was a shrewd decision because it would disrupt the Turks' main tactical advantage: their famous archery barrage. But the wind suddenly betrayed Sadaqa and began to blow in the opposite direction. So when Sadaqa's cavalry charged, it was into a hailstorm of arrows. The Turks had also deployed themselves in such a way that a canal lay between them and the advancing Arab cavalry squadrons. Consequently, the Arab charge stalled, and Sadaqa's forces were shot down. It was a disaster, and Sadaqa himself died from an arrow wound.[33]

Dubays participated in this defeat, and the memory of his father's death exercised a powerful influence on his later career. In the wake of the battle, he was taken prisoner and, recognizing the weakness of his position, made peace with Mohammed. Still, Dubays was itching to make trouble for his Turkish masters. His chance came in 1118, when Mohammed died and the Seljuk sultanate once again descended into civil war. There were a series of confrontations between Mohammed's sons and his brother Sanjar over the sultanate, and Dubays sought to elevate his own position in this contest by playing the rival parties off against each other. He did so with some skill for a time, but it was a dangerous game. In

1120 his position became perilous when his candidate for the sultanate, Mohammed's son Mas'ud, suffered defeat in battle. Dubays was suddenly on the losing side in a Seljuk civil war, just as Ilghazi had been all those years before. Now it was his turn to flee to the sanctuary of the Jazira. He gathered his men, sent his women into hiding in Iraq's marshlands, and headed north.[34]

Once in the Jazira, Dubays made common cause with Ilghazi, knowing him to be a famous rebel who had supported his father.[35] Dubays may have felt safe in the far north, yet even there his enemies tried to reach him. It was the caliph in Baghdad, al-Mustarshid, rather than the new Turkish sultan, Mahmud II, who now bore him the greatest enmity, perceiving Dubays as a threat to his own rising power. The caliph wrote to Ilghazi, asking him to break his association with the Arab leader and send him away. Although Ilghazi did not agree to the caliph's request, the letter seems to have persuaded Dubays that it was time to return to Iraq to confront his enemies.

In about 1122 Dubays raised a new army and set out for Baghdad. Thus began a period of intense warfare in northern Iraq. Rather like his father, Dubays won his first major battle but lost his second, in March 1123. His army was destroyed near his family's lands in al-Hilla. He only narrowly escaped from his army's collapse by swiftly crossing the Euphrates. Riding with what forces he could muster, he returned once again to the north, an angry but not a beaten man.[36]

On reaching northern Syria, Dubays immediately set about building a new power base. He knew both that Aleppo had a large Shia population and that there were long-standing tensions between this community and their Turkish masters. Consequently, he used his own status as a major Arab Shia leader to try to plot the overthrow of Ilghazi's son Timurtash.[37] These designs ultimately came to nothing, but they worried Timurtash sufficiently for him to seek support against Dubays by making Baldwin's release conditional on the king's joining forces with him against the new threat.

Unfortunately for Timurtash, his plan backfired spectacularly. Rather than fighting Dubays, Baldwin and Joscelin broke their promise and allied themselves to the rebel Arab leader through the offices of the Banu Uqayl in Qalat Jabar. Then, in October 1124, the Franks and the Arabs staged a combined assault on Aleppo.[38]

The decision to launch a combined assault on Aleppo opened new opportunities for the Franks. For Baldwin, it raised a very real chance to finally take control of this vital city, a vision that in turn dangled the prospect—yet again—of the wholesale conquest of northern Syria. His attempts in recent years to regain the momentum of earlier Frankish conquest in the north had been rewarded. The balance of power had tipped in the Franks' favor, and Aleppo was again vulnerable.

By the time Dubays's men joined forces with the Franks outside the walls of Aleppo, the Arab army had already scored an early victory, meeting Timurtash in battle and driving him out of the province.[39] The city was suddenly confronting a serious combined attack without its ruler, and Baldwin was eager to bring his long struggle over the city to a conclusion. He appears to have struck a deal with Dubays by which the Franks would control the Aleppan region and Dubays would rule Aleppo itself as the Franks' governor. It was unusual to start a siege in October—campaigning tended to take place in the spring and summer—but then, these were not usual circumstances. Baldwin was determined to act immediately, and to this end the besiegers built houses outside Aleppo's ramparts to protect themselves against the cold.

Baldwin's army outside Aleppo's walls was a powerful coalition. In addition to Dubays's men, it included troops sent by the Banu Uqayl of Qalat Jabar. This Arab clan was a long-standing ally of the Banu Mazyad, and they probably realized that destroying Turkish authority in Aleppo would help stave off the rising tide of Turkish power that was choking Arab rulers across the land. The army also contained various rebel Turks, including a member of Ilghazi's family and, perhaps most curiously, a son of the late Aleppan ruler Ridwan. Viewed along either ethnic or religious lines, the 1124 siege of Aleppo was a bizarre affair: a Frank-led coalition including Arabs, Turks, and probably Armenians, besieging a city with a mixed population governed by an absent Turkish ruler.

The siege that followed was vicious. It was conducted in the depths of winter. The Aleppan populace starved, and it was rumored that some resorted to cannibalism; sickness spread through the city. Its garrison of only five hundred men looked insufficient to hold off the powerful coalition outside the walls. The besiegers sought to increase the citizens' miseries, hoping to drive them to capitulate. Tombs were opened, and the dead were subjected to mockery within sight of the walls. The defenders kept up their side of this grisly conversation by publicly torturing any prisoners who fell into their hands. At the outset of the siege, Dubays had hoped that the citizens would view him favorably and support him and his allies in their attempt to seize the city. However, the brutality of the struggle destroyed any credibility Dubays may ever have had with the populace, who derisively shouted his name from the walls.[40] The horrors perpetrated by the combatants during this winter siege reflect how entrenched the struggle over Aleppo had become. The conflict had degenerated into a horrific orgy of violence.

As their predicament deteriorated, the Aleppan people searched yet again for a protector. Their ruler Timurtash was their most obvious hope, but he was not prepared to march to their aid. He had retreated to his father's town of Mardin and was intent on staying there. By this stage he may well have come to view Aleppo as a poisoned chalice and shuddered at the thought of reentering the contest for its possession. Consequently, he allowed himself to be diverted by the news that the ruler of the nearby town of Mayyafariqin had died and, rather than heading west to Aleppo, set out in the opposite direction to secure this more promising prize.[41] No help would be coming from him.

The Turkish warlord Aqsunqur, however, proved to be a more reliable source of support. By this stage he had risen in status, becoming the ruler of the prosperous city of Mosul (a position he had formerly held until 1115 or 1116). He had two strong reasons for wanting to march to Aleppo's aid. First, he had long wanted to gain control over the city. He had attempted to take control in 1116, but the citizens had refused to admit him. Now, however, with their backs to the wall, they were perfectly prepared to encourage his candidature.[42]

A second pressing motive for intervening in the siege was his hatred for Dubays. The feeling was entirely mutual. The two men loathed each other. In 1108 Aqsunqur had fought against Dubays's father during his last, fatal, battle, and in the wake of the encounter he had presented Sadaqa's severed head to Sultan Mohammed.[43] Dubays had held a grudge ever since. Aqsunqur had later commanded armies in the name of both the sultan and the caliph in their wars against Dubays. He had become Dubays's leading antagonist, and their ongoing struggle had only further entrenched their shared enmity. Now, in late 1124, Dubays was weak, isolated, and far from home. There was a real opportunity here for Aqsunqur to dispatch his enemy once and for all.

For these reasons, when the Aleppan messengers reached Aqsunqur offering him their city, he decided to march to their assistance even though he was seriously ill at the time. He mustered a force of seven thousand men and four thousand camels and set out first for Rahba, writing to Tughtakin asking for help, and then headed for Bales and the Aleppan region.[44]

The news that Aqsunqur was en route for Aleppo took some time to reach the besiegers. Dubays initially learned only that Aqsunqur was ill, and he rejoiced in the mistaken belief that sickness would prevent his long-standing foe from lifting the siege. Dubays then taunted the Aleppans for putting their faith in such a savior. Eventually this celebration was shown to be premature. Reports began to arrive that Aqsunqur's army would soon reach the besiegers' camp. Dubays reacted aggressively to the threat, advising his Frankish allies to march out and attack Aqsunqur as he tried to cross the Euphrates.[45]

This was a reasonable suggestion for two reasons. First, armies were often vulnerable when traversing major rivers because it took time to move a large army from one bank to another. An army attacked midway through the maneuver could be taken off guard and destroyed before it could gather its forces on the nearside bank. The Franks themselves had suffered just such a defeat when crossing the Euphrates in 1110. Second, Aqsunqur's army was large, but not overwhelmingly so. The allied forces outside Aleppo were probably at least a match for the oncoming Turkish foe.

However, Baldwin did not agree to Dubays's plan. He would not march against Aqsunqur. He was probably weighing the potential consequences of failure against the opportunities raised by success. Typically, the Franks did not like fighting big battles so far from their own borders, and any temptation Baldwin may have felt to adopt this head-on approach would have been tempered by consideration of the catastrophic consequences of a rout. If his army was defeated, his surviving forces would have to march—possibly for days through flat enemy territory while being harried by Turkish cavalry (who were exceptionally well suited for this kind of pursuit). He might also have known that Aqsunqur had called on Tughtakin for reinforcements, which could appear at any time. Moreover, even if he succeeded in battle against Aqsunqur, the allied army could easily suffer too many casualties to be able to resume the siege of Aleppo, and in that case, their victory would be both perilous and pointless.

Instead, in January 1125, Baldwin decided to lift the siege, and he retired back toward al-Atharib and the Antiochene frontier. Dubays could not maintain the siege on his own, and he too left the field. Aqsunqur had outmaneuvered him again, and the Aleppan people welcomed the Turkish commander as their new ruler. This was a galling outcome for Dubays, so he set out eastward and laid waste to Aqsunqur's lands around Mosul.[46] He was determined to leave some teeth marks on his foe even if he could not defeat him in person. He later sought out another claimant to the Seljuk sultanate and opened a new front in his rebellion against the sultan and caliph.

After his abortive siege, Baldwin returned to Antioch and from there to Jerusalem. He reached the holy city in April 1125, after an absence of nearly two years. He had proved himself to be an able defender of the northern Franks, but he had failed in his main offensive objective: the conquest of Aleppo. That struggle was now finally over. The Franks had come so close to winning on so many occasions, but now their hopes lay in ruins.

Theoretically, Turkish authority over the city was still contestable; Aqsunqur's position remained weak. He had only recently taken power, and the city's population had been reduced to dire straits. Baldwin probably had the material resources to raise a new army and launch yet another siege, but politically this was no longer possible. He had been away from his kingdom for too long. Jerusalem was his main responsibility, and it could no longer be neglected. He would also have known that there were many among Jerusalem's nobility who resented his continual absence.

In 1120 the nobles had expressed their discontent by attempting to prevent Baldwin from traveling north with the kingdom's great standard, the True Cross (a large fragment of the Cross of Christ, discovered shortly after the First Crusade). More worryingly, during Baldwin's absence, a noble faction had begun to conspire against him, even offering the throne to Count Charles of Flanders. Legally speaking, Baldwin's position as king was vulnerable, and he had originally taken the throne despite the existence of a more legitimate candidate.[47] It is not clear how much Baldwin knew of the plotters' scheme, but he probably realized that something was afoot. He needed to resecure his position at home. Any appetite he might once have felt for hurling his armies against Aleppo's walls was spent.

This did not mean that he was prepared to neglect his responsibility to defend Antioch. Indeed, no sooner had he returned to Jerusalem than he had to raise a new force to defend Antioch against a major attack led by Aqsunqur. Still, his conduct during this, one of his most successful expeditions, reflects his changing priorities.

The campaign began when Aqsunqur joined forces with Tughtakin and their combined army advanced into Antiochene territory where, in early May 1125, they forced the surrender of the fortress of Kafartab. Then the Turkish leaders moved quickly to besiege the nearby stronghold of Azaz. Aqsunqur was an active commander, and he swiftly erected twelve catapults with which to hammer the walls while miners set to work undermining them. This news sent Baldwin hurrying north again, collecting the count of Tripoli en route and joining forces with the northern Franks at Antioch.

By this time, Azaz's defenders were growing concerned that the sheer size of the combined Aleppan and Damascene army would deter Baldwin from trying to lift the siege. Consequently, a Frankish knight in the garrison volunteered to perform an audacious act of bravery. He mounted a fast horse and galloped straight out of the town's gates, bursting through the enemy guards blockading his path and leaping over a defensive ditch created by the besiegers. He broke through the Turkish army and headed straight for Antioch to encourage Baldwin to march to their aid as swiftly as possible. He rode carrying a sword in one hand and a concealed carrier pigeon, clasped against his chest, in the other. Amazingly, he was not caught, and on reaching Antioch he was able to release the pigeon to send back news that help was on its way. But when the bird returned to Azaz, it landed in the Turkish camp rather than at the castle, and Aqsunqur ordered that its message be changed to one ordering the garrison's immediate surrender. Fortunately for the Franks, the garrison sensed something amiss in the new message and chose to disregard the instruction.[48]

Baldwin was closing fast on Azaz by this point. He first reached the ancient town of Cyrrhus—a magnificent classical site with a great Roman amphitheater—where he deposited his baggage train before advancing on the Turkish siege works outside Azaz. Baldwin's army was small, but it contained a powerful force of heavy cavalry (perhaps over a thousand knights) and a strong Armenian contingent. Nevertheless, there was no escaping the fact that Aqsunqur's forces were far larger, and the Turks responded to the advancing Christians by encircling their small army and pinning it down. The confrontation quickly turned into a battle of attrition. The Turks managed to corral the Franks in a tight space, riding around their battle lines and preventing them from gathering food. They also sought to dishearten Baldwin and his men by launching repeated small attacks against their lines and shouting great war cries. This was a bad start for the Franks, yet Baldwin saw a chance to use the Turks' own tactics against them.

After three days of relentless pressure, Baldwin's army cut a path away from Azaz and toward the nearby stronghold of al-Atharib. To all appearances the king was a beaten man seeking refuge. In reality, he was baiting a trap. He had managed to get a message through to the garrison at Azaz instructing them to send up a smoke signal when the Turks set out in pursuit of his departing army. Baldwin's force marched for two miles before smoke discolored the spring sky. The Turks had been convinced that the Franks were in full retreat, and they dashed toward the withdrawing Christian army. As they closed on their enemy, the Frankish knights—alerted to their presence by the Azaz garrison—suddenly wheeled round, gave a great trumpet call, and charged straight at their pursuers. The Turks had no chance to evade hand-to-hand combat and simply plowed into—and probably under—the oncoming heavy cavalry. The resulting melee destroyed the Turkish army and created thousands of casualties.[49]

This was a substantial victory won against the combined might of two of Turkish Syria's most capable commanders. Had he wished, Baldwin could have followed up on his success by marching on Aleppo, but what he did instead betrays a perceptible change of mood. He did not seek to capitalize on his victory. Instead, he signed a truce with Aqsunqur and then returned south. As far as Antioch was concerned, Baldwin had moved from the offensive to the defensive. The struggle for Aleppo was over. Baldwin needed to focus on Jerusalem. He may have been the victor, but he had yielded the fight.

Baldwin must have been aware that his tenure as temporary ruler of Antioch was coming to an end. Bohemond II was coming of age and would be arriving soon. The burden of defending two states simultaneously was almost over.

In some respects the Kingdom of Jerusalem (if not its overworked ruler) had been the true beneficiary of the intensive fighting to the north. The Jerusalemites may have been deprived of their king's leadership for long periods, but many of Jerusalem's enemies had also committed their resources to the ongoing struggle for Aleppo and had consequently held back from attacking the kingdom. The most important of these was Tughtakin. From 1119 to 1125 he had frequently found himself marching north, both to support his Turkish allies and to pursue his own schemes. These entanglements ensured that he was rarely in a position to take advantage of Baldwin's absences from Jerusalem. On only one occasion during this period did he launch a limited—and unsuccessful—attack against the kingdom, and ironically this was at a time when Baldwin was actually present.

These small encounters aside, the war for Aleppo seems to have had the effect of sheltering the Kingdom of Jerusalem. The wars between Antioch and Aleppo sucked in the Near East's combatant factions while allowing other areas to live in relative peace. With Tughtakin and Baldwin engaged to the north, the Kingdom of Jerusalem could continue to grow stronger, build new villages, welcome pilgrims, and encourage settlers. Castles were being constructed, trade was burgeoning, and the port cities were bustling with activity. Increasingly, Jerusalem was the region's dominant military power, and Tughtakin was consistently wary about risking an encounter with Baldwin's army (at least without the support of major allies).

Another longstanding threat to Jerusalem was Fatimid Egypt to the south. The Fatimids were less cautious than Tughtakin and were better prepared to take advantage of Baldwin's absences. In the spring of 1123, shortly after messengers arrived reporting Baldwin's captivity, a large Fatimid army crossed the Sinai and camped at Ascalon, supported by a fleet of eighty ships. From there they advanced up the coast to vigorously besiege the important pilgrim port of Jaffa. Jaffa's garrison was not large, and the Fatimid infantry made several assaults on the walls. Their attacks were beaten off only with the greatest of difficulty, and chroniclers report that the townswomen played a vital role in Jaffa's defense, bringing rocks and water to the defenders on the ramparts.[50]

The siege concluded soon afterward. The kingdom's constable, Eustace Grenier, gathered its army at Qaqun, to the north of Jaffa, and advanced south along the coastal plain. The Fatimid army seems to have made some attempt to meet them in battle, but the engagement soon became a rout, and the Egyptians were forced to withdraw with heavy losses. In the years that followed the Egyptians launched several forays out of Ascalon, but these were generally small-scale raids and were not pressed home with much enthusiasm.

Confronted by few external challengers, the Kingdom of Jerusalem was in a position to take the offensive—despite the king's absence—and in 1124 the Jerusalemites achieved a long-desired goal: the conquest of Tyre. By 1124 Tyre was the sole port on the Levantine coast between Jaffa in the south and the Principality of Antioch in the north to remain in Muslim hands. It was one of the few natural harbors on the largely featureless eastern Mediterranean coastline. The city itself was built on a promontory that stuck out into the sea, creating a natural shelter for shipping. It was accessible from the land on only one side, which rendered it highly defensible. Efforts had been made previously to conquer the city, and in 1108 Baldwin I had besieged it for a month, but at that time he had despaired of breaking through its formidable ramparts and had allowed himself to be bought off by the defenders. In 1111 Baldwin I made another serious attempt to take Tyre, besieging it for almost five months from land and sea. His engineers constructed two massive siege towers with which to assail the walls, but he was eventually beaten off when the defenders, who were supported by Tughtakin's men, managed to burn both towers. With the failure of his second effort, he abandoned the attempt and resorted instead to the construction of a fortress to the south of the city, at Scandalion. This fort served to blockade Tyre and curb the raids launched by its citizens.

Scandalion may have helped fence off Tyre and its inhabitants, but the city continued to pose a naval menace to the Kingdom of Jerusalem. This was a major danger to the Crusader States, whose survival was contingent on the regular arrival of fleets from western Europe bearing both trade goods and people. The Italian cities of Venice, Genoa, and Pisa were the Crusader States' most prominent allies among Christendom's maritime powers. They played a vital role in supporting the commercial life of the East, and their warships continually sought to protect the sea-lanes across the eastern Mediterranean.[51]

The destruction of Fatimid naval power was a priority because it would ensure the safe passage of ships traveling from southern Europe to the Crusader States. This goal could be achieved in two ways. One was to seek out and destroy Fatimid warships and squadrons while they were at sea. Naval encounters did take place from time to time, with the earliest taking place at the time of the First Crusade, and the Italians scored several notable victories. The other approach was to capture the Fatimids' naval bases at port cities such as Jaffa, Acre, Tyre, Beirut, and Tripoli. The Fatimids fought using galleys, but these warships required lots of thirsty rowers who consumed a great deal of water (about two gallons, or eight liters, per day).[52] If all the ports along the Levantine coast were to fall into Frankish hands, the Fatimids would be unable to rewater their ships north of Ascalon (which was not a port), substantially reducing their cruising range.

If they could conquer these harbors, the Franks could also prevent the Fatimids from acquiring the timber necessary for shipbuilding. Egypt had no suitable forests of its own and depended on supplies from Lebanon or the mountains of northern Syria. The Fatimids had previously been careful to safeguard the passage of timber to their lands and had inserted specific clauses to this effect in treaties with the Kingdom of Jerusalem.[53] The conquest of Tyre, however, would enable the Franks to cut off this supply entirely, as it was the last Fatimid port on this stretch of coastline.

The Franks finally had a chance to break through Tyre's formidable defenses in 1124 with the arrival of a major fleet from western Christendom. Since the disaster at the Field of Blood, the Crusader States had been writing to powerful nobles across Europe asking them to send aid to the East. The Venetians had been contacted for help in 1120. Doge Domenico Michiel had responded favorably to this request and had encouraged his fellow Venetians to raise a new force for the defense of the Crusader States. The pope also supported the venture and sent the fleet a papal banner, causing other crusaders to rally to the cause. The Venetians had proven themselves to be enthusiastic crusaders in previous years, and they had dispatched several fleets to the eastern Mediterranean since the time of the First Crusade.

A large fleet set sail from the city of Saint Mark on August 8, 1122, traveling down the Adriatic and then east toward the Holy Land; it made landfall at Acre in May 1123. The Venetians carried with them perhaps fifteen thousand warriors and also some horses, the first mounts to be transported from western Christendom to the Crusader States by sea.[54] This was a substantial army, and it scored an important victory almost immediately. Only a short while before the Venetians' arrival, the army of Jerusalem had beaten off the Fatimid siege of Jaffa, but the supporting Egyptian fleet of eighty vessels was still at sea. Doge Domenico seized this chance and set out in pursuit. The Venetians had a long-established reputation as skillful mariners, but the doge proved especially adept in the clash that ensued. He advanced south toward Ascalon and attacked at first light. The Egyptians were taken by surprise and were insufficiently prepared to offer concerted resistance. Many of the Venetian vessels managed to ram their opponents amidships, capsizing them, and the doge's vessel is said to have struck the ship carrying the Fatimid fleet commander. The result was a catastrophic defeat for the Egyptian fleet. The surrounding sea turned red with blood, and shortly afterward the incoming waves began to pile corpses on the shore. The Venetian fleet continued to prowl south, scooping up any Fatimid ships they encountered.

It was a stunning victory, but it was not the Venetians' main military achievement. Once the fleet reached the shelter of Acre's harbor, the doge set out to fulfill his long-standing desire to visit Jerusalem's sacred sites. He celebrated Christmas in Jerusalem, and soon afterward he attended a council with the nobility of Jerusalem to talk of war and trade. The outcome of these discussions was a bargain struck between the doge and the barons of Jerusalem (led by the patriarch) wherein the Venetians would assist the Kingdom of Jerusalem to conquer Tyre, and in return they would receive a slew of trading and property rights across the territories under Baldwin II's control, most importantly, one-third of the city of Tyre and its hinterland.

The siege of Tyre began on February 16, 1124. The city's fortifications were formidable: on its landward side it was protected by three rows of walls, and on its sea-facing side there were two lines of fortifications. The Christian forces were aware that a relief army from Damascus might be sent to lift the siege, so they built a ditch around the circumference of their encampment. The eastern Franks then set about creating siege machines, including a siege tower and several catapults, while the Venetians built more siege weapons. Then the bombardment began, and the catapults continued without stop throughout the siege. The people of Tyre responded to this barrage with their own catapults, which created a cross fire of falling rocks, temporarily driving the Christians away from their machines. In time, the crusaders steadily gained the upper hand in this missile duel, and the air was filled with dust as Tyre's outer defenses began to collapse.[55]

Both the Damascenes and the Fatimids learned of the siege, and Tughtakin set out to relieve the city. Even Balak in the north is said to have contemplated going to Tyre's defense. They all knew how much the city's fall would advance the Frankish cause. The Fatimid forces in Ascalon launched a series of attacks during the siege, including one against Jerusalem itself, seemingly in the hopes of panicking the Frankish leaders and causing them to abandon their assault upon Tyre. But they achieved little more than to kill a few peasants working in the fields outside the city. Jerusalem's citizens sallied out and drove off the Fatimids, who then withdrew.

Tughtakin's forces, meanwhile, attempted to raise the siege, and there were rumors of a new Fatimid fleet on the way. The crusaders responded to these dangers by breaking their army into three sections. The doge set his men to launching their galleys, which had been pulled up on the beach, and they sailed south to patrol for Fatimid naval forces. The remaining Franks divided themselves between those who would maintain the siege and those who would leave the encampment to confront the Damascenes. In the event, their enemies held back. Tughtakin refused battle, and the Venetians discovered no advancing fleet.[56]

This news raised the army's spirits, and their morale received another boost when a messenger arrived from Count Joscelin of Edessa. This rider reported that Balak was dead, and he opened a bag and lifted aloft Balak's severed head as proof. This revelation caused quite a stir, and stories that Joscelin had killed the Turkish commander in single combat began to circulate.[57]

By late June, and after many months of bombardment and starvation, the resolve of the people of Tyre weakened, and they began to contemplate a negotiated surrender. Tughtakin brokered the agreement: in return for control of the city, the Frankish leaders agreed not to harm the townsfolk and to permit those who wished to depart to leave with all their movable goods. Many among the rank and file, however, were angered at the thought that they would not be able to loot the city. When the combined Frankish army entered Tyre on June 29, they respected their promise, and many among the Franks had only praise for the stalwart resistance offered by the citizens. When they opened Tyre's granaries, they found only five measures of wheat, a fact that earned their respect because it showed that the city really had fought to the point of starvation.

With the conquest of Tyre, the regional balance of power shifted still further. The Kingdom of Jerusalem was looking ever more powerful, far outstripping its Frankish rivals in military force, land-holdings, and revenue. The newly won city of Tyre was a major asset. Antioch's position was less favorable. Its frontiers were battered, but its core territories were largely intact. Nevertheless, it had not grown as the Kingdom of Jerusalem had, and it had known few moments of peace. The Turkish rulers of the adjacent regions had also demonstrated a frustrating ability to unite their forces at the right moment to prevent the principality's expansion— especially where Aleppo was concerned. This was not a result of good planning or coordination on their part, nor did warriors such as Ridwan, Ilghazi, Tughtakin, Balak, and Aqsunqur necessarily perceive the Franks as a greater threat than their own Turkish rivals. Still, between them, they had managed to keep the Franks out of Aleppo, and the Aleppan populace, who had contemplated voluntarily handing themselves over to Roger of Antioch in 1118, were by 1125 deeply entrenched in their opposition to the Franks.

Following his victory over Aqsunqur, Baldwin II's return to the Kingdom of Jerusalem was marked by a decisive shift in target. He fully understood the strategic need to capture at least one of his enemies' major centers of power: Aleppo, Damascus, or Cairo. Aleppo was now firmly out of reach.[58] Instead, Damascus lay squarely in his sights, and Jerusalem was in a position to bring considerable force to bear on the city. Unlike Aleppo, Damascus could be attacked directly from his own kingdom, without needing to pass through Antioch. It also lacked the same heavy fortifications that had protected Aleppo so effectively.

Almost as soon as he returned home, Baldwin sent out raiding parties into Damascene territory. After the Christmas celebrations in 1125, Baldwin announced that he would assemble the kingdom's full armed strength and march east. Heralds traveled throughout the land gathering men and arms. The muster was set for Safforie, a settlement lying in the lush, rolling hills to the north of Nazareth. Then Baldwin led his kingdom's full might east toward the frontier town of Tiberias. They crossed the River Jordan and entered enemy territory. He was confident, and for the first time in many years, he was actively seeking a full-scale battle during an offensive, rather than a defensive, campaign.

Meanwhile, news had arrived in Damascus of the Christian attack, and Tughtakin gathered his army and put out a request for volunteers. Turkmen arrived in large numbers, and eager young warriors thronged the streets. Even the Assassins joined his force. They set out to meet the oncoming Christian army. Battle was brewing and conflict was imminent. The struggle for the Near East had entered a new phase. The battle for Aleppo was finished, but the Franks' drive to conquer their foes' inland cities would continue. A new strategy was in formation. The struggle for Damascus would go on for over two decades. The center of conflict had pivoted south. A new game was opening, and the pieces were moving.

While Baldwin was shifting his strategic objectives south, the long-awaited Bohemond II was preparing himself for the journey to Antioch. On his arrival he would finally assume his late father's title as prince of Antioch. He had been preparing for this task all his young life, yet this was also his first visit to the East. The world of the eastern Mediterranean was very different from the kingdoms of western Christendom, and new arrivals—whether crusaders, pilgrims, or settlers—needed to suddenly come to terms with their new environment. It is worth considering, therefore, what Bohemond II, and the many thousands of other pilgrims and crusaders who had taken ship for the Levant, would have expected to find when they finally arrived in that distant outpost of Christendom, the Crusader States.

Writing in the Abbey of Saint-Evroult in Normandy, the famous writer and monk Orderic Vitalis once recorded a remarkable tale. He wrote that the viscount of Baghdad, a man named Balad, had traveled to Aleppo and married the daughter of King Ridwan. Balad had become the city's ruler and waged war against the Christians. He enjoyed early success and captured Count Joscelin and King Baldwin, who were traveling to Edessa to celebrate Easter. He imprisoned his captives in a castle called Carpetram. There, they were held prisoner for over a year under the watchful guard of 350 knights. During their captivity, the imprisoned Franks were compelled to labor ceaselessly, carrying water from the Euphrates, with their feet bound in shackles. They endured these tasks cheerfully, and Baldwin won favor with the guards, who treated him with respect. The other Franks fared less well and the Turks, when the mood took them, selected one from their number, tied him to a post, and shot him with arrows. Eventually the Franks and some Armenian prisoners rose up against their jailors and seized the castle. They then burst into the town around the castle, killing all the pagans. News of their deeds began to spread among the neighboring lands, and Baldwin's Armenian wife sent some troops to aid him.

At this point, Joscelin set out from Carpetram looking for help. On his journey toward Christian territory, however, he was waylaid by a Turkish peasant, who recognized him and offered to help. The peasant had formerly served Joscelin and was returning to Christian territory because he preferred it to his Turkish homelands. Joscelin borrowed clothes from the peasant, and to complete his disguise, he carried the Turk's six-year-old daughter in his arms.

Shortly after Joscelin's departure, it was discovered that Balad's three wives were holed up in a tower in the castle. One sent a dove to summon her husband home. Balad received the news and hurried back to besiege the castle. Shortly after his arrival, Balad remonstrated with Baldwin, telling him that it was unchivalrous to hold his wives captive. Baldwin was concerned by this slight on his honor, so he summoned a council of his men to discuss whether the wives should be freed, but it was Queen Fatima, one of Balad's wives, who broke into their deliberations and decided the matter. She encouraged the men to put away any knightly impulse that might cause them to release her and the other wives. She steered them instead to offer the greatest resistance to her tyrannous husband, challenging them to put their faith in God, inspiring them by recalling the endurance of the defenders of ancient Troy during the Trojan wars. She reminded them of the nobility of their Frankish race and reassured them that she and the other wives were content in their custody. Then all three wives asked to be baptized as Christians.

Baldwin was not unmoved by these entreaties, but eventually he capitulated to Balad's demands and surrendered the ladies, who were returned to their husband richly attired and escorted by five noble Christian warriors. Having handed over the wives, the five knights were taken prisoner by Balad and sent to the king of the Medes and later to the caliph and the sultan. They subsequently distinguished themselves in service to the Persians and the Medes, drawing admiring glances from the daughters of kings. After many adventures, they were granted leave to return to Christian territory, and they arrived among their countrymen garbed in silk robes and bearing a golden arrow, a special gift from the sultan. Meanwhile, Baldwin decided to surrender the citadel, to the disgrace of all Christians, and his men were executed. When he learned this news, Joscelin broke out in loud lamentation, but the deed was done.

There was then a great battle between Balad and Joscelin at the town of Monbec. On the eve of the battle, Balad's sister sought out her brother. She was a powerful sorceress, and she warned him that he would be killed in the coming battle, in combat with a knight named Geoffrey the Monk. This news alarmed Balad, who offered Geoffrey two asses carrying sacks of gold if he would stay away from the battlefield. Geoffrey, however, was not moved by Balad's offer and swore that he was willing to sacrifice himself for God. Battle then commenced; nine hundred Frankish knights bravely fought off three hundred thousand enemy warriors, and Balad was killed in combat with Geoffrey. So "the horns of the Gentiles were broken as God thundered and the Christians lifted up their heads and rendered praise to the unconquered Lord of hosts."[59]

So the tale goes . . .

As is evident here, communication between the Crusader States and western Christendom was not great during the medieval period. Messengers and returning pilgrims had to traverse hundreds of miles of treacherous sea simply to reach the ports of southern Europe. Some then had to take the long roads north, across the Alps and through Christendom's deep forests, to reach northern France, Germany, or England; others secured passage on coastal vessels or riverboats. Whether by land or by boat, however, there is no disguising the fact that this was a long and difficult journey. News would often have passed through many hands before reaching northwestern Europe. It is easy to imagine a scenario in which a knight returning from the wars of Antioch might inform a merchant in the busy hubbub of Acre about the fighting to the north between Baldwin II of Jerusalem and Balak; the merchant would tell a sailor, who would tell a knight returning to western

Christendom, who would tell a tradesman in Brindisi in Apulia in southern Italy, who would write the report down and send it to his local bishop, who would tell an archdeacon in conversation at a church council, who would tell his neighbors in northern France. This imagined scenario reflects the complex path by which much information reached the peoples of western Europe.

Orderic may have been drawing on written reports that derived directly from the Crusader States themselves, but even so—whether as a result of his own imagination or that of his informants—his tale of Baldwin II's captivity in Kharput acquired beautiful queens eager for baptism, a sinister sorceress, Christian heroes winning favor at the sultan's court, and hoards of gold. Nor is it surprising that the role of the Armenian fighters who actually seized Kharput was substantially diminished while the heroism of the Frankish knights was decidedly enhanced.

The mixture of factual report and fantasy in Orderic's tale provides a snapshot of the kinds of information available to knights in western Christendom about the distant Crusader States. Stories like Orderic's account of Baldwin II's imprisonment show what they thought it would be like "out there." These were the kinds of reports that shaped the preconceptions and expectations of crusaders, pilgrims, and merchants setting off for distant Jerusalem. Certainly many legends were in circulation about the world of the East, some rooted loosely in theology and others in the reports of travelers. It was "known," for example, that to the east of the River Jordan lay the four rivers of Paradise, including the Tigris and Euphrates. To the north lay the iron gates of the Caucasus where Alexander the Great had imprisoned the peoples of Gog and Magog until the end-times. On the journey to the East lay cities of fabulous wealth, especially Constantinople, whose colossal walls encompassed a city far greater than anything most pilgrims would have seen before. In the East itself were lions, wild asses, porcupines, crocodiles, and hyenas that sought out the dead. Other reports from the region only amplified its mysteriousness; fantastical tales were received in England, such as a Muslim fable describing how mice in the East like to urinate on those who have been bitten by leopards.[60]

Another conviction that steadily gained ground in western Europe was the belief that the Franks in the Crusader States had, generation by generation, become softened and corrupted by their exposure to the decadent world of the East, that they had adopted "Saracen" culture and weakened themselves in the process. For this reason the eastern Franks acquired the slighting nickname *Pullani* (colts).[61]

Such stories provide brief insights into what the thousands of travelers might have expected to find when they reached the distant Crusader States. Certainly, huge numbers of men and women set out for the Holy Land in these years, and their journeys were strongly encouraged by the Frankish rulers. Bohemond II, future prince of Antioch, would have been among the best informed of such new arrivals. He had been surrounded by his father's old guard since birth, so he would have had some idea of what to expect when he assumed his father's title.

Bohemond II had been raised in Taranto (in southern Italy) by his royal mother Constance, and Frankish authors speak favorably both of his appearance and of his character. They report that he was tall, handsome, and blond; that he was a courageous and capable ruler; and that he had a royal bearing.[62] Eastern Christian writers also comment favorably on his virtues.[63]

Bohemond landed with a fleet of twenty-two ships near Antioch in the autumn of 1126. He was around eighteen years old and had already been knighted. His long-anticipated arrival was met with considerable rejoicing, and Baldwin II of Jerusalem—custodian of Antioch—showed his favor for the young man by granting him the hand of his daughter Alice in marriage. Baldwin was clearly eager to cast off the burden of Antioch's defense, and he ordered the fodder needed for his return journey to Jerusalem on the very night Bohemond arrived.[64] He was going home.

In his short reign, Bohemond II proved himself to be a capable and ruthless warrior. His first act was to retake Kafartab, which had been taken previously by Aqsunqur. In 1127, he also plundered Aleppo's hinterland and briefly gathered his forces outside its ramparts before allowing himself to be bought off. He lacked the resources to make an earnest attempt on the city's walls, so his intention was presumably to conduct a raid and exact tribute.[65]

———————

Aleppo was receding rapidly as a viable Frankish target, and any prospect of an attack on the city diminished even further in 1128. A new power was rising in northern Syria, a new warlord whose achievements would far exceed those of his forebears. Men such as Ridwan, Tughtakin, Ilghazi, Balak, Dubays, and Aqsunqur had existed in a landscape where multiple rulers, each holding a handful of towns, had competed both against each other and against their Frankish, Armenian, and Arab neighbors. The whole region of the Jazira and northern Syria had been a network of family feuds, temporary friendships, animosities, and ethnic or religious tensions. Sometimes the various powers worked together for some common purpose; often they did not. Even so, this colorful, violent, and furiously complex world would soon vanish forever, to be replaced by a new bloc forged by a man named Zangi.[66]

Zangi's early career bore many similarities to those of his predecessors. He was born in northern Syria in about 1084 into a Turkmen family. His father, Aqsunqur, the Turkish governor of Aleppo and a slave-soldier belonging to the sultan Malik Shah, was murdered by the Seljuk ruler Tutush in 1094. Zangi's mother had been killed a short time previously, so Zangi was orphaned at about the age of ten.

From that point he was raised in Mosul by the Turkish commander Karbugha (the man who tried to relieve the siege of Antioch in 1098), and after Karbugha's death, several of the city's subsequent governors continued to support him as he grew into adulthood. During this time he participated in campaigns against the Franks, and he was present at the great Turkish victory of Harran in 1104. In these early years he earned a reputation as a capable soldier. He became embroiled in the infighting over the sultanate, which took place following the death of Sultan Moham-med in 1118. He supported the winning faction and was soon bask-ing in the patronage of his new master, Sultan Mahmud II (sultan 1118–1131). Zangi was given land in Iraq, and in 1123 he played an important role in the battles fought against the Arab ruler Du-bays. In the years that followed, as tensions rose between the Seljuk sultan and the caliph, he fought for the sultan against the caliph's armies, scoring a notable victory in 1126. He then became *shihna* of Baghdad, just as Ilghazi had before him.

His major rise to power occurred the next year. Mosul needed a new *atabeg*, and, after his supporters had paid a few hefty bribes, the role was offered to Zangi in the autumn of 1127. Mosul was an important city, and it provided him with the resources to conquer a large portion of the Jazira and northern Syria over the following years. Town after town fell to his assaults, and he acquired others through diplomacy or the threat of force; many warlords, whether Arab, Turk, or Kurd, came under his dominion. Aleppo was one of his early acquisitions: he took control in January 1128 and arrived in person in June. The troublesome Aleppans were not quiescent under his rule, and there were rumors of potential rebellion even toward the end of Zangi's life. Nonetheless, he gave the city a de-gree of stability and order that it had lacked for decades. With the two great cities of Aleppo and Mosul under his control, he was in a position to outcompete most of his rivals, and he continued to absorb lands held by lesser chieftains. Few were able to resist his military and political might, and in Syria he soon secured control of both Hama and Homs. Only Damascus proved strong enough to evade his grasp (and then only with the greatest of difficulty).

Over the next fifteen years, Zangi showed only occasional inter-est in the Franks.[67] Aleppo, and therefore the Antiochene frontier, were left under the control of an appointed governor. There was some raiding between the Franks and Zangi's deputy, but few serious confrontations. Indeed, soon after taking control of Mosul in 1127, Zangi made peace with the Franks of Edessa. His main preoccupations were similar to those of so many of his predecessors: the perpetual infighting over the sultanate taking place in Iran and Iraq and his own desire to bring the Jazira to heel. When he did attack Antiochene or Edessan territory, he was generally successful; for example, in 1130 he managed to conquer the fortress of al-Atharib while beating off a Frankish relief army. But he did not assertively follow up on this victory, and after briefly besieging the hilltop stronghold of Harim, he allowed himself to be bought off. He made some conquests along the border in later years, but he seems to have been content to maintain the status quo, simply making sure that the Franks kept their heads down. Before 1144, his attacks were launched solely against Frankish frontier fortifications, never against major targets such as big ports or larger cities.

With Zangi's rising dominance across the region, Aleppo was permanently out of reach for the Franks, Turkmen chiefs, or anyone else. The city was no longer a quarrelsome and isolated metropolis surrounded by Frankish states and Turkmen tribesmen. Now it was the base for Zangi's large regional power, which far eclipsed the authority of his Turkish predecessors. Neither Antioch nor Edessa had the strength to conquer the city using their own resources alone. At times there was some discussion about a new campaign against Aleppo, but later rulers of Antioch recognized that such a campaign would be impossible without massive external support. The Frankish conquests in the north were over. The best they could hope for now in the face of Zangi's rising influence was to maintain their current position.

During the fifteen-year period from 1128 to 1143, only one attack was made on Aleppo, when the Byzantine emperor invaded northern Syria in 1138. He *did* have the power to wrest Aleppo from Zangi's hands—although whether the Franks could have retained it once he had withdrawn is more doubtful—but he made only a halfhearted and unsuccessful lunge toward the city and achieved nothing.

The geopolitics of the region had changed substantially since the end of the First Crusade. Formerly Antioch had dominated the northern region and jockeyed for position against its southern rival, the Kingdom of Jerusalem. Now, following the debacle at the Field of Blood and given the southern kingdom's sustained growth in recent years, Antioch was no match for Jerusalem. Nor could it compete with Zangi.[68] Fortunately for Antioch, Zangi simply was not interested enough in the Frankish territories to stage a major campaign against them. Nevertheless, it is important to note that it was now Zangi's disinterest, rather than Antioch's military power, that ensured the principality's survival; the balance of power had shifted permanently, and never again would the Franks of northern Syria be strong enough to seek hegemony over Syria.

Thus, with Zangi's rise and Baldwin II's strategic pivot south to face Damascus, a chapter was closing in the history of the crusader struggle for the Near East. Far from being a lucrative target for aspiring Frankish commanders, Aleppo was now to play its part in bringing about the destruction of the Crusader States.

CHAPTER 5

AFTERMATH

1128–1187

THE LENGTHY STRUGGLE for Aleppo represented the Franks' first concerted effort to drive their frontiers inland by attempting the conquest of one of their enemy's major centers of power. Their failure to achieve that goal stands as an important turning point in the history of the Crusader States, ending their expansionist wars of conquest in the north. Even so, the Franks' ambition to seize an enemy capital persisted, and over the following decades, the Kingdom of Jerusalem made two further efforts to achieve this objective, setting its sights initially on Damascus and then on Cairo.

Like the earlier struggle for Aleppo, which had come to nothing, these two later campaigns to expand the Crusader States were similarly unsuccessful. Understanding the reasons for their failure will help to provide an answer to the broader question of why the Franks never succeeded in achieving their ambition to expand their territories inland and conquer the Near East.

To begin, however, it is worth considering the broader positon of Crusader States in about 1150.

Every year, as the northern world begins to sense the advent of autumn, tens of thousands of birds from across Europe and Russia take flight for the warmer climes of the south, cramming the skies. For the most part they prefer not to fly for long distances over the Mediterranean, so they are funneled over land bridges and narrow stretches of ocean that will take them to Africa: at Gibraltar in the west and along the shores of the Levant in the east. This was an annual event in the Crusader States, one in which, for a time, the natural world temporarily asserted its presence over the affairs of man. In some years the air was so filled with birds that one Armenian writer described their flying chevrons as doing battle for possession of the skies.[1] Among the various migrating birds heading south was (and is) the white stork, which, having crossed Bulgaria and Asia Minor, traveled down the length of the Crusader States in mid-August, from Antioch in the north to the Kingdom of Jerusalem's Egyptian border in the south. It is interesting to speculate about what the birds migrating south in the year 1150 would have seen.

Having crossed the immensity of Anatolia, these migrating storks would have approached the Principality of Antioch and seen in the distance a densely settled state protected by a string of powerful strongholds. The first barriers they encountered, however, would have been the Amanus range. This line of wooded slopes represented a natural frontier and was also home to several Armenian monasteries in the Black Mountain region that were built by pious founders who valued the isolation of this lofty wilderness. These sacred spaces of contemplation and prayer, along with others spread across the principality, played host to conversations and debates between western European monks and their Eastern Christian counterparts.[2]

Once they had passed beyond the Amanus, the storks would have entered the principality itself, a land of craggy ridges and broad valleys. There they would have seen the estates and farms of the Antiochene Franks, whose vineyards covered the hillsides and whose crops rippled along the valley floors. The Franks were intensive farmers and they had the good fortune to arrive during a period when the region was becoming more humid and therefore more fertile. They raised cereal crops and other foodstuffs as well as cotton, designed for export to southern Europe.[3]

Antioch itself rose majestically above the Orontes River; its fortifications, built by Emperor Justinian, ran up the valley side to a mighty citadel at the summit of Mount Silpius. This was one of the great cities of the classical world, founded in about 300 BC, and it was here that the name "Christian" was first coined. Antioch later became one of the patriarchates (the early Christian church established five patriarchates for its most important bishoprics). Its walls were over seven miles long, and within them were churches representing many branches of Christianity: Catholic, Armenian, Greek, or Syriac. The city was an intellectual center, and theologians and philosophers from many civilizations sought it out to exchange ideas, including an English thinker named Adelard of Bath.

Lying to the northeast of the city was the great lake of Antioch, whose banks were populated by Christian fishermen famous for catching vast quantities of eels, which were then exported by the thousands to neighboring states, where they were a much-coveted delicacy.[4]

To the southwest of Antioch was the small port of Saint Symeon lying next to the mouth of the Orontes River. In the other direction from Antioch, twenty miles to the east along the road to Aleppo, stood the embattled frontier fortress of Harim, surveying the landscape from the summit of its great mound.[5] Further south was Antioch's main port of Latakia, and beyond that were the coastal towns of Jabala and Tortosa and the frontiers of the County of Tripoli. The Franks intensively farmed the coastal strip south of Latakia, and the area contained a complex network of villages and estates. Many were centered on small, defensive towers, which dotted the region between the Mediterranean and the mountains inland.[6]

Soaring south, the storks would have crossed the highlands and the much-feared Alawite Mountains and the strongholds of the Assassins and then flown on to reach the fertile plains of the Homs Gap and the northern marches of the County of Tripoli. To their east was the great fortress of Krak des Chevaliers, draped with the proud banners of the Knights Hospitaller, protecting the county's vulnerable frontier facing Homs. Then ahead, the land rose again toward the massif of Mount Lebanon and, at the gateway of the narrow strip of land sandwiched between the mountains and the sea, the bustling port city of Tripoli.

Tripoli itself would have been crammed with ships, some preparing to winter in the port, with perhaps a few hoping to slip out before the onset of the winter gales, bearing goods to Christendom brought overland to the city from as far afield as India and China. Many languages could be heard in this great emporium as Italian merchants rubbed shoulders with traders from distant lands. Other smaller vessels traversed the Levantine coast, hugging the shoreline, connecting the Crusader States and carrying passengers, trade goods, and soldiers. Surrounding Tripoli was a fertile strip, where rivers rushing down from the mountains passed through high-sided valleys and finally into fertile farmlands on the coastal plain.

Flying high over the coast road, heading south, the storks would then have crossed into the Kingdom of Jerusalem at the port of Beirut—famous for its glassware—and after passing over the large pine forest to the south of the town, would have found a flourishing rural society.[7] Away from the frontier lands, the kingdom had been swelled by peace and constant construction. The Turks by this stage were a relatively distant threat to the kingdom's heartlands, and many newly constructed buildings were only lightly fortified; they had no reason to anticipate serious attack.

As the Lebanese mountains faded away behind them, to be replaced by the rich and rolling hills of the Kingdom of Jerusalem, a pattern of estates emerged. Well planned and productive, they were proof that the Frankish settlers, generally from France, had swiftly adapted themselves to their new surroundings. The hill country of Galilee was often neatly terraced, and fields of vines and olives were watered by a complex system of irrigation channels. On the flatter land and on the coastal plain there were cereal crops—especially wheat and barley—and groves of fruit trees.[8] Sugarcane was cultivated in large plantations, both for local consumption and for export. Western European markets had a sweet tooth but little local supply of sugar.[9] They would pay a pretty price for it in Pisa, Genoa, or Marseilles, and an even greater one in London and Paris. The Franks of the Crusader States energetically set about growing and gathering sugarcane to supply this demand, transporting it to the great port cities so that it could be refined, molded, and dispatched to the West in trade.

The storks would have passed over a landscape of strongly built farmsteads, small villages, towers, and castles, all connected by a lattice of roads. The larger settlements were centered on small churches—often with thick walls, and which served as centers of worship and places of refuge. Such villages were often home to both Franks and Eastern Christians. Typically Franks settled among their coreligionists and rarely put down roots in those areas of the Latin East where the population was either predominantly Muslim or nomadic.[10] For their part, rural Islamic communities tended to have little communication with their Frankish overlords, paying their taxes and generally being left undisturbed. When a Muslim traveler from Spain visited the Kingdom of Jerusalem in the 1180s, he was appalled by the relaxed relationship between the local Muslims and their Frankish overlords, observing with concern that in many respects they were at greater ease under the Christians than their coreligionists were under the Turks.[11]

Gliding down the coastline, the storks would have overflown the Kingdom of Jerusalem's powerful northern ports. They would already have passed Tyre, conquered in 1124 and filled with traders, many from Venice. Tyre was famous for its textiles, for its glass, and for a purple dye extracted from sea snails. Further south was Acre, situated, like Tyre, on a promontory jutting into the sea. This was the commercial heart of the kingdom, and the city was polluted and overcrowded. The sea itself was slick with filth that drifted around the margins of this mercantile metropolis. On the city's southern flank was its great harbor, where tens of great ark-like "round ships" could take shelter on a coastline that offered few havens to anxious seafarers. Within its walls, the city itself was permanently under construction, and houses rose three and four stories above its crowded streets.[12] There were many churches and a mosque, primarily used by visiting Muslim merchants. Acre did not sleep. Even in times of war the volume of trade passing through its gates from Muslim territories and lands further east scarcely slackened.

This city, like many others, was characterized by a merging of many cultures and traditions. Both the Muslim call for prayer and the sound of church bells could be heard over its many courts. Muslims were allowed to practice their religion freely across the Crusader States, except in Jerusalem itself.[13] For their part, the Franks frequented bathhouses, scarcely known in the West but a familiar sight in Islamic cities, and Muslims, Jews, and members of other religions bought goods and wares from the Italian merchants' shops that lined the city's streets.

Passing Acre, situated on the western margins of its great plain, filled with estates and bustling roads, the storks would then have soared up past Haifa and over the higher ground of Mount Carmel until they reached the coastlands around the port of Jaffa. This, the first harbor taken by the crusaders in the Holy Land, was a vital waypoint for the tens of thousands of pilgrims who traveled each year to reverence the places where Jesus had lived, died, and been resurrected. From Jaffa, the winding paths to Jerusalem, so perilous in the early years of the kingdom, had been made safe by the ceaseless labors of the Knights Templar and by the steady growth of the kingdom. Now the roads into the highlands to the east were full of pious groups on the last leg of their journey to Jerusalem.

Small villages were strung out along the line of the road, containing arcades of shops selling food, trinkets, and the necessaries of life.[14]

Then there was Jerusalem, wreathed by the healthy air of the hill country and surrounded by orchards and vineyards. It presented a very different spectacle from the hubbub of the mercantile cities of the coast. There were traders and artisans here too, and many labored to serve the ongoing pilgrim traffic. Silversmiths and goldsmiths produced pilgrim badges and devotional items that could be reverently carried back to distant Lombardy, Champagne, and England by pilgrims who had spent years seeking the holy city. New public works catered to this spiritual traffic, among them a newly constructed covered market and sewage and drainage works.[15] These were impressive structures, yet they were dwarfed by the churches. In recent years the city had flourished as masons labored to transform Jerusalem into a place of such beauty that pilgrims could   so it was hoped—glimpse the majesty of its spiritual significance. Splicing artistic influences and building techniques from the West, Armenia, Byzantium, and even the Islamic world, these churches were among the Crusader States' greatest treasures and architectural achievements. Rising above the city's towers and roofs was the Temple Mount, a holy site containing the Temple of the Lord (the Dome of the Rock), topped by its great golden cross, which stood beside the headquarters of the Knights Templar (the al-Aqsa Mosque). Just to the south of the city was Bethlehem, birthplace of Christ, whose great Church of the Nativity was another site of veneration, drawing visitors from regions as disparate as Ethiopia, Georgia, and Scandinavia. Its twelve copper bells, including one shaped like a mighty dragon, sounded out loudly across the land.[16]

After Jerusalem, the storks would have left the fertile lands of the north and passed into the desert, with the bitter waters of the Dead Sea lying just to the east, and beyond them the kingdom's distant holdings across the River Jordan, dominated by their fortresses at Kerak and Montreal. The area directly south of Jerusalem had once all been frontier territory, long fought over by the crusaders and their Egyptian foes. For decades the Egyptians, operating out of their frontier city of Ascalon on the coast south of Jaffa, had posed a threat to the Franks' control of Jerusalem. However, the menace of a Fatimid invasion had long receded, and in the 1130s the Kingdom of Jerusalem had created a trio of fortresses to blockade Ascalon. The southern frontier was looking increasingly secure, and Christian farmers and settlers were building new estates along the fertile strip between the desert and the sea. This was also Bedouin territory, and the Franks often cooperated with their nomadic neighbors, allowing them to graze their herds on the kingdom's borders, and worked with them to patrol the kingdom's southern marches. Nevertheless, they were unpredictable allies.

The white storks flying over the Levant were looking at a string of three Frankish territories that remained significant regional powers. Even so, for all their bustling ports, their mighty commercial revenues, the powerful military orders of the Knights Templar and the Knights Hospitaller, their fortresses and impressive army, storm clouds were hanging over the Crusader States. The northern defenses were crumbling, and the County of Edessa had fallen.

———◦———

The Franks' failure to conquer Aleppo had permanently ended their attempt to achieve supremacy across the Syrian region. Then, after 1128, with Aleppo firmly under Zangi's control and pumping its resources into his (and not the Franks') coffers, Zangi had assembled a colossal territorial bloc in Syria and the Jazira, making him the dominant power in the area. By the 1140s the Antiochene Franks fully recognized that they lacked the strength to challenge Zangi's hegemony, and they made scarcely any attempt on Aleppan territory, aside from an occasional raiding expedition.[17] As discussed in Chapter 4, Zangi was rarely interested in campaigning against the Franks, being more concerned with the ongoing disputes over the sultanate and the Jazira.[18] Even so, in late 1144 Zangi launched a sudden major offensive against the County of Edessa, culminating in the conquest of the city of Edessa itself. This stunning blow came as a huge shock to the Franks, and it was the beginning of the end for the county. In 1150 the county's remaining Frankish inhabitants were evacuated. The first Crusader State had fallen.

By this time, Jerusalem was uncontested in its status as the predominant Christian power in the area. It was also the only Frankish country strong enough to wage offensive war against its major Turkish rivals with any hope of achieving significant, long-term advances. Two leading combatants were emerging: Zangi in the north and the Kingdom of Jerusalem in the south. The remaining smaller players steadily came to acknowledge this geopolitical reality by aligning themselves with one or the other, looking for sanctuary and protection. The smaller Frankish states, some Bedouin tribes, and occasionally the Armenians and the Assassins looked to Jerusalem. The smaller Turkish states, the Turkmen tribes, and some Arab dynasties looked to Zangi.

Although the Franks' regional dominance was being increasingly contested, their aspiration to conquer a major inland city, and thereby to gain the upper hand, remained their overriding priority. The Frankish territories, strung out along hundreds of miles of the Levantine coastline, were perilously vulnerable to attack, and for the most part their lands penetrated only a short way inland. Their rulers recognized the fragility of their position and understood that this could not be accepted in the long term. Their survival depended on further expansion inland, so, with the failure of the war for Aleppo, Damascus steadily crystallized as their new target.

By the late 1140s, the Kingdom of Jerusalem had been trying to get hold of Damascus for years. Initially the Franks had hoped to conquer the city by force, so in 1126 and 1129 King Baldwin II staged two large-scale attacks on Damascene territory. There was also frequent fighting over the fertile Hawran region to the south of the city. Damascus depended on Hawran for its arable crops, so retaining it was vital to the city's security. The Frankish assaults met with varying degrees of success, but on no occasion did Jerusalem get close enough to besiege Damascus's walls.

The Franks changed their approach in the 1130s, temporarily suspending their attempts to seize Damascus by force and trying instead to draw the city diplomatically into their sphere of influence. This was a logical move. Damascus was becoming increasingly isolated, and Zangi was hovering on its northern borders, looking for an opportunity to swoop down and take control. That was a serious threat for the Franks: if Zangi added Damascus to his already-considerable landholdings, he would be unstoppable. Zangi attacked Damascus directly in 1135 and 1139; at other times he contested control of the towns of Baalbek, Hama, and Homs, which lay between his own territories and those of Damascus. The Damascenes needed allies in those years, and the Franks had every reason to offer aid. The Frankish-Damascene entente kept the city out of Zangi's growing empire, but the rulers of Jerusalem remained keen to seize the city for themselves. Damascus would be a prize as great as Aleppo and would substantially enhance the Crusader States' regional position.

The Franks did not get a chance to make another serious attempt to conquer Damascus until 1148, and by then the strategic situation had changed significantly, for several important reasons. First, Zangi had been murdered two years earlier, in 1146, while trying to seize the Arab stronghold of Qalat Jabar. The Damascene author Ibn al-Qalanisi reported that Zangi had been assassinated while in a drunken stupor by one of his eunuchs.[19] His sons inherited his various landholdings. From the Frankish perspective, the most important of Zangi's heirs was his second son, Nur al-Din, who took control in Aleppo. Nur al-Din was an exceptionally capable ruler and military commander, and in time he would become devout in his observance of Sunni Islam and strongly committed to the pursuit of jihad against the Franks. In his deep dedication to Islam, he differed sharply from his father, and this dissimilarity manifested itself clearly in the building programs conducted by father and son. Whereas Zangi had shown scarcely any interest in the construction of religious buildings,[20] Nur al-Din was an enthusiastic builder, constructing and endowing tens of mosques, madrasas, and shrines, as well as other sites. These institutions stressed his pious credentials, reinforcing his spiritual authority with the populace and building support for holy war.[21] The reconquest of Jerusalem became a leading goal of his rule, and in 1168 he boldly commissioned the construction of a *minbar* (a pulpit) for the symbolic purpose of installing it in Jerusalem after its future conquest. This was a powerful propaganda statement, one that focused his supporters' attention on the struggle for the holy city.[22]

A second major shift that took place shortly before 1148 was the collapse of the Frankish-Damascene alliance. This relationship broke down in 1147, and there had already been considerable fighting over the crucial agricultural region of Hawran. With the outbreak of war between these former allies, the Damascenes switched their allegiance to Nur al-Din, marking an important shift in the region's geopolitics.

The third important development, which gave the Crusader States the resources they needed to stage a renewed assault on Damascus, was the advent of the Second Crusade. This colossal military undertaking had been launched in 1145 by Pope Eugenius III in response to the fall of Edessa. Over the following months, preachers and letters had crisscrossed Christendom, seeking recruits for the new campaign and challenging knights and nobles to prove themselves worthy of their illustrious forebears who had conquered Jerusalem during the First Crusade. The response to the call had been enormous, and two major rulers, Louis VII of France and Conrad III of Germany, had taken the cross and marched east with large armies to support the Crusader States.

In the early phases of the Second Crusade, there had been a real chance that these great armies would substantially realign the balance of power in the Near East in favor of the Franks. But both armies suffered enormous casualties while trying to cross Anatolia.

Conrad's force ran into trouble shortly after leaving Byzantine territory. It was poorly equipped with archers, and the Turks wore the army down by hovering on its flanks and raining arrows down upon the Germans while using their nimble ponies to evade any attempt by the Christian cavalry to engage them in hand-to-hand combat. The French army penetrated somewhat deeper into Turkish territory, but they suffered badly from a sudden Turkish onset when they were trying to cross a high mountain pass.

Ultimately, only a fraction of either of these two major armies reached the Crusader States, but the crusader reinforcements were still sufficient, when combined with the local Frankish forces, to attempt the conquest of a major city. Although retaking Edessa had been the crusade's original target, that goal was rapidly becoming impractical. The county had disintegrated too far to be easily rebuilt, and King Louis argued with the Antiochene ruler, Raymond of Poitiers, soon after his arrival in Frankish territory, destroying any possibility of a cooperative venture in the north. Consequently, the decision was taken to stage an advance on Damascus.

The campaign against Damascus began reasonably well. The combined Christian army reached the city's outskirts and began fighting its way through the outlying orchards to reach the main city walls. What happened next is not entirely clear. For some reason, having reached the walls, the Franks suddenly shifted their main encampment to the north, to a location that had no water. It seems that they had hoped to find the city poorly defended on that quarter, but that proved not to be the case. They then attempted to return to their former position but found it blocked by enemy forces. News then reached them that reinforcements from Nur al-Din would be arriving shortly, so the Franks were forced to raise the siege and return to Christian territory.

The Second Crusade thus fizzled out in an astonishingly lackluster denouement. It was followed by a storm of controversy as frustrated participants and commentators singled out scapegoats and sought to assign blame. Some pointed the finger at the local

Frankish barons, claiming they had been bribed by the Damascenes to lift the siege. The suggestion was also made that there had been discord among the crusaders over who should rule Damascus once it had fallen into Christian hands. Nevertheless, when the hubbub of blame and accusation had settled down, the political reality set in: a promising attempt to conquer Damascus had failed. Yet again the Franks had failed to drive a road inland and seize a major center of Turkish power.[23]

After the withdrawal of the Second Crusade, some Damascenes must have seen Nur al-Din as a savior: the man who drove away the crusaders and protected the city. That should have put him in a strong position to aspire to take Damascus for himself, yet when he attempted to do so in 1149 he was firmly rebuffed, and the Damascenes resumed their entente with the Franks. For the next few years, Nur al-Din periodically harassed Damascus, encamping on its estates, despoiling its farmlands, and assailing its inhabitants with demands that they launch a jihad against their Frankish allies. These bullying tactics eventually bore fruit. In April 1154, after Nur al-Din blocked the city's grain supply and won a skirmish against its troops outside the city walls, he managed to strong-arm his way through one of the main gates and take control. He was finally in.[24]

The conquest of Damascus was a critical event. Nur al-Din now had two of the region's most powerful cities in his grasp, and that consolidation of power dramatically enhanced his position. His victory also quashed the Franks' long-cherished hope of taking the city for themselves. They had been trying to get inside the walls of Damascus for over two decades, and, as with their former efforts to secure Aleppo, they had come close to achieving that aim, first during the 1120s and then during the Second Crusade. That struggle was now over, and Nur al-Din had emerged as the victor.

———•———

The Franks would not get another chance to make a serious strike against an enemy center of power for over a decade after the failure of the Second Crusade. In the meantime, Nur al-Din pummeled the Crusader States time and again. With the Damascene territories firmly linked to his original Aleppan power base, he now shared a lengthy land border with the Kingdom of Jerusalem as well as with the northern Crusader States. Unlike the earlier rulers of Aleppo and the Jazira, he had the resources to engage the full might of Jerusalem's field army, not simply expeditionary forces sent to relieve the pressure on Antioch.

Even so, the Kingdom of Jerusalem's military remained arguably the strongest force in the Near East at that time, and it could deliver heavy blows. In addition, the kingdom continued to gather strength, even as Nur al-Din grew in power to the northeast. In 1153 Jerusalem's forces finally conquered the Fatimid city of Ascalon, severely reducing the threat of land-based attacks from Egypt and allowing the Franks to settle the fertile coastal strip immediately surrounding the city. Jerusalem's rulers could now concentrate their efforts on Nur al-Din, just as he was steadily focusing on the Franks.[25]

For all his zeal, Nur al-Din achieved little in his struggle against the Franks before 1164. Most of his campaigning tended to concentrate on the Frankish frontier outposts, which represented gateways to the hinterlands beyond. On the Antiochene frontier, the fortress of Harim was endlessly contested by both powers.[26] On the border between the Kingdom of Jerusalem and Damascus, the town of Baniyas was repeatedly attacked. The Franks, for their part, launched swinging raids across Nur al-Din's territories, but they lacked the strength to tackle his main centers of power.

The fortunes of war swung repeatedly from one side to the other. Nur al-Din did make some limited advances, particularly in the north, and won a major victory over the Antiochenes in 1149, but he also suffered two big battlefield defeats, one at the hands of the Kingdom of Jerusalem in 1158 in the Hawran region and the other near the great Hospitaller fortress of Krak des Chevaliers in 1163.

The latter defeat was especially humiliating. Like so many others, it was a cavalry victory: as in the Battle of Tell Danith in 1115, the Franks sent out a flying column of horsemen who caught the Turks unprepared and stormed through their camp. Nur al-Din was almost killed in the encounter and only narrowly escaped. Apparently, when he learned of the approaching Frankish charge, he mounted his horse while he was still inside his main tent. The Franks knew where he was and were galloping straight for him. He urged his horse to flee only to find that it was still hobbled (horses are hobbled with a strap to prevent them from straying). A Kurdish bodyguard leaped down from his own steed and cut his master's horse free. By this time the Christian heavy cavalry were only seconds away, but Nur al-Din managed to gallop away from the destruction of his army; his loyal Kurdish bodyguard was cut down before he had a chance to remount.[27]

The 1163 defeat also reflected another shift in the nature of conflict in the Near East. The Frankish forces in this encounter were led by a Templar knight, and the battle itself took place near a Hospitaller fortress. The military orders were a rising power in the Frankish states. By now they were formal institutions of the church, and their brethren took religious vows, committing themselves to the protection of Jerusalem (and for the Hospitallers, to the care of the sick). Both orders possessed considerable reserves of knights and infantry, and they were steadily being entrusted with some of the most embattled frontier fortresses across the Crusader States (Krak des Chevaliers, the fortress controlling the one clear invasion route into the County of Tripoli, being a case in point). The Templars and Hospitallers had the advantages of being both colossally rich and well represented in western Christendom. In recent decades, thousands of benefactors from across Europe, noble and nonnoble alike, had heaped donations on the orders, wishing to support both their work for the defense of the East and, in the case of the Hospitallers, their great hospital in Jerusalem. The orders had become wealthy, and they used their funds to assemble networks of hundreds of estates across western Christendom. These outposts, known as "commanderies," served as supply bases for the Crusader States, and their staffs recruited local warriors to join the orders or to take up the cross for the distant wars of Jerusalem. They also raised money to send directly to Jerusalem, not only drawing income from their own assets but also cultivating local donors and securing further benefactions. Combining wealth with a deep-seated commitment to the defense of the Holy Land, Templar and Hospitaller knights were among the most elite forces of their day, and they added a new cutting edge to the Frankish armies.[28]

By 1163 the Kingdom of Jerusalem and Nur al-Din had been thumping each other for years, yet neither had gained a decisive advantage. Nur al-Din had strengthened his territorial position as much as possible, and the Kingdom of Jerusalem was energetically seeking new crusaders from western Christendom and allies from Constantinople, but neither had yet found a way to break the deadlock and take the other's main centers of power. But a new opportunity was about to appear.

———•———

For King Amalric of Jerusalem (king of Jerusalem 1163–1174), 1167 was a year of great triumph, one that finally turned the tables on Nur al-Din. Amalric's predecessors may have labored in vain to break Aleppo and Damascus, but Amalric had finally gained control over a far greater prize: Egypt. Such an achievement would have been unthinkable only a few years before, but in August 1167 the great banner of the Kingdom of Jerusalem was flying from the highest point of Alexandria's majestic Pharos lighthouse, one of the great wonders of the ancient world. Egypt had become essentially a client state. It was militarily enfeebled and dependent for its survival on the Kingdom of Jerusalem. Egypt's vizier, Shawar—the effective ruler—had just agreed to pay the colossal sum of one hundred thousand dinars annually in tribute to the kingdom. Nur al-Din's Turkish army, which had contested control of the country, had been expelled. Christian knights were assigned to garrison Cairo's main gates, and a permanent Frankish representative would be posted to the city. The Kingdom of Jerusalem had just gained an advantage in its war with Nur al-Din, one that could prove decisive.[29]

The struggle for Egypt had begun in 1163. Egypt was in full political meltdown at that time, and its enemies were legion. Ascalon had fallen to the Franks in 1153, and in 1154 the Sicilians—a rising naval power—had sacked the coastal town of Tinnis. In recent years, the Fatimid army's Turkish and Sudanese troops had been wracked by infighting, and there had been a series of political coups. The most recent one took place in 1162 when Shawar, then the governor of Qus, launched a successful rebellion against the current vizier. After defeating and decapitating his foe, Shawar installed himself as vizier—only to be cast out of office in yet another coup by a rival named Dirgham.[30]

The Franks had been well aware of the trouble brewing in the Nile delta, but they only intervened militarily when the Egyptians failed to render their annual tribute to the Kingdom of Jerusalem. This regular payment had begun during the reign of Amalric's predecessor, Baldwin III, and it was sufficiently valuable for a default in payment to provoke an immediate invasion. Amalric then defeated the Fatimid army and forced Dirgham to promise an even larger tribute.

At the same time, the ousted vizier Shawar fled to Nur al-Din asking him to send a force to restore him to the vizierate. Nur al-Din acceded to this request, and he too dispatched a force to Egypt, led by a Kurdish commander named Shirkuh. The Turkish army began its campaign by sprinting daringly out from Damascus, across the Kingdom of Jerusalem, and into Egypt. Having arrived safely, Shirkuh swiftly completed his mission. He killed Dirgham, massacred his followers, and reinstated Shawar. Temporarily, this must have seemed like a great success to Nur al-Din's men, but any celebration was short-lived. Once Nur al-Din's Turks had restored Shawar to power, the new vizier denied that he was under any

obligation to the Turks and demanded Shirkuh's immediate departure. This betrayal enraged Shirkuh, who immediately attacked the
town of Bilbeis in northeast Egypt, possibly seeking to establish a
base near the frontier closest to his master's lands.

Shawar cannot have been surprised that Shirkuh would not
meekly retire from Egypt, but he had lacked the force necessary to throw him out. Consequently, he turned to the Franks
for assistance. Fearful that Nur al-Din and Shirkuh might seize
Cairo—and alarmed at the news carried by Shawar's emissaries—
Amalric quickly launched another campaign and drove Shirkuh
out of Egypt.

Egypt was then relatively quiet until 1167, when Shirkuh persuaded Nur al-Din, against his better judgment, to launch another
campaign against Cairo. On this occasion Shirkuh headed straight
for the city, making camp at Giza, near the pyramids. His purpose
could not have been plainer: he was intent on direct conquest. The
Franks reacted swiftly and sent their own army south. They joined
forces with the Egyptian army, and together their combined armies
forced Shirkuh's withdrawal from the city, pushing him south
along the line of the Nile. With the Turks on the run, the Franks
set out in pursuit. They then fought an indecisive battle in the desert, which compelled the Franks to retire north toward Cairo.

Shirkuh's next move was to travel north to seize the major port
of Alexandria, but he found himself besieged by the Franks. At this
point his campaign began to collapse, and he was eventually forced
to make peace with the Franks and return to Syria. For their part,
the Egyptians accepted a treaty that essentially rendered them a
tributary state.

Consequently, in the summer of 1167, Amalric could reasonably claim a great victory. The Fatimids' continued existence now
depended on the Kingdom of Jerusalem's protection, and Shirkuh's
aspirations had again been thwarted. But this achievement had
come at a price. While Amalric was campaigning in Egypt in 1164,
Nur al-Din took advantage of his absence to invade the Principality

of Antioch, and on August 10 he soundly defeated its prince in battle at Artah. A few months later he attacked the Kingdom of Jerusalem, taking its frontier stronghold of Baniyas. He took the initiative again in the summer of 1167, ravaging the County of Tripoli while Amalric was in Egypt. Sacrificing the defense of the northern Crusader States was a bitter price to pay for control over Egypt, but Amalric probably felt that the risk warranted the reward. Certainly he could reasonably have told himself that hegemony over Egypt would give him the resources to fully repay Nur al-Din for these incursions.

In his history of the Crusader States, the famous historian William of Tyre expressed himself with a red fury when he recalled what happened next. He railed that although the 1167 agreement had given the Kingdom of Jerusalem all it needed from Egypt—peace, revenue, and trade—the Franks' greed had not been satisfied.[31]

In late October 1168 Amalric gathered his forces for a fourth campaign into Egypt, seeking the complete overthrow of the Fatimid regime. This highly controversial endeavor would utterly destroy Amalric's advantageous entente with Shawar, all in the hope of securing direct control over the entire region. The Templars initially refused to participate in the risky and disreputable scheme. The Hospitallers were more willing, and Amalric enthusiastically marked out the parts of Egypt they could claim for themselves after the Fatimids were overthrown. Admittedly, the king's motives may not have been undiluted greed. There were rumors in the Kingdom of Jerusalem that Shawar was once again plotting with Nur al-Din. Moreover, the Byzantines were leaning on Amalric to complete his conquest, and several Egyptian nobles are said to have written to Amalric encouraging him to take charge.[32]

Amalric's true motives are unclear, but his campaign's outcome is certain. He advanced into Egypt and conquered Bilbeis in early November, subjecting the town to a thorough sack. Then he moved on to Cairo, where he began to construct the siege weapons nec-essary to assault the walls. Shawar responded skillfully. He prom-ised Amalric vast amounts of money in return for his withdrawal, and he managed to keep the negotiations going long enough for Shirkuh to arrive with reinforcements. When, in late December, Amalric learned that Shirkuh was approaching Egypt, he returned to Bilbeis, hoping to meet him in battle and prevent him from join-ing Shawar. Shirkuh simply evaded the Franks and reached Cairo. Finding themselves wrong-footed, the Franks had no choice but to withdraw.

When Shirkuh reached Cairo, he assassinated Shawar and be-came vizier himself, taking possession of Egypt in Nur al-Din's name. In 1169 the Franks invaded yet again, but achieved nothing. A third struggle for possession of a major center of power had again ended in ignominious defeat for the Franks. Nur al-Din now con-trolled Egypt.

By 1171 Nur al-Din had Aleppo, Damascus, and Cairo under his control, a major achievement. Over the preceding six decades, the Franks had contested control of each of these cities, but they had lost to the Turks on each occasion. Nur al-Din now had the upper hand, and he was ready to move in force against the Kingdom of Jerusalem. The war for the Near East entered its final phase, which would culminate with the overthrow of the Kingdom of Jerusalem.

In October 1171, Nur al-Din learned that his Egyptian forces had moved against the Frankish fortress of Montreal in Jordan. Founded in 1115, this important castle drew substantial revenue from the merchants traveling through the region to reach Egypt. Nur al-Din's lieutenant in Egypt was now Saladin, Shirkuh's nephew (Shirkuh had died in 1169).

Nur al-Din responded to Saladin's advance by moving south, seeking to combine their forces and strike a crushing blow against the Franks. The time was right for such a venture because Nur al-Din effectively had the Franks surrounded. Except in the extreme north, he controlled all their landward frontiers, and with the money and troops from his colossal landholdings, he could realistically contemplate a frontal assault on the kingdom.

Despite its potential, the campaign was a nonevent. Soon after Nur al-Din departed from Damascus, Saladin withdrew, claiming that problems in Egypt required his attention. The excuse may have been the plain truth, but he may have feared, as was later claimed, that if he met Nur al-Din in person he would be replaced as ruler of Egypt. Either way, rumors started to circulate that tensions were developing between the two men. In the years that followed their relationship became even more strained. Despite Saladin's gifts and protestations of loyalty, Nur al-Din came to fear that Saladin was turning renegade, seeking to break away and become an independent power. By 1174 it was becoming clear that only force would enable Nur al-Din to gain any meaningful control in Egypt.[33]

Nur al-Din never got the chance to rein in his subaltern. He died of illness in 1174 before his army was ready to march against Saladin. Nur al-Din was the most persistent enemy the Franks had ever faced, but he had won their admiration too. Amalric also won the respect of his foes, and when he died, in the same year as Nur al-Din, Saladin wrote a letter of condolence to the new Frankish king, Baldwin IV.[34]

—————•—————

Saladin was born to a family of Kurdish ethnicity in 1138 in the town of Tikrit (in northern Iraq), which was then governed by his father Ayyub in the name of the Seljuk sultan. That year, his family entered Zangi's service, and his father was given control of the castle of Baalbek in the Biqa Valley. Ayyub and his brother Shirkuh later served with Nur al-Din. During this time, Saladin grew steadily in authority, and his uncle Shirkuh learned to rely upon him during the 1167 Egyptian campaign. Saladin replaced his uncle as vizier of Egypt on March 26, 1169.

Initially he ruled Egypt in the name of the Fatimid caliph, but in 1171 he abolished the Fatimid caliphate (Shia) and proclaimed instead the Abbasid caliphate (Sunni) in the *khutbah*. Saladin swiftly built up his authority across Egypt, using his family members to impose control across the land, winning favor with the populace, gathering money, and ruthlessly crushing both political and military opposition.[35]

By late 1174, his position was sufficiently secure in Egypt to enable him to lead a small force of horsemen through Frankish territory and into Syria. He wanted to intervene in the chaos following Nur al-Din's death, and his target was Damascus. This was a risky and gutsy move. The city's new ruler was Nur al-Din's son and heir al-Salih, but the boy was only eleven years old and was currently in Aleppo. Saladin had a chance to take control, but it would require delicate diplomacy. He could not appear to be usurping the place of his master's heir, so he presented himself instead as a pious protector of Nur al-Din's family and interests, wishing to take charge only to save the city and maintain the jihad against the Franks. The gamble worked. His demand was met with uncertainty and dissension among the Damascene elites, but many in the army sided with Saladin, allowing him to take possession. He entrenched himself as its ruler by showering gold on the populace.

Directly after taking Damascus, Saladin set out for the north to try to take control of Nur al-Din's remaining lands. Within a few months he had captured Homs (although not, initially, its citadel) and Hama, but Aleppo evaded his grasp. Al-Salih himself tearfully begged the Aleppan populace to defend his birthright against Saladin, and they responded to his call. Saladin then took Baalbek, driving back the Franks who were rumored to have been called on to assist the beleaguered Aleppans. Saladin furiously denounced his enemies for making treaties with the Franks—but he did the same thing himself shortly afterward.

While Saladin was strengthening his position around Hama and Homs, the various branches of Zangi's family (the Zangid dynasty), who ruled Syria and the Jazira, were converging to swat away this new threat. Their combined army was formidable, and they were keen to put a stop to Saladin's ambitions. Nevertheless, when this allied force met Saladin on April 13, 1175, they were soundly defeated and were forced to yield their rights to the lands Saladin had already taken. The following year, in April 1176, there was a second big battle between Saladin and the Zangids, and this too was a clear defeat for Nur al-Din's heirs. Saladin then attempted to negotiate his way through Aleppo's gates, but he encountered only defiance from al-Salih. Consequently, following in the footsteps of the Franks during the 1110s and 1120s, he set about conquering the surrounding towns, applying more and more pressure on the city to strengthen his position.

Overall, Saladin's actions in the years following Nur al-Din's death focused squarely on the overthrow of his former master's heirs; he waged campaign after campaign against their remaining regional strongholds. He made little effort to fight the Franks in these early years and generally sought to hold them off with diplomacy. However, 1177 was an exception to this pattern: that year, Saladin tackled Jerusalem directly, invading out of Egypt and across the kingdom's southern border while the Franks' main army was waging war in the north. Saladin's army reached Ascalon on November 23, 1177, and encountered little resistance during his initial advance. The remaining Frankish forces were too few to bar his path, and they took shelter inside the walls of Ascalon and Gaza. Emboldened by this lack of resistance, Saladin became overconfident and made a critical error: he allowed his troops to fan out and to start despoiling the coastal plain. Baldwin IV's few remaining forces launched a sudden cavalry charge that swept through the Turks' scattered companies and routed Saladin's army. This encounter, known as the Battle of Montgisard, was not merely a military setback; it was a disaster. There was no friendly stronghold to which Saladin could retreat, and his surviving troops had to cross out of the Kingdom of Jerusalem and all the way across the Sinai Desert to reach safety. Moreover, his fleeing troops were harassed as they fled homeward, first by the victorious Christian knights and then by the Bedouin, who preyed upon them as they crossed the desert.

In following years Saladin enjoyed more success in his wars against the Franks, but, as Nur al-Din had found in the 1150s, his forces tended to batter the frontier rather than landing a blow that would truly weaken his foe. He also energetically pursued his wars against al-Salih and against the Zangid dynasty, launching expeditions against them and their allies both in the Jazira and in northern Syria. But again, although he tended to win in these encounters, he had yet to secure either of the two big bastions of power in these regions: Aleppo and Mosul.

His opportunity to claim the former finally came in November 1181 when al-Salih fell ill and died. Saladin moved swiftly to take control. Although he was not immediately successful—there was infighting among Aleppo's elites—Saladin continued to work for the city's overthrow. In 1182 his army traversed the Jazira, strengthening his position and weakening the Zangids wherever possible. He blockaded Mosul but did not press his attack home in earnest. In 1183 Saladin's persistent campaign of attrition against the Zangids' position was finally rewarded. In May of that year, following ongoing skirmishing with the populace, the Zangids finally conceded Aleppo to Saladin. On June 12 Saladin's standard was hoisted above the city's citadel; the "eye of Syria" was now in his hands.[36] More than that, all the main centers of power surrounding the Crusader States—Egypt, Damascus, and Aleppo—were now under Saladin's control. Three years later he gained authority over Mosul as well. The end was approaching.

Contemplating these years of war and intrigue, historians have gone back and forth trying to understand Saladin's character and behavior. His determination and boldness are beyond dispute. He was a politician of the highest caliber, and his ability to mix diplomatic pressure with military force was both effective and impressive. He was, however, as several historians have pointed out, perhaps only a competent soldier, not a brilliant one, and he tended to suffer badly when confronted by a commander of real tactical ability.[37]

An ongoing question is whether Saladin truly believed his own rhetoric. Was he a genuine heartfelt advocate of the jihad? Or was his pious commitment to holy war merely a polished facade covering his own selfish ambitions? Certainly there were many occasions when his actions seemed to contradict his professed devotion to holy war.[38] It is quite possible, however, that Saladin had so convinced himself that it was his right, and his alone, to rule the Near East and to lead the faithful in a jihad against the Franks that his conspicuous personal ambition and professed piety had merged into a single entity. Perhaps in his eyes, he *was* the jihad, and his personal motives and the interests of the Muslim world were therefore one and the same. This was not hypocrisy; it was a belief that he alone had been marked out for a special destiny. According to this script, his coreligionists had a duty to give way to his authority, and those who barred his path automatically made themselves viable targets. Likewise, when he himself deviated from the ideals he espoused— such as condemning fellow Muslims for making treaties with the Franks but then doing so himself, or claiming to fight jihad but concentrating his efforts on fighting fellow Muslims, or presenting himself as al-Salih's defender but then attacking his interests both in word and in deed, or claiming a right to cities or territories with the thinnest of excuses—he could justify such acts by captioning them as the necessary means of achieving his end goal. Such beliefs made Saladin a very dangerous man.

By 1186, no single ruler had amassed so much power in the Near East for almost a century. Moreover, with Muslim Syria and the Jazira firmly under his control, the Kingdom of Jerusalem was now in his sights. Saladin had spent years fighting to build up his territories, devoting the majority of his energies to fighting fellow Muslims. Now he needed to prove that there was some real substance to his endless assurances that he would destroy the Franks and retake Jerusalem. The political house of cards he had created was founded squarely on propaganda promising a glorious jihad, promises that were still unfulfilled. He had to act.

———•———

It cannot have been a happy gathering when the nobility of the Kingdom of Jerusalem assembled in council on the evening of July 2, 1187. The kingdom had mustered its army in full strength at the small castle of Safforie to fend off yet another assault by Saladin. The sultan's huge army lay to the east. He had crossed the River Jordan the previous day and laid siege to the town of Tiberias. The issue under discussion was whether the army should march out to confront him or remain in its current position. The general consensus was that they should stay exactly where they were. The most strident voice advocating this course of action was Count Raymond of Tripoli. Raymond urged the assembled nobles to wait until reinforcements could arrive to bolster their ranks. In the meantime, he suggested that they should hold Saladin off by blocking his line of advance and entrenching their own position so that he would be discouraged from staging an attack on their lines.

It was good advice. It would keep Saladin's superior force at arm's length without risking the uncertainties of a major encounter. It would also build political pressure—already considerable—on Saladin himself, who had tried repeatedly to invade the Kingdom of Jerusalem but had achieved very little. Being stalled yet again far outside Jerusalem's core territories would not look good for him, damaging his credentials as the leader of the jihad.

Raymond's strategic assessment was undoubtedly impartial because it ran contrary to his personal interests. Tiberias was his town, and the garrison was commanded by his wife Eschiva. His children were also within its walls, so his advice placed them all in harm's way (although he was holding on to the thin hope that his family could take boats onto Lake Tiberias and hold out until reinforcements could arrive).[39]

This may have been good military counsel, but the new king of Jerusalem, Guy of Lusignan (Baldwin IV died in 1185, and his heir, Baldwin V, died soon afterward, in 1186), was not in a position to make military decisions based solely on tactical concerns. He had only recently become king, and his ascension to power had been deeply controversial. The Kingdom of Jerusalem was riven by noble squabbles, and Guy had only been able to take the throne through a political sleight of hand. His support base was limited, and the nobles gathered at Safforie included both allies and enemies. Guy had to weigh the count of Tripoli's military good sense against the fact that when he had been the kingdom's regent in 1183, he had been disgraced for pursuing a similar course of action. On that occasion, he had allowed his army simply to block a major advance by Saladin without giving battle; the decision had cost him his regency.[40]

It did not look good to refuse battle. This was a world where knights were born and raised on tales of daring, risk, and adventure. They also believed that God would grant them victory in battle, especially against non-Christian enemies. Guy would have known that while his nobles were debating policy, the army's knights were celebrating the thought of saving the ladies of Tiberias. What would they think of him as their king if he sat in Safforie with one of the largest armies the kingdom had ever mustered and simply watched the town burn? Of equal importance was the fact that two of his closest allies, the Templar master and the lord of Kerak, were pushing for him to march on Tiberias. They argued vigorously for this aggressive strategy in open debate, heckling the count of Tripoli, for whom the Templar master had a strong personal dislike.

Finally, the king made his decision and ended the debate: they would not risk marching on Tiberias. A few hours later, however, after Guy had retired to his tent for the night, the Templar master came to him in private and persuaded him to change his mind. The army would march on Tiberias in the morning after all.

On July 3, 1187, the army of the Kingdom of Jerusalem began its advance. The armies were unbalanced in numbers. The
Franks deployed twelve hundred heavy cavalry and about fifteen
thousand light cavalry and infantry. Saladin possessed about thirty
thousand troops.[41] Still, the commanders on both sides would have
been aware that the Christian heavy cavalry could overrun much
larger forces if they were used effectively. The battle began when the
Christian army moved forward in close formation toward Tiberias.
The Turkish forces did not initially try to block its advance; rather,
they sought to slow it down. These were desolate lands, with few
springs, and in the July heat the Turks wanted to keep the Franks
away from water. King Guy did not reach Tiberias the first day, so
he was forced to make camp for the night. The following day the
Franks woke to find themselves surrounded, and they tried unsuc-
cessfully to break through to Tiberias. Saladin maintained a steady
pressure on the Christian army, and exhaustion, dehydration, and
superior numbers slowly began to have their effect. The army crumpled and the survivors made their stand in an old Iron Age fort
known as the Horns of Hattin.[42]

The Battle of Hattin was a disaster for the Crusader States. King
Guy had stripped the Kingdom of Jerusalem of defenders to raise
an army big enough to confront Saladin, but by nightfall on July 4
almost the entire force was either dead or in captivity. The kingdom
now had too few soldiers to raise a new army or to maintain its
borders. In the months that followed, the kingdom collapsed, and
its towns and strongholds fell like dominoes to Saladin's advancing
army. Jerusalem was taken in October. Tyre alone among the kingdom's cities managed to hold out. Saladin also drove north, sacking
both the County of Tripoli and the Principality of Antioch, which
were in no position to oppose him now that Jerusalem's army had
fallen. Saladin's sweeping victories fundamentally shifted the balance of power in his favor, and now there was a very real prospect
that the Crusader States would be utterly annihilated.

When news of the defeat reached western Christendom, the papacy promptly launched a massive new campaign: the Third Crusade. The response was overwhelming, and vast numbers of knights from across Christendom took the cross, determined to retake Jerusalem from Saladin. Armies set out from across western Christendom, and soon a new war was brewing in the Near East, one that would pit Saladin against his most famous opponent: Richard I, "Lionheart," king of England. The Franks on the Levantine mainland still had a future, and their lands in the Levant would briefly revive in the thirteenth century before finally being overthrown in 1291. However, that does not detract from the importance of 1187. The great crusader kingdom of Jerusalem had been reduced from a preeminent Near Eastern power to a tiny territory consisting of only one city.

Looking back across the history of the Crusader States, from the conquest of Jerusalem in 1099 to its fall in 1187, one can clearly identify three phases when the crusaders had a real chance to expand inland from the coastline and consolidate their rule across the Near East through the conquest of either Aleppo, Damascus, or Cairo. If nothing else, the mere fact that they were able to strike at these centers of power so repeatedly proves that the demise of the Frankish position in the Levant was not a foregone conclusion. Complete victory remained a realizable outcome at least until the 1170s.

Of these three moments, it was the struggle for Aleppo that came closest to victory. By 1118 the Franks already possessed much of Aleppo's hinterland and many of its satellite towns. They were able to apply direct pressure to the city itself for a prolonged period; this was very different from the later assaults against Damascus (1148) and Cairo (1168), which were both one-off lunges. In addition, they had good relationships with important regional allies during the struggle for Aleppo, including the Banu Uqayl of

Qalat Jabar, Dubays, and the Armenians. During this contest, the Franks could also draw upon the long-standing momentum of conquest built up during and after the First Crusade. On this occasion they came within a hair's breadth of driving inland and achieving a position of regional dominance. Consequently, the struggle for Aleppo, and the Battle of the Field of Blood in particular, have to be considered vital turning points in the struggle for the Near East, representing critical moments that blunted the Frankish advance.

Still, victory continually eluded them, at Aleppo and then again in their later attacks on Damascus and Egypt. Indeed, the history of the Crusader States and their rulers' military ambition to achieve regional conquest is a curious tale of repeated near misses. Why did all three of these attempts to drive inland fail? Each was launched with a solid chance of success, but they all ended badly. So why did the Crusader States prove so consistently incapable of breaking down their enemies' centers of power?

The answer to this must lie, on the one hand, within the specific events surrounding each campaign. As we have seen already, it is vital to understand the cut and thrust, the move and countermove, of the various protagonists engaged in each struggle. So in each case, these attacks and their reasons for failure are unique, specific to the individual campaign.

Yet on the other hand, there is a curious symmetry to these thwarted wars of conquest. In each case, prior to the main attack, the Franks struck up a strong and reciprocal rapport with the city's urban elites: Aleppo was virtually an Antiochene protectorate in 1117–1118, the Kingdom of Jerusalem had a long history of cooperation with Damascus prior to 1148, and Egypt had agreed to be a Frankish protectorate in 1167. Then, in each case, the Franks broke off the relationship and commenced offensive operations.[43] In each case they then besieged the city, waiting outside the walls without making a serious attempt at a frontal assault. Then, as Turkish reinforcements began to arrive, whether from Aqsunqur in 1125, Nur al-Din in 1148, or Shirkuh in 1168, the

Franks—astonishingly—showed only a slight willingness to put up a fight. In 1125 they did not seek to engage Aqsunqur, even though Dubays wanted to fight. In 1148, outside Damascus, the Franks did not seek to fight their way back from a waterless area to a more advantageous position. In 1168, Amalric did try to intercept Shirkuh as he advanced upon Cairo, but he did not seek to continue his attack once Shirkuh's forces reached the Egyptian capital. And last, in all cases, the Franks retreated.

The parallels among these endeavors are striking, and they raise the possibility that there may have been broader issues in play that consistently inhibited the Franks from pressing home their sieges. One such broader issue may have been the sheer size of the cities. These were the largest cities in the region. It is impossible to establish precise population figures, but numbers around the six-figure mark for Damascus and Aleppo and a much higher six-figure mark for Cairo seem reasonable. Consequently, the urban population would have been many times larger than the besieging forces. It is nowhere stated explicitly, but perhaps when the Frankish commanders contemplated the reality of securing permanent dominion over these centers of power and the risks and resources entailed, they were daunted by the sheer enormity of the task. Cities had devoured assaulting contingents whole in the past. In 1153, at the siege of Ascalon, a Templar force assaulted the city through a newly formed breach in the wall, crossed into the city, and simply disappeared.[44] Perhaps the thought of a conquering Frankish army crossing the enemy's ramparts only to scatter itself within a maze of narrow alleyways filled with hostile eyes and knives in the dark sent shudders down commanders' spines, and this may explain why determined assaults on the walls were not launched at any of these sieges.

Another common factor may have been a fundamental weakness in the Franks' basic strategic approach to conquering big enemy cities. They seem to have considered the idea of assaulting a city militarily to be incompatible with the idea of working with collaborating factions among the local population. For example, at Aleppo, the Franks first worked with the city's elites, adopting the role of protector, but then jettisoned this policy for one of outright hostility. A similar pattern can be seen in their attacks on Damascus and Cairo; in both cases they had previously worked alongside local factions, before changing their stance and attacking. This was an obviously flawed approach in that the later "assault" phase entirely negated any advantage derived from the earlier "negotiation" phase.

The Turks were substantially more sophisticated in the strategies they used to break into big cities; they often effectively combined military force with political pressure, and they recognized the importance of securing goodwill among the urban population. It has to be remembered that during this same period, Turkish or Kurdish commanders repeatedly strong-armed their way into Aleppo, Damascus, and Cairo, sometimes more than once, just as their Frankish neighbors conspicuously failed in all their own attempts. The Turks tended to be far more effective at exploiting existing divisions within the cities' urban elites, using the local quarrels to win allies and supporters among the population: divide and rule. The manipulation of internal alliances coupled with the application of external military pressure (generally brought about by strangling the city's food supply) gave them considerable leverage. The Turks also seem to have had a gift for staging round after round of negotiations during their sieges, often finding face-saving excuses that would allow the urban population's representatives to justify capitulation. It may also have helped that the Turkish commanders tended to be at least nominally Muslim and could therefore appeal to a common faith, although it has to be noted that urban populations were also prepared to talk to Frankish commanders. Once within the walls, the Turks often proved equally adept at winning the populace's support—or at least submission—either by lowering taxes or, conversely, by brutally purging the city's leaders: a carrot-and-stick approach.

Comparing the Frankish and Turkish approaches to the conquest of cities, therefore, reveals several major deficiencies in the standard Frankish game plan. They do not seem to have evolved the same hybrid tactics used so effectively by the Turks, simultaneously applying external military pressure while seeking to take advantage of internal civic infighting. Although it is true that at Aleppo in 1125 Baldwin II had the support of several Turkish and Arab leaders, he or they seem to have been ineffective in their attempts to use that support to create rifts and divisions among the urban population. Instead, in the winter siege of 1124–1125, the allied Frankish-Arab army's rather clumsy attempts at psychological warfare and intrigue served only to unify the populace in their opposition to their besiegers.

A final common factor connecting these campaigns could perhaps be captioned as a "fear of the consequences of failure." Again comparing the relative strengths and weaknesses of Frankish and Turkish armies, it swiftly becomes apparent that the Franks were extremely ill-suited for wars of conquest conducted deep within Turkish territory. If they were to advance on an enemy city, fight a major battle against a Turkish relief army, and lose, they would immediately find themselves facing complete annihilation. Their defeated Frankish army would have to return to friendly territory, mostly on foot, while suffering endless attacks from Turkish light cavalrymen, who were highly suited to this kind of pursuit. If the Turks, by contrast, were to suffer a defeat and fail to seize a major city, they could simply scatter, immediately evading any lumbering Frankish pursuit. In short, the consequences of failure were asymmetric for the two sides. For these reasons, Frankish commanders had to be exceptionally cautious when striking at enemy centers of power because they could not risk suffering a major battlefield defeat far from their own borders. They had no choice but to be risk averse in such circumstances. This may help explain why they took so few risks in combat during the sieges of Aleppo, Damascus, and Cairo, and why they were skittish about fighting relief armies.

It may by extension go some way to explaining why they were so consistently unsuccessful.

The Franks' best chance—according to their very limited strategic toolbox—at forcing the submission of a major city was an ultra-slow process. It required them to maintain prolonged control of all the surrounding territory and neighboring towns and fortifications. Only then could the city be isolated and any relieving armies be engaged in battle with the reassurance that they possessed strong places of retreat should matters take a turn for the worse. The city could then slowly be ground down until it was so weak that it could no longer offer resistance. This approach could work. It was the method the Franks used to get into Tyre and later into Ascalon. Nevertheless, it was cumbersome, expensive, and painstakingly slow, often taking many decades to complete. Also, isolating inland cities such as Aleppo and Damascus, which possessed excellent supply lines connecting them to the Turkish heartlands in Iraq, was a substantially harder task than blockading the more isolated coastal cities. This martial logic was also predicated on the belief that a city's urban population would have to be cowed en bloc, rather than divided through political intrigue and chicanery—again, a much harder task.

The Franks did not even get close to achieving this kind of position during their assaults on Damascus and Cairo, but they were at the point of forcing a blockade around Aleppo by 1118. By this stage, they held many of the surrounding towns and fortifications and were almost at the point of isolating the city from its main avenues of support. This consideration underlines the importance of the Franks' failure to secure Aleppo between the years 1118 and 1125.

Overall, between 1099 and 1187 the Franks instigated three long-term attempts to strike inland and conquer their enemies' centers of power. They failed on every occasion. Among these three endeavors, the struggle for Aleppo came closest to success. For this reason, the Franks' failure to achieve this goal must sit squarely within any attempt to explain their inability to conquer the Near Eastern region. It also underscores the importance of the Battle of the Field of Blood, which broke the Frankish noose around the city just as it was tightening.

AFTERWORD

WHILE WRITING ABOUT the Field of Blood and the wars fought over Aleppo from the vantage point of the twenty-first century, it is natural to reflect on the current state of northern Syria. At this moment, our screens are filled with haunting images of a shattered Aleppo circled by many combatant factions. The human cost of war, which was bad enough at the time of the Crusades, is now far greater, the product of a higher population density, the enhanced killing power of modern weapons, and a readiness to take human life that is at least equal to that of the crusading era (in some cases I suspect it is greater today).

Reflecting on this present situation, it is natural to ponder comparisons between these two murderous contests for this much-coveted city. Almost nine hundred years of history separate the two wars, yet there are some striking similarities. It is again a struggle in which Arabs, Turks, and Kurds are locked in a complex political game played out both around the negotiating table and on the battlefield. The protagonists again include proponents of jihad mixed with other factions whose motives include money, power, political stability, or, for many, survival. The West is again caught up in a conflict that it only partially understands and in which its attempts to achieve a degree of control are immediately skewed as multiple local factions seek to twist its interventions to their own advantage. And again, there is no easy political resolution to the conflict.

These significant parities serve as reminders that the political, ethnic, and religious fault lines dividing the region are deep and historic. They will not be solved easily—if they are to be solved at all. The entrenched hostilities, rivalries, and alliances that play their part in shaping the conflict have been handed down from generation to generation. They are inextricably entwined in the fabric of society.

In recent years, considerable pressure has been placed on policy makers, particularly in western Europe and the United States, to "solve" the problems of the Middle East. Such pressure has been exerted by commentators from all shades of the political spectrum. Yet this assessment vastly overestimates the West's power and influence. The West has played its part in shaping the course of recent events and undoubtedly has the potential to play a part in resolving the pressing problems confronting the region (if resolution is possible). Nevertheless, it is essential to recognize that many of the core issues at play predate the modern world, and most predate the Crusades. Indeed, many of these tensions were old even when the Crusades were young.

It might be possible to ease tensions temporarily with a photo-opportunity handshake of politicians making peace, and it might be possible for international institutions such as the United Nations to play some role in separating the embattled factions. Nevertheless, a long-standing resolution can only take place at a grassroots level when these historic hostilities are finally confronted by all factions and at all levels of society with an eye to reconciling their differences. We can but hope.

As for the Crusades and the wars of the Latin East, they are in the strange position of simultaneously being both irrelevant and highly relevant to the modern Middle East. Let me explain what I mean. For those interested in the causes of modern-day events and the long-standing roots of conflict, the Field of Blood, or indeed the Crusades as a whole, scarcely register as direct causes. The medieval struggle for the Near East took place a very long time ago; almost nine hundred years separate us from the Field of Blood. In the intervening period, empires have risen and fallen, trade routes have sprung up and collapsed, leaders have shaped their people's history and then died, and both Christendom and Europe, on the one hand, and the empires of the Muslim world, on the other, have had many other neighbors and concerns to divert their attention. The Crusades are simply one strand among thousands of others in the warp and weft of events that have shaped the modern world. True, the Crusades persisted long after the eradication of the Frankish presence on the Levantine mainland in 1291, but they were often waged on other frontiers, such as the Baltic or against heretics, and were frequently launched in Christendom's defense rather than as aggressive campaigns.

Yet from another perspective, the Crusades remain all around us. The propagandists of jihad have seized on these historic wars, manipulating their memory to establish precedents for their own violence. This is weaponized history: the use of the past to create a narrative that drives violence in the present. Time and again terrorists and jihadists have announced that their atrocities have been guided by the desire to fight "crusaders," although increasingly the designation of being a "crusader enemy" has broadened to encompass just about anyone standing in their path. Worryingly, I have also started to hear tales of far-right movements in the West drawing on crusading-themed ideas.

The irony of all such violent arguments is, of course, that the actual twelfth-century struggle between the Franks and the Turks only occasionally bore a resemblance to an interreligious conflict of the kind touted by modern-day advocates of hate. Both the Turks and the Franks had far more complex agendas than straightforward sectarian violence, and they were prepared to cooperate with one another when their interests coincided. Their worldviews were also broad enough that they could respect and even admire their opponents. Some even became friends with their foes. War in the Middle Ages could be brutal, but when the fighting was done, there remained space for the combatant factions to engage in trade, conversation, and diplomacy. As we have seen, there were occasions during the crusading period when warriors could seek out their enemies after the fighting was done and share stories about their deeds on the battlefield, confident in the knowledge that they would receive their enemy's welcome and hospitality.

This point deserves attention. The word "medieval" in modern parlance has become a term of abuse, conveying ideas of barbarity, ignorance, superstition, and backwardness. We condemn the worst of contemporary wars by describing them as being fought in "medieval" conditions, or we might observe that violence has reached "medieval" proportions. Even so, the crusaders and their Turkish and Arab counterparts, during these so-called dark ages, could find space for respect, cooperation, and even friendship across the fault lines of war. There is little enough of that today.

ABBREVIATIONS

The following abbreviations are used throughout the notes. Where available, references have been made to modern English translations so that the sources are as accessible as possible (although translations are not available for every source used in this work).

AA Albert of Aachen. *Historia Ierosolimitana: History of the Journey to Jerusalem*. Edited and translated by S. B. Edgington. Oxford Medieval Texts. Oxford, 2007.

AC Anna Comnena. *The Alexiad*. Translated by E. R. A. Sewter. With an introduction by P. Frankopan. London, 2009.

ASC Anonymous. "Syriac Chronicle." Translated by A. Tritton. *Journal of the Royal Asiatic Society* 65 (1933): 69–101.

FC Fulcher of Chartres. *A History of the Expedition to Jerusalem, 1095–1127*. Translated by F. R. Ryan. New York, 1969.

GF *Gesta Francorum: The Deeds of the Franks and the Other Pilgrims to Jerusalem*. Edited and translated by R. Hill. Oxford Medieval Texts. Oxford, 1962.

GN Guibert of Nogent. *The Deeds of God Through the Franks: Gesta dei per Francos*. Translated by R. Levine. Woodbridge, UK, 1997.

IAA(1) Ibn al-Athir. *The Annals of the Saljuq Turks: Selections from al-Kāmil fī'l-Ta'rīkh of 'Izz al-Dīn Ibn al-Athīr*. Translated by D. S. Richards. Studies in the History of Iran and Turkey, 1000–1700 AD. Abingdon, UK, 2002.

IAA(2) Ibn al-Athir. *The Chronicle of Ibn al-Athir for the Crusading Period from al-Kamil fi'l-Ta'rikh.* Translated by D. S. Richards. 3 vols. Crusade Texts in Translation 13, 15, and 17. Aldershot, UK, 2006–2008.

IQ Ibn al-Qalanisi. *The Damascus Chronicle of the Crusades.* Translated by H. A. R. Gibb. New York, 2002.

KAD Kemal al-Din. "Extraits de la Chronique d'Alep." *Recueil des Historiens des Croisades: Historiens Orientaux.* Vol. 3. Paris, 1884.

ME Matthew of Edessa. *Armenia and the Crusades: Tenth to Twelfth Centuries. The Chronicle of Matthew of Edessa.* Translated by A. E. Dostourian. New York, 1993.

OV Orderic Vitalis. *The Ecclesiastical History of Orderic Vitalis.* Edited and translated by M. Chibnall. 6 vols. Oxford Medieval Texts. Oxford, 1969–1990.

RA Raymond d'Aguilers. *Historia Francorum qui ceperunt Iherusalem.* Translated by J. H. Hill and L. L. Hill. Philadelphia, 1968.

RC Ralph of Caen. *The Gesta Tancredi of Ralph of Caen: A History of the Normans on the First Crusade.* Translated by B. S. Bachrach and D. S. Bachrach. Crusade Texts in Translation 12. Farnham, UK, 2010.

UIM Usama ibn Munqidh. *The Book of Contemplation: Islam and the Crusades.* Penguin Classics. London, 2008.

WC Walter the Chancellor. *The Antiochene Wars: A Translation and Commentary.* Translated by T. Asbridge and S. B. Edgington. Crusade Texts in Translation 4. Aldershot, UK, 1999.

WT William of Tyre. *A History of Deeds Done Beyond the Sea.* Translated by E. A. Babcock and A. C. Krey. 2 vols. New York, 1943.

NOTES

PROLOGUE

1. For the full text in English translation, see *The "Chanson des Chétifs" and "Chanson de Jérusalem": Completing the Central Trilogy of the Old French Crusade Cycle*, trans. C. Sweetenham, Crusade Texts in Translation 29 (Farnham, UK, 2016), 67–172.

2. See also T. Asbridge, "How the Crusades Could Have Been Won: King Baldwin II of Jerusalem's Campaigns Against Aleppo (1124–5) and Damascus (1129)," *Journal of Medieval Military History*, ed. C. J. Rogers and K. DeVries, 11 (2013): 73–74.

3. T. Asbridge, "How the Crusades Could Have Been Won," 73–93.

CHAPTER 1: THE RIVAL ARCHITECTS OF THE CRUSADER STATES (1100–1110)

1. AA, 533.

2. FC, 139.

3. Ibid., 134. See also AA, 237.

4. J. France, *Victory in the East: A Military History of the First Crusade* (Cambridge, 1994), 246.

5. *The Chronicle of the Third Crusade: The Itinerarium Peregrinorum et Gesta Regis Ricardi*, trans. H. Nicholson, Crusade Texts in Translation 3 (Aldershot, UK, 1997), 234.

6. AA, 533–537, 563; FC, 137–142; IQ, 51; IAA(2), 1: 47; WT, 1: 422–424.

7. For an introductory discussion on the launch of the First Crusade, see P. Frankopan, *The First Crusade: The Call from the East* (London, 2012), chaps. 6 and 7; T. Asbridge, *The First Crusade: A New History* (Oxford, 2004), chaps. 1 and 2.

8. See N. Morton, *Encountering Islam on the First Crusade* (Cambridge, 2016), chap. 2.

9. AC, 304–305.

10. France, *Victory in the East,* 209.

11. Ibid., 192–196.

12. FC, 90.

13. AA, 175; FC, 91; ME, 169. For discussion, see C. MacEvitt, *The Crusades and the Christian World of the East: Rough Tolerance* (Philadelphia, 2008), 65–71.

14. For detailed discussion of the siege of Antioch, see France, *Victory in the East,* chaps. 7 and 8.

15. This story is told by many authors, but for a sample, see AA, 277–279; GF, 44–47.

16. OV, 5: 325.

17. Several sources report their appearance. See, for example, GF, 69. For discussion, see E. Lapina, *Warfare and the Miraculous in the Chronicles of the First Crusade* (University Park, PA, 2015), 37–53.

18. For discussion of the role played by the Holy Lance in this battle, see T. Asbridge, "The Holy Lance of Antioch: Power, Devotion and Memory on the First Crusade," *Reading Medieval Studies* 33 (2007): 3–36.

19. KAD, 582–583.

20. France, *Victory in the East,* 288–296.

21. M. A. Köhler, *Alliances and Treaties Between Frankish and Muslim Rulers in the Middle East: Cross-Cultural Diplomacy in the Period of the Crusades,* trans. P. M. Holt, ed. K. Hirschler, The Muslim World in the Age of the Crusades (Leiden, 2013), 44–57.

22. B. Z. Kedar, "The Jerusalem Massacre of July 1099 in the Western Historiography of the Crusades," *Crusades* 3 (2004): 15–75.

23. AA, 553.

24. Geoffrey of Malaterra, *The Deeds of Count Roger of Calabria and Sicily and of His Brother Duke Robert Guiscard,* trans. K. Baxter Wolf (Ann Arbor, MI, 2005), 57–58.

25. Caffaro, *Caffaro, Genoa and the Twelfth Century Crusades,* trans. M. Hall and J. Phillips, Crusade Texts in Translation 16 (Farnham, UK, 2013).

26. For discussion of the Fatimid army, see Y. Lev, "Regime, Army and Society in Medieval Egypt, 9th–12th Centuries," in *War and Society in the Eastern Mediterranean, 7th–15th Centuries,* ed. Y. Lev (Leiden, 1997), 115–152; Y. Lev, "Army, Regime and Society in Fatimid Egypt, 358–487/968–1094," *International Journal of Middle Eastern Studies* 19, no. 3 (1987): 337–365.

27. RA, 115.

28. R. Burns, *Damascus: A History* (Abingdon, UK, 2005).

29. AA, 511.

30. Al-Muqaddasi, *The Best Divisions for Knowledge of the Regions*, trans. B. Collins (Reading, UK, 2001), 132.

31. For further discussion of the geopolitical importance of Damascus and Aleppo, see T. Asbridge, "How the Crusades Could Have Been Won: King Baldwin II of Jerusalem's Campaigns Against Aleppo (1124–5) and Damascus (1129)," *Journal of Medieval Military History*, ed. C. J. Rogers and K. DeVries, 11 (2013): 93.

32. GN, 159. Asbridge has also considered the role played by Aleppo in the Franks' long-standing geopolitical ambitions. In a recent article he argued that it was Baldwin II of Jerusalem who first actively sought the "actual conquest" of Aleppo, unlike his predecessors who were more interested in tribute taking. Asbridge, "How the Crusades Could Have Been Won," 83. Nevertheless, in two earlier publications he raised the possibility that Antioch had been considering a frontal assault on the city under the earlier ruler Roger of Salerno. T. Asbridge, "The Significance and Causes of the Battle of the Field of Blood," *Journal of Medieval History* 23, no. 4 (1997): 213; T. Asbridge, *The Creation of the Principality of Antioch, 1098–1130* (Woodbridge, UK, 2000), 69.

33. KAD, 589.

34. For discussion of the southern Italian / Sicilian Normans, see J. J. Norwich, *The Normans in Sicily* (London, 1970).

35. S. Edgington, "Espionage and Military Intelligence During the First Crusade, 1095–1099," in *Crusading and Warfare in the Middle Ages*, ed. S. John and N. Morton, Crusades—Subsidia 7 (Farnham, UK, 2014), 78.

36. Asbridge, *The Creation of the Principality of Antioch*, 47–51.

37. RC, 162–163.

38. Ibid., 164.

39. IAA(2), 1: 76.

40. Ibid., 1: 79.

41. RC, 165; FC, 177–178; AA, 693.

42. AA, 693.

43. ME, 193.

44. IAA(2), 1: 80.

45. FC, 179.

46. The Turkmen are frequently mentioned in the surviving sources, but they are difficult to define as a group. In this book the term "Turkmen" is used to denote Turkish warriors who still maintained their tribal nomadic lifestyle.

47. OV, 6: 105.

48. Ibid., 6: 109.

49. ME, 212.

50. KAD, 597.

51. Ibid., 595.

52. ME, 202.

53. *Nāsir-e Khosraw's Book of Travels (Safarnāma)*, trans. W. M. Thackston Jr., Persian Heritage Series 36 (Albany, NY, 1986), 12–13.

54. IAA(2), 1: 104.

55. AA, 777–779; William of Malmesbury, *Gesta Regum Anglorum*, ed. and trans. R. A. B. Mynors, R. M. Thomson, and M. Winterbottom, vol. 1, Oxford Medieval Texts (Oxford, 1998), 701.

56. K. Lewis, *The Counts of Tripoli and Lebanon in the Twelfth Century: Sons of Saint-Gilles* (Abingdon, UK, 2017), 41–49.

57. For discussion, see J. France, *Western Warfare in the Age of the Crusades, 1000–1300* (Ithaca, NY, 1999), 117–118.

58. The debate over what motivated the crusaders is a very old one. For a summary of this discussion, see N. Housley, *Contesting the Crusades, Contesting the Past* (Oxford, 2006), 75–98.

59. For discussion, see D. S. Bachrach, *Religion and the Conduct of War, c. 300–c. 1215* (Woodbridge, UK, 2003).

60. RC, 22.

61. S. D. Goitein, "Geniza Sources for the Crusader Period: A Survey," in *Outremer: Studies in the History of the Crusading Kingdom of Jerusalem* (Jerusalem, 1982), 312.

62. D. M. Metcalf, *Coinage of the Crusades and the Latin East in the Ashmolean Museum Oxford*, 2nd ed. (London, 1995), 28.

CHAPTER 2: RIDING THE STORM (1111–1118)

1. "Sultan" was his name and should not be confused with the title of "Turkish sultan."

2. I am indebted to Kevin Lewis for his advice on this point. K. Lewis, *The Counts of Tripoli and Lebanon in the Twelfth Century: Sons of Saint-Gilles* (Abingdon, UK, 2017), 33.

3. IQ, 90, 92.

4. IAA(1), 226.

5. C. Hillenbrand, "Ibn al-'Adim's Biography of the Seljuq Sultan, Alp Arslan," in *Actas XVI Congreso UEAI* (Salamanca, 1995), 239–241.

6. KAD, 577.

7. The members of Arab tribes tended to be related or otherwise connected to a great historic predecessor. "Banu Kilab," for example, means "House of Kilab."

8. "The History of David King of Kings," in *Rewriting Caucasian History: The Medieval Armenian Adaptation of the Georgian Chronicles,* trans. R. W. Thomson (Oxford, 1996), 316.

9. GF, 81; RA, 84.

10. For discussion and differing opinions on how the Muslim world viewed western Europe prior to and during the Crusades, see B. Lewis, *The Muslim Discovery of Europe* (London, 1982); D. König, *Arabic-Islamic Views of the Latin West: Tracing the Emergence of Medieval Europe* (Oxford, 2015).

11. UIM, 145, 148.

12. Ibid., 76–77.

13. F. Daftary, *The Ismāʿīlīs: Their History and Doctrines* (Cambridge, 1990).

14. IQ, 72–73; UIM, 244–245.

15. AA, 739–741.

16. UIM, 77–78.

17. IQ, 114.

18. IAA(2), 1: 154.

19. IQ, 111.

20. KAD, 600.

21. IQ, 118.

22. Ibid., 118.

23. See B. S. Bachrach and D. S. Bachrach, "Ralph of Caen as a Military Historian," in *Crusading and Warfare in the Middle Ages: Realities, Representations. Essays in Honour of John France,* ed. S. John and N. Morton, Crusades–Subsidia 7 (Farnham, UK, 2014), 94.

24. UIM, 80–81.

25. For a review of the possible reasons for the Turks' migration, see A. C. S. Peacock, *The Great Seljuk Empire,* Edinburgh History of the Islamic Empires (Edinburgh, 2015), 25.

26. IAA(2), 1: 111–117.

27. KAD, 606–608.

28. Ibid., 608.

29. WC, 90, 92.

30. Ibid., 92–93.

31. Ibid., 95.

32. UIM, 85.

33. WC, 96–104; IAA(2), 1: 172–173; ASC, 86.

34. KAD, 606.

35. Ibid., 611.

36. OV, 6: 129–131.

37. N. Morton, *Encountering Islam on the First Crusade* (Cambridge, 2016), 42–55.

38. IAA(2), 1: 155.

39. AA, 339.

40. GF, 42.

41. See, for example, IQ, 149, 271; UIM, 131–132; WC, 90, 164; OV, 6: 113.

42. See N. Morton, "The Saljuq Turks' Conversion to Islam: The Crusading Sources," *Al-Masāq: Journal of the Medieval Mediterranean* 27, no. 2 (2015): 109–118.

43. IAA(1), 294.

44. RA, 89.

45. For further discussion on the political context, see M. Köhler, *Alliances and Treaties Between Frankish and Muslim Rulers in the Middle East: Cross-Cultural Diplomacy in the Period of the Crusades*, trans. P. Holt, ed. K. Hirschler, The Muslim World in the Age of the Crusades (Leiden, 2013), 1–174.

46. *The Sea of Precious Virtues (Bahr al-Favā'id): A Medieval Mirror for Princes*, trans. J. S. Meisami (Salt Lake City, UT, 1991), 56.

47. König, *Arabic-Islamic Views of the Latin West*, 11.

48. *Constitutiones canonicorum regularium ordinis Arroasiensis*, ed. L. Milis and J. Becquet, Corpus Christianorum: Continuatio Mediaeualis 20 (Turnhout, Belgium, 1970), 213.

49. "Notitiae duae Lemovicenses de Praedicatione crucis in Aquitania," in *Recueil des historiens des croisades: Historiens occidentaux*, vol. 5 (Paris, 1895), 351.

50. S. R. Candby et al., *Court and Cosmos: The Great Age of the Seljuqs* (New York, 2016), 146.

51. A. J. Boas, *Domestic Settings: Sources on Domestic Architecture and Day-to-Day Activities in the Crusader States*, Medieval Mediterranean 84 (Leiden, 2010), 20–31.

52. N. Kenaan-Kedar, "Decorative Architectural Sculpture in Crusader Jerusalem: The Eastern, Western, and Armenian Sources of a Local Visual Culture," in *The Crusader World*, ed. A. Boas (Routledge, 2016), 609–623.

53. N. Hodgson, "Conflict and Cohabitation: Marriage and Diplomacy Between Latins and Cilician Armenians, c. 1097–1253," in *The Crusades and the Near East: Cultural Histories*, ed. C. Kostick (Abingdon, UK, 2011), 83–106.

54. UIM, 153–154.

55. R. Ellenblum, *Frankish Rural Settlement in the Latin Kingdom of Jerusalem* (Cambridge, 1998), 84.

56. P. Mitchell, "Intestinal Parasites in the Crusades: Evidence for Disease, Diet and Migration," in Boas, *The Crusader World*, 593–606.

57. Morton, *Encountering Islam,* 98–102.

58. Badr al-Din Mahmud (al-Ayni), "Genealogy and Tribal Division," in *The Turkic Peoples in Medieval Arabic Writings,* trans. Y. Frenkel, Routledge Studies in the History of Iran and Turkey (Abingdon, UK, 2015), 67.

59. *The Sea of Precious Virtues,* 57, 215.

60. Ibid., 57.

CHAPTER 3: THE BATTLE (1119)

1. H. E. Mayer, "The Succession to Baldwin II of Jerusalem: English Impact on the East," *Dumbarton Oaks Papers* 39 (1985): 139–147; A. Murray, "Baldwin II and His Nobles: Baronial Factionalism and Dissent in the Kingdom of Jerusalem, 1118–1134," *Nottingham Medieval Studies* 38 (1994): 60–85.

2. IAA(2), 1: 196.

3. KAD, 614.

4. See also T. Asbridge, *The Creation of the Principality of Antioch, 1098–1130* (Woodbridge, UK, 2000), 74.

5. KAD, 614–615.

6. For a good introduction to Tughtakin, see T. El-Azhari, "Tughtigin (d. 1128)," in *The Crusades: An Encyclopaedia,* ed. A. Murray (Santa Barbara, 2006), 4: 1204–1205.

7. It is possible that the literacy rate in the region was in the double digits—very rare for the world at this time and far higher than in medieval Europe. K. Hirschler, *Medieval Damascus: Plurality and Diversity in an Arabic Library. The Ashrafiya Library Catalogue,* Edinburgh Studies in Classical Islamic History and Culture (Edinburgh, 2016), 2.

8. IQ, 183–186.

9. IAA(2), 1: 16.

10. IQ, 49.

11. Ibid., 56–57; IAA(2), 1: 72–73, 80–81.

12. IAA(2), 1: 39–40.

13. Ibid., 1: 116.

14. AA, 535.

15. IAA(2), 1: 146, 164.

16. C. Hillenbrand, "The Career of Najm al-Dīn Il-Ghazi," *Der Islam* 58, no. 2 (1981): 254–259.

17. IAA(2), 1: 56.

18. Ibid., 1: 173.

19. Ibid., 1: 197.

20. C. Hillenbrand, *The Crusades: Islamic Perspectives* (Edinburgh, 2006), 104–108.

21. See al-Sulami, *The Book of the Jihad of 'Ali ibn Tahir al-Sulami (d. 1106): Text, Translation and Commentary*, ed. and trans. N. Christie (Aldershot, UK, 2015).

22. WC, 161; GN, 165; Ibn al-Furat, *Ayyubids, Mamlukes and Crusaders: Selections from the Tārīkh al-Duwal wa'l-Mulūk*, ed. and trans. U. Lyons and M. C. Lyons (Cambridge, 1971), 2: 45–46; C. Hillenbrand, "What's in a Name? Tughtegin—'The Minister of the Antichrist'?," in *Fortresses of the Intellect: Ismaili and Other Islamic Studies in Honour of Farhad Daftary*, ed. Omar Ali-de-Onzaga (London, 2011), 469–471.

23. AA, 771; WC, 163; WT, 1: 544.

24. S. R. Candby et al., *Court and Cosmos: The Great Age of the Seljuqs* (New York, 2016), 66, 70.

25. WC, 150; AA, 771; ASC, 99. Hillenbrand, "What's in a Name?," 467–469.

26. WC, 86, 90, 101, 134.

27. Ibid., 161.

28. AA, 837; FC, 204.

29. IAA(2), 1: 160.

30. AA, 837; ASC, 85.

31. Usama ibn Munqidh, *The Book of Contemplation: Islam and the Crusades*, Penguin Classics (London, 2008), 131.

32. Asbridge, *The Creation of the Principality of Antioch*, 165–166.

33. William of Malmesbury, *Gesta Regum Anglorum*, ed. and trans. R. A. B. Mynors, R. M. Thomson, and M. Winterbottom, vol. 1, Oxford Medieval Texts (Oxford, 1998), 695.

34. FC, 227.

35. WC, 111–113; AA, 841–843.

36. WC, 112–113.

37. There is an ongoing debate surrounding the willingness of medieval commanders to give battle. For a starting point to this conversation, see J. Gillingham, "Richard I and the Science of War in the Middle Ages," in *Anglo-Norman Warfare*, ed. M. Strickland (Woodbridge, UK, 1992), 194–207; J. France, "The Crusades and Military History," in *Chemins d'Outre-Mer: Études d'histoire sur la Méditerranée médiévale offertes à Michel Balard*, ed. D. Coulon et al. (Paris, 2004), 345–352; R. C. Smail, *Crusading Warfare: 1097–1193*, 2nd ed. (Cambridge, 1995), 138–139.

38. WC, 115.

39. R. Ellenblum, *Crusader Castles and Modern Histories* (Cambridge, 2007), 170–177.

40. C. Yovitchitch, "Bosra: Eine Zitadelle des Fürstentums Damaskus," in *Burgen und Städte der Kreuzzugszeit*, ed. M. Piana (Petersberg, Germany, 2008), 169–177.

41. D. M. Metcalf, "Six Unresolved Problems in the Monetary History of Antioch, 969–1268," in *East and West in the Medieval Eastern Mediterranean I: Antioch from the Byzantine Reconquest until the End of the Crusader Principality*, ed. K. Ciggaar and M. Metcalf (Leuven, Belgium, 2006), 285.

42. WT, 2: 514–515.

43. H. Kennedy, *Crusader Castles* (Cambridge, 1994), 84–96.

44. J. Phillips, *The Crusades: 1095–1204*, 2nd ed. (Abingdon, UK, 2014), 105.

45. Kennedy, *Crusader Castles*, 97.

46. WC, 115–118.

47. Ibid., 119–120.

48. ASC, 87.

49. IAA(2), 1: 204; IQ, 160; ME, 223; KAD, 616.

50. IAA(2), 1: 214–215.

51. KAD, 617.

52. Ibid., 617.

53. J. France, "Warfare in the Mediterranean Region in the Age of the Crusades, 1095–1291: A Clash of Contrasts," in *The Crusades and the Near East: Cultural Histories*, ed. C. Kostick (Abingdon, UK, 2011), 9–26.

54. Ibn Fadlan, *Ibn Fadlan and the Land of Darkness*, trans. P. Lunde and C. Stone, Penguin Classics (London, 2012), 20.

55. Translation of Abu'l-Hasan 'Ali al-Harawi's work, taken from N. Christie, *Muslims and Crusaders: Christianity's Wars in the Middle East, 1095–1382, from Islamic Sources* (Abingdon, UK, 2014), 147.

56. For discussion, see Candby et al., *Court and Cosmos*, 145; A. C. S. Peacock, *Early Seljūq History: A New Interpretation*, Routledge Studies in the History of Iran and Turkey (Abingdon, UK, 2010), 76.

57. IAA(2), 1: 204; IQ, 160; ME, 224.

58. WC, 128.

59. IAA(2), 2: 185.

60. UIM, 71.

61. J. France, *Western Warfare in the Age of the Crusades, 1000–1300* (Ithaca, NY, 1999), 26.

62. *Decrees of the Ecumenical Councils*, vol. 1, *Nicaea I–Lateran V*, ed. N. P. Tanner (London and Washington, 1990), 203.

63. WC, 128–129.

64. Ibid., 128.

65. Ibid., 127.

66. William of Malmesbury, *Gesta Regum Anglorum*, 1: 695.

67. OV, 6: 131.

68. WC, 132.

69. IQ, 160.

70. Bar Hebraeus, *The Chronography of Gregory Abû'l Faraj: The Son of Aaron, the Hebrew Physician Commonly Known as Bar Hebraeus*, trans. E. Wallis Budge (Oxford, 1932), 1: 249.

71. WC, 136; KAD, 620; IAA(2), 1: 205; WC, 151, n204. For a thorough assessment of the full territorial losses suffered by Antioch, see T. Asbridge, "The Significance and Causes of the Battle of the Field of Blood," *Journal of Medieval History* 23, no. 4 (1997): 303–304; Asbridge, *The Creation of the Principality of Antioch*, 80.

72. IQ, 161.

73. WC, 144.

74. KAD, 620; FC, 228.

75. WC, 150.

76. Ibid., 153–154. The armies of both Jerusalem and Antioch bore great crosses into battle as their standards. The Jerusalemite cross contained within it the bulk of the True Cross of the Crucifixion that was discovered soon after the First Crusade, and the Antiochene cross contained a fragment of the "True Cross."

77. ME, 224.

78. See, for example, ME, 224.

79. KAD, 621.

80. See WC, 156–171; KAD, 622; UIM, 131–132.

81. WC, 165.

82. IAA(2), 1: 204–205.

83. ME, 223.

84. Asbridge, *The Creation of the Principality of Antioch*, 80.

85. Ibid., 80–81.

86. See Asbridge, "The Significance and Causes of the Battle of the Field of Blood," 306.

87. J. Phillips, *Defenders of the Holy Land: Relations Between the Latin East and the West, 1119–1187* (Oxford, 1996), 14.

88. WC, 77–84.

89. Phillips, *Defenders of the Holy Land*, 14.

90. For discussion of the council, see B. Z. Kedar, "On the Earliest Laws of Frankish Jerusalem: The Canons of the Council of Nablus, 1120," *Speculum* 74, no. 2 (1999): 310–335; M. E. Mayer, "The Concordat of Nablus," *Journal of Ecclesiastical History* 33, no. 4 (1982): 531–543.

91. M. Barber, *The New Knighthood: A History of the Order of the Temple* (Cambridge, 1994), 9.

CHAPTER 4: FIELDS OF BLOOD (1120–1128)

1. The History of David King of Kings," in *Rewriting Caucasian History: The Medieval Armenian Adaptation of the Georgian Chronicles,* trans. R. W. Thomson (Oxford, 1996), 333; IQ, 164; ME, 226.

2. KAD, 627–629.

3. Ibid., 629.

4. Ibid., 630.

5. IAA(2), 1: 261, 231.

6. KAD, 632.

7. AA, 177–179.

8. IQ, 50–51.

9. IAA(2), 1: 76.

10. Ibid., 1: 93–94; ME, 215.

11. KAD, 631.

12. ASC, 90–91; FC, 237; IAA(2), 1: 232; ME, 228.

13. ME, 229; FC, 239–240; IQ, 167.

14. KAD, 636.

15. ASC, 92.

16. WT, 1: 540.

17. C. MacEvitt, *The Crusades and the Christian World of the East: Rough Tolerance* (Philadelphia, 2008).

18. However, as T. L. Andrews points out, the notion that the Franks were their prophesied saviors seems to have faded over time, at least for the important Armenian writer Matthew of Edessa. T. L. Andrews, *Matt'ēos Uřhayec'i and His Chronicle: History as Apocalypse in a Crossroads of Cultures* (Leiden: Brill, 2017), 121–138.

19. For further discussion, see MacEvitt, *The Crusades and the Christian World of the East.*

20. ME, 230.

21. FC, 249.

22. ASC, 93; WT, 1: 544.

23. ASC, 93.

24. Ibid., 94.

25. IQ, 169–170; KAD, 640.

26. ASC, 94; FC, 262–263; KAD, 641–642.

27. ME, 232.

28. Translation taken from C. Hillenbrand, *The Crusades: Islamic Perspectives* (Edinburgh, 2006), 110.

29. UIM, 132.

30. V. Klemm, *Memoirs of a Mission: The Ismaili Scholar, Statesman and Poet, Al-Mu'ayyad Fi'l-Din Al-Shirazi* (London, 2003), 82.

31. IAA(2), 1: 37–124.

32. Ibid., 1: 124.

33. Ibid., 1: 129.

34. Ibid., 1: 210–213.

35. WC, 150; KAD, 626–628.

36. IAA(2), 1: 242–244.

37. KAD, 644.

38. IAA(2), 1: 244.

39. KAD, 645.

40. Ibid., 647.

41. Ibid., 647–648.

42. IAA(2), 1: 254.

43. Ibid., 1: 129.

44. FC, 274.

45. ASC, 96.

46. ME, 234.

47. A. Murray, "Baldwin II and His Nobles: Baronial Factionalism and Dissent in the Kingdom of Jerusalem, 1118–1134," *Nottingham Medieval Studies* 38 (1994): 69–75.

48. ASC, 97.

49. Ibid., 97.

50. FC, 240–241.

51. J. Pryor, *Geography, Technology and War: Studies in the Maritime History of the Mediterranean, 649–1571* (Cambridge, 1988), 114.

52. J. Pryor, "A View from the Masthead: The First Crusade from the Sea," *Crusades* 7 (2008): 102.

53. Guibert of Nogent, "Un épisode de la lutte entre Baudouin Ier et les habitants d'Ascalon," in *Guitberti Abbatis Sanctae Marie Novigenti: Historia quae inscribitur Dei gesta per Francos et cinq autres textes,* ed. R. B. C. Huygens, Corpus Christianorum Continuatio Mediaeualis 127A (Turnhout, Belgium, 1996), 255.

54. For discussion of this crusade, see D. E. Queller and I. B. Katele, "Venice and the Conquest of the Latin Kingdom of Jerusalem," *Studi Veneziani* 12 (1986): 15–43; J. Riley-Smith, "The Venetian Crusade of 1122–1124," in *I Communi italiani nel regno crociato di Gerusalemme,* ed. G. Airaldi and B. Z. Kedar (Genoa, 1986), 337–350.

55. WT, 2: 10–11.

56. Ibid., 2: 14.

57. Ibid., 2: 16.

58. T. Asbridge, "How the Crusades Could Have Been Won: King Baldwin II of Jerusalem's Campaigns Against Aleppo (1124–5) and Damascus (1129)," *Journal of Medieval Military History,* ed. C. J. Rogers and K. DeVries, 11 (2013): 73–93.

59. This story and the translated passage can be found in OV, 6: 109–127; quoted passage on 127.

60. William of Malmesbury, *Gesta Regum Anglorum*, ed. and trans. R. A. B. Mynors, R. M. Thomson, and M. Winterbottom, vol. 1, Oxford Medieval Texts (Oxford, 1998), 524; UIM, 124.

61. William of Newburgh, "The History of William of Newburgh," in *The Church Historians of England*, trans. Rev. J. Stevenson, vol. 4, part 1 (London, 1856), 535.

62. OV, 6: 135; WT, 1: 33.

63. ME, 237; ASC, 99.

64. UIM, 133.

65. KAD, 656.

66. For an authoritative and recent biography of Zangi, see T. El-Azhari, *Zengi and the Muslim Response to the Crusades: The Politics of Jihad* (Abingdon, UK, 2016).

67. Ibid., passim.

68. Indeed, Andrew Buck has suggested that the principality reached its greatest territorial extent in 1130. See A. D. Buck, *The Principality of Antioch and Its Frontiers in the Twelfth Century* (Woodbridge, UK, 2017), 21.

CHAPTER 5: AFTERMATH (1128–1187)

1. ME, 231.

2. J. J. S. Weitenberg, "The Armenian Monasteries in the Black Mountain," in *East and West in the Medieval Eastern Mediterranean I: Antioch from the Byzantine Reconquest until the End of the Crusader Principality*, ed. K. Ciggaar and M. Metcalf (Leuven, Belgium, 2006), 90.

3. S. K. Raphael, *Climate and Political Change: Environmental Disasters in the Medieval Levant* (Leiden, 2013), 32.

4. B. Major, *Medieval Rural Settlements in the Syrian Coastal Region (12th and 13th Centuries)*, Archaeolingua Central European Archaeological Heritage Series 9 (Oxford, 2015), 136; H. E. Mayer, *Varia Antiochena: Studien zum Kreuzfahrerfürstentum Antiochia im 12. und frühen 13. Jahrhundert* (Hannover, 1993), 164–165.

5. A. D. Buck, "The Castle and Lordship of Hārim and the Frankish-Muslim Frontier of Northern Syria in the Twelfth Century," *Al-Masāq: Journal of the Medieval Mediterranean* 28, no. 2 (2016): 113–131.

6. Major, *Medieval Rural Settlements in the Syrian Coastal Region*.

7. See D. Jacoby, "Frankish Beirut: A Minor Economic Centre," in *Crusader Landscapes in the Medieval Levant: The Archaeology and History of the Latin East*, ed. M. Sinibaldi, K. J. Lewis, B. Major, and J. A. Thompson (Cardiff, 2016), 263–276.

8. For the key study on Frankish rural settlement, see R. Ellenblum, *Frankish Rural Settlement in the Latin Kingdom of Jerusalem* (Cambridge, 1998). A. J. Boas, "Domestic Life in the Latin East," in *The Crusader World,* ed. A. J. Boas (London, 2016), 553–554.

9. A. Boas, *Domestic Settings: Sources on Domestic Architecture and Day-to-Day Activities in the Crusader States,* Medieval Mediterranean 84 (Leiden, 2010), 136.

10. Ellenblum, *Frankish Rural Settlement in the Latin Kingdom of Jerusalem,* 283. This work has been foundational in offering this bird's-eye view of the Kingdom of Jerusalem.

11. *The Travels of Ibn Jubayr: A Mediaeval Spanish Muslim Visits Makkah, Madinah, Egypt, Cities of the Middle East and Sicily,* trans. R. Broadhurst (London, 1952), 316–317.

12. Boas, *Domestic Settings,* 217–218 and passim; Boas, "Domestic Life in the Latin East," 545.

13. B. Z. Kedar, "The Subjected Muslims of the Frankish Levant," in *The Crusades: The Essential Readings,* ed. T. Madden (Malden, MA, 2002), 233–264.

14. E. Yehuda, "Frankish Street Settlements and the Status of Their Inhabitants in the Society of the Latin Kingdom of Jerusalem," unpublished paper.

15. A. J. Boas, *Jerusalem in the Time of the Crusades* (Abingdon, UK, 2001).

16. D. Pringle, *The Churches of the Crusader Kingdom of Jerusalem: A Corpus,* vol. 3, *The City of Jerusalem* (Cambridge, 2007), 397–434; Boas, "Domestic Life in the Latin East," 561–562.

17. A. D. Buck, *The Principality of Antioch and Its Frontiers in the Twelfth Century* (Woodbridge, UK, 2017), 36.

18. T. El-Azhari, *Zengi and the Muslim Response to the Crusades: The Politics of Jihad* (Abingdon, UK, 2016), passim.

19. IQ, 271.

20. El-Azhari, *Zengi and the Muslim Response to the Crusades,* 137–143.

21. For discussion, see D. Talmon-Heller, *Islamic Piety in Medieval Syria: Mosques, Cemeteries, and Sermons under the Zangids and Ayyūbids (1146–1260)* (Boston, 2007); N. Christie, *Muslims and Crusaders: Christianity's Wars in the Middle East, 1095–1382, from the Islamic Sources* (Abingdon, UK, 2014), 36–41; El-Azhari, *Zengi and the Muslim Response to the Crusades,* 137–141.

22. C. Hillenbrand, *The Crusades: Islamic Perspectives* (Edinburgh, 2006), 151–152.

23. For discussion, see J. Phillips, *The Second Crusade: Extending the Frontiers of Christendom* (New Haven, 2007).

24. IQ, 318–319.

25. WT, 2: 230–234.

26. Buck, "The Castle and Lordship of Ḥārim," 113–131.

27. IAA(2), 1: 141; WT, 2: 306.

28. For an introduction to the military orders, see N. Morton, *The Medieval Military Orders* (Abingdon, UK, 2014).

29. The main accounts for the wars between King Amalric of Jerusalem and Nur al-Din over Egypt are IAA(2), 1: 138–184; WT, 2: 302–369.

30. B. A. Catlos, *Infidel Kings and Unholy Warriors: Faith, Power and Violence in the Age of Crusade and Jihad* (New York, 2014), 234–235.

31. WT, 2: 350–358.

32. H. Nicholson, *The Knights Templar: A New History* (Stroud, UK, 2005), 69–70; WT, 2: 350; IAA(2), 2: 172; WT, 2: 348.

33. IAA(2), 2: 198–199, 221.

34. M. C. Lyons and D. E. P. Jackson, *Saladin: The Politics of the Holy War* (Cambridge, 2001), 75.

35. For an excellent account of Saladin's early rise to power, see ibid.

36. Quotation taken from Lyons and Jackson, *Saladin*, 199.

37. See, for example, P. Lock, *The Routledge Companion to the Crusades* (Abingdon, UK, 2006), 250.

38. For a selection of recent and/or influential views on this topic, see Christie, *Muslims and Crusaders*, 48–52; Lyons and Jackson, *Saladin*, passim; J. Phillips, *Holy Warriors: A Modern History of the Crusades* (London, 2009), 165; T. Asbridge, *The Crusades: The Authoritative History of the War for the Holy Land* (New York, 2010), 335–336; Hillenbrand, *The Crusades*, 175–195.

39. "The Old French Continuation of William of Tyre, 1184–1197," in *The Conquest of Jerusalem and the Third Crusade: Sources in Translation*, ed. and trans. P. Edbury, Crusade Texts in Translation 1 (Aldershot, UK, 1998), 36–38.

40. WT, 2: 471–501.

41. These estimates are loosely based on those offered by Martin Hoch in "Hattin, Battle of," in *The Crusades: An Encyclopedia*, ed. A. Murray (Santa Barbara, 2006), 2: 559.

42. For a detailed account of the Battle of Hattin, see B. Z. Kedar, "The Battle of Hattin Revisited," in *The Horns of Hattin*, ed. B. Z. Kedar (Jerusalem, 1992), 190–207. For a more recent study, see J. France, *Great Battles: Hattin* (Oxford, 2015).

43. In some cases the attack destroyed the former relationship established between the Franks and the urban population; in other cases the relationship had already collapsed a short time before.

44. WT, 2: 227.

FURTHER READING

There are many very helpfully written books, both on the Crusader States and on the Muslim world of the medieval Near East. In what follows I have supplied references to some of the most useful and influential. These texts have been chosen because they represent some of the most recent and comprehensive summaries of the archaeological and textual sources. I have also supplied references to many of the key primary sources written during the medieval period that provide insight into the ideas and perspectives that were circulating at the time of the Crusades.

GENERAL INTRODUCTIONS

Asbridge, T. *The Crusades: The Authoritative History of the War for the Holy Land.* New York, 2010.

Jotischky, A. *Crusading and the Crusader States.* 2nd ed. Abingdon, UK, 2017.

Phillips, J. *Holy Warriors: A Modern History of the Crusades.* London, 2009.

Riley-Smith, J. *The Crusades: A History.* 3rd ed. London, 2014.

Tyerman, C. *God's War: A New History of the Crusades.* London, 2006.

NORTHERN SYRIA AND THE CRUSADER STATES

Asbridge, T. *The Creation of the Principality of Antioch, 1098–1130.* Woodbridge, UK, 2000.

Barber, M. *The Crusader States.* New Haven, CT, 2012.

Köhler, M. A. *Alliances and Treaties Between Frankish and Muslim Rulers in the Middle East: Cross-Cultural Diplomacy in the Period of the Crusades.* Translated by P. M. Holt. Edited by K. Hirschler. Leiden, 2013.

MacEvitt, C. *The Crusades and the Christian World of the East: Rough Tolerance.* Philadelphia, 2008.

Phillips, J. *Defenders of the Holy Land: Relations Between the Latin East and the West, 1119–1187.* Oxford, 1996.

———. *The Second Crusade: Extending the Frontiers of Christendom.* New Haven, CT, 2007.

THE TURKISH, FATIMID, AND MUSLIM WORLD AT THE TIME OF THE CRUSADES

Azhari, T. el-. *Zengi and the Muslim Response to the Crusades: The Politics of Jihad.* Abingdon, UK, 2016.

Christie, N. *Muslims and Crusaders: Christianity's Wars in the Middle East, 1095–1382, from the Islamic Sources.* Abingdon, UK, 2014.

Hillenbrand, C. *The Crusades: Islamic Perspectives.* Edinburgh, 2006.

Mallet, A., ed. *Medieval Muslim Historians and the Franks in the Levant.* The Muslim World in the Age of the Crusades 2. Leiden, 2014.

Mecit, S. *The Rum Seljuqs: Evolution of a Dynasty.* Routledge Studies in the History of Iran and Turkey. Abingdon, UK, 2014.

Peacock, A. C. S. *The Great Seljuk Empire.* Edinburgh History of the Islamic Empires. Edinburgh, 2015.

ARCHAEOLOGICAL STUDIES ON THE CRUSADER STATES

Boas, A. J. *Crusader Archaeology: The Material Culture of the Latin East.* 2nd ed. Abingdon, UK, 2017.

———. *Domestic Settings: Sources on Domestic Architecture and Day-to-Day Activities in the Crusader States.* Medieval Mediterranean 84. Leiden, 2010.

Ellenblum, R. *Frankish Rural Settlement in the Latin Kingdom of Jerusalem.* Cambridge, UK, 2002.

Major, B., *Medieval Rural Settlements in the Syrian Coastal Region (12th and 13th Centuries).* Archaeolingua Central European Archaeological Heritage Series 9. Oxford, 2015.

SOURCES IN TRANSLATION ON THE CRUSADER STATES AND THEIR NEIGHBORS

Albert of Aachen. *Historia Ierosolimitana: History of the Journey to Jerusalem.* Edited and translated by S. B. Edgington. Oxford Medieval Texts. Oxford, 2007.

al-Sulami. *The Book of the Jihad of 'Ali ibn Tahir al-Sulami (d. 1106): Text, Translation and Commentary.* Translated by N. Christie. Farnham, UK, 2015.

Anna Comnena. *The Alexiad.* Translated by E. R. A. Sewter. With an introduction by P. Frankopan. London, 2009.

Anonymous. "Syriac chronicle." Translated by A. Tritton. *Journal of the Royal Asiatic Society* 65 (1933): 69–101.

Caffaro. *Caffaro, Genoa and the Twelfth Century Crusades.* Translated by M. Hall and J. Phillips. Crusade Texts in Translation 16. Farnham, UK, 2013.

Fulcher of Chartres. *A History of the Expedition to Jerusalem, 1095–1127.* Translated by F. R. Ryan. New York, 1969.

Ibn al-Athir. *The Chronicle of Ibn al-Athir for the Crusading Period from al-Kamil fi'l-Ta'rikh.* Translated by D. S. Richards. 3 vols. Crusade Texts in Translation 13, 15, and 17. Aldershot, UK, 2006–2008.

Ibn al-Qalanisi. *The Damascus Chronicle of the Crusades.* Translated by H. A. R. Gibb. New York, 2002.

Letters from the East: Crusaders, Pilgrims, and Settlers in the 12th–13th Centuries. Translated by M. Barber and K. Bate. Crusade Texts in Translation 18. Aldershot, UK, 2010.

Matthew of Edessa. *Armenia and the Crusades: Tenth to Twelfth Centuries. The Chronicle of Matthew of Edessa.* Translated by A. E. Dostourian. New York, 1993.

Niketas Choniatēs. *O City of Byzantium: Annals of Niketas Choniatēs.* Translated by H. J. Magoulias. Byzantine Texts in Translation. Detroit, 1984.

Odo of Deuil. *De profectione Ludovici VII in orientem: The Journey of Louis VII to the East.* Edited and translated by V. G. Berry. Columbia Records of Civilization. New York, 1948.

Orderic Vitalis. *The Ecclesiastical History of Orderic Vitalis.* Edited and translated by M. Chibnall. Vol. 6. Oxford Medieval Texts. Oxford, 1978.

Revised Regesta Regni Hierosolymitani. http://crusades-regesta.com/. This website contains a searchable database of legal documents and letters concerning the Crusader States from 1098 to 1291. Summaries of each document are provided in English.

Usama ibn Munqidh. *The Book of Contemplation: Islam and the Crusades.* Penguin Classics. London, 2008.

Walter the Chancellor. *The Antiochene Wars: A Translation and Commentary.* Translated by T. S. Asbridge and S. B. Edgington. Crusade Texts in Translation 4. Aldershot, UK, 1999.

William of Tyre. *A History of Deeds Done Beyond the Sea.* Translated by E. A. Babcock and A. C. Krey. 2 vols. New York, 1943.

INDEX

Eethan Laughlin

NICHOLAS MORTON IS a senior lecturer at Nottingham Trent University in the UK. He has published widely on themes connected to the Crusades, the military orders, and the Seljuk Turks and is the author or editor of five books on these topics. He also coedits two book series, Rulers of the Latin East and The Military Religious Orders.